LIVES OF THE MASTERS

The Third Karmapa Rangjung Dorje

MASTER OF MAHĀMUDRĀ

Ruth Gamble

Shambhala

Shambhala Publications, Inc.
4720 Walnut Street
Boulder, Colorado 80301
www.shambhala.com

FRONTISPIECE: Third Karmapa, Rangjung Dorje; Eastern Tibet; 19th century; Pigments on cloth; Rubin Museum of Art; Gift of Shelley & Donald Rubin Foundation; F1996.3.1 (HAR 407)

Cover art: Robert Fenwick May, Jr.
Cover design: Gopa & Ted2, Inc.

9 8 7 6 5 4 3 2 1

FIRST EDITION
Printed in Canada

♾ This edition is printed on acid-free paper that meets the American National Standards Institute z39.48 Standard.
♻ This book is printed on 100% postconsumer recycled paper.
For more information please visit www.shambhala.com.

Shambhala Publications is distributed worldwide by Penguin Random House, Inc., and its subsidiaries.

LIBRARY OF CONGRESS CATALOGING-IN-PUBLICATION DATA
Names: Gamble, Ruth, 1972– author. | Rang-byung-rdo-rje, Karma-pa III, 1284–1339.
Title: The Third Karmapa Rangjung Dorje: master of Māhamudrā / Ruth Gamble.
Description: First edition. | Boulder: Shambhala, [2020] | Series: Lives of the masters | Includes bibliographical references and index.
Identifiers: LCCN 2019051721 | ISBN 9781611807080 (trade paperback)
Subjects: LCSH: Rang-byung-rdo-rje, Karma-pa III, 1284–1339. | Kar-ma-pa lamas—Tibet Region—Biography.
Classification: LCC BQ7950.R367 G36 2020 | DDC 294.3/923092 [B]—dc23
LC record available at https://lccn.loc.gov/2019051721

Contents

Series Introduction

BUDDHIST TRADITIONS are heir to some of the most creative thinkers in world history. The Lives of the Masters series offers lively and reliable introductions to the lives, works, and legacies of key Buddhist teachers, philosophers, contemplatives, and writers. Each volume in the Lives series tells the story of an innovator who embodied the ideals of Buddhism, crafted a dynamic living tradition during his or her lifetime, and bequeathed a vibrant legacy of knowledge and practice to future generations.

Lives books rely on primary sources in the original languages to describe the extraordinary achievements of Buddhist thinkers and illuminate these achievements by vividly setting them within their historical contexts. Each volume offers a concise yet comprehensive summary of the master's life and an account of how they came to hold a central place in Buddhist traditions. Each contribution also contains a broad selection of the master's writings.

This series makes it possible for all readers to imagine Buddhist masters as deeply creative and inspired people whose work was animated by the rich complexity of their time and place and how these inspiring figures continue to engage our quest for knowledge and understanding today.

KURTIS SCHAEFFER, *series editor*

Preface

We collect felt cases for our texts,
But they don't make reading them more comfortable.[1]

RANGJUNG DORJE, *1296, age 13*
Khyung Dzong, Tsurpu

MY RELATIONSHIP with Rangjung Dorje's stories and songs is now more than a decade old. I was first handed a copy of his Collected Works on a CD-ROM the year I started graduate school. At that stage, I was not as interested in his life as I was in his songs. I scanned the names of the texts on the disc, looking for one that included the word *gur*, the honorific Tibetan word for "song," and I was excited to find several collections of them.[2] The "songs" I was looking for did not have accompanying melodies. They were lyrics written and often performed by a lineage of Vajrayāna Buddhist yogis who lived in medieval India (where they employed genres called *dohā*, or couplets, and *gītī*, or songs) and Tibet (where they were called *gur* or the nonhonorific *lu*).[3]

I had been fascinated by the songs of this genre since I was a teenager and read the life story of the *Mahāmudrā* yogi Milarepa. Milarepa was famous for his songs, and many of them had been woven into his life story. His songs' combination of spiritual pursuit and irreverence, the balance they struck between discipline and play, struck an immediate chord with me. They dealt with the hard truths of death and loss and the suffering of life, but they were also funny and (importantly for a teenager growing up in a conservative society) they contained social criticism that was biting. The hard truths Milarepa spoke about life and death were much easier to face because of his humor, and—in the story at least—his satire made tyrannous religious and political patriarchs quake. Among my diverse cultural references, Milarepa hovered like a fast-quipping, awakened superhero. He could fly, his consorts were mountains, and he even had theme songs. After these encounters with Milarepa, I was always on the lookout for more yogi songs.

By the time I was handed the CD, I also knew something about the Karmapas. I had met the Seventeenth Karmapa, Orgyen Trinle, in Tibet when I was a teenager and he a child, and I remet him in India when he was a teenager and I was studying Tibetan. I had found him always curious, kind, and funny, but I was also disturbed by the restrictions he had to endure because of his religious and political position.

After meeting Orgyen Trinle, I had tried to read the sanitized, standardized forms of the Karmapas' life stories, but I kept tuning out as I read them. Many have said that it was my karma not to connect with those stories. But it also had something to do with the way they were presented. My experiences and culture had bombarded me with text and taught me not to believe so easily. Later versions of the Karmapas' life stories, it seems to me anyway, were written for an already-devoted audience who had limited access to the written word and merely wanted a narrative sketch to accompany their lineage prayers.

When I scanned the table of contents of Rangjung Dorje's Collected Works on the CD, I noted that there were also a few works called *namthar*, a term that usually refers to spiritual biographies.[4] I was not expecting much from them. I thought they would be formulaic versions of his life, placed at the start of his Collected Works by its collator as a form of introductory homage.

My first surprise was that they were a series of autobiographies. My second surprise was the content of these autobiographies.

Rather than the formulaic tales of a life I was expecting, they were often raw and revealing insights into an often difficult but fundamentally resilient life. Reading and translating his stories and songs was like opening a time capsule; it was always fascinating but not always comfortable.

In these works, Rangjung Dorje expressed enough self-doubt for me to relate to him. He was someone, like many of us, who was an outsider that had to work hard to achieve his goals and construct an identity for himself. He was someone who had to negotiate ethical dilemmas in difficult times and someone who had made a pact with peace. He came from a more desperate family than even Milarepa. Milarepa's story is a story of lost wealth and prestige. Rangjung Dorje came from nothing and had nothing to lose. His early life was replete with stories about his father getting drunk and bragging about him in a town and about his mother walking hundreds of kilometers to find a place to stay soon after she gave birth to him.

Rangjung Dorje's story also provided fascinating insights into a very different world from mine, the world of a recognized reincarnate, whose sometime-discomfort, sometime-thriving relationship with his reincarnate status reminded me of not just the Seventeenth Karmapa but of many other people in similar situations. And then there were his visions. Rangjung Dorje's story and songs may have resonated with me, but they also transported me to a version of the world that was very foreign to me. His stories and songs mixed the common with the otherworldly.

I have been fascinated constantly with these stories and songs since I encountered them, but it has not always been a comfortable relationship. One of my teachers, Geshe Pema Tsering, told me to treat all texts as a mirror. When I look at these texts, I see a lot about myself, and most of it makes me uncomfortable. Rangjung Dorje asks his readers to give up all of life's comforts, relationships, and distractions. I am struggling to do something basic like reduce my carbon footprint.

The texts let me down sometimes too. I still, for example, feel uncomfortable reading the third-to-last song in the *Collected Songs of Rangjung Dorje*, as it is particularly scathing toward a group of women practitioners. This is the only time that Rangjung Dorje turns his harsh social criticism toward subaltern people. Is his harshness a sign of respect? Or is it a reminder of very different social norms than the ones I live within?

Mainly, however, the texts make me examine my own views, both my own self-obsessions and those which seem external to me. It is a long journey from the times and places in which the texts were composed to the times and places in which I view them. This examination is not only existential, a deconstruction of the self, subjects, and objects; it is also cultural.

It is easy to approach these texts reductively, to only focus on the elements within them that sit easily within dominant, contemporary perspectives. I was brought up in a colonial culture and society that was threatened by different points of view; the very existence of different cultures threatened (and still threatens) its legitimacy. Within this culture, I was taught how to be reductive. If I were to adopt its dominant, consumerist view in my approach toward Rangjung Dorje's texts, I would only engage with their political and material elements and expect constant self-interest from their protagonists. This politically cynical, lowest-common-denominator approach is a comfortable, well-attested stance, but I don't think it shows enough respect for these texts or their composer.

Instead, in what follows, I have tried as much as possible, to read Rangjung Dorje's texts in their context. I was raised on the unceded lands of the Murri Nation, and thanks to the kindness of their elders, I grew up with stories of a living landscape and glimpsed other ways to see the world. My interactions with these ways of seeing are still childish compared to the ways in which the people who told me these stories interact with them. But they were enough for me to recognize that a multiplicity of perspectives is possible, and if we are to undo even some of the devastation of the worldwide colonial project, they are also necessary. This exposure—and perhaps my gender and social background—also means that I cannot approach these works with the confident dismissal of the otherworldly that sometimes permeates academic writing on Tibetan lifeways either. If it seems I am not being critical enough of Rangjung Dorje for the readers' taste, please accept this explanation for my approach rather than dismissing the book's contents as hagiography. I am hoping it strikes a middle path between the two extremes of normalized Western reduction of other cultures and the traditional formulaic praises I found difficult to read.

This book is my second book on Rangjung Dorje, and it contains more translations of his words than the first. Like the first book, it is still, by its nature, a work of cultural as well as literary and linguistic interpretation. My desire to take his worldview as a starting point to understand his writing cannot negate the power differentials implicit in translating a story into English. It is impossible to close the chasm between thirteenth- and fourteenth-century Tibet and the contemporary globalized Anglosphere. I am keenly aware of how things can be misinterpreted across these spaces and that ultimately translation is impossible. Please, therefore, do not take the following biography or the translations that follow it to be definitive. They are an interpretation and are always open to improvement. There is more in Rangjung Dorje's life and works than I have the capacity to see. Hopefully, this story and these translations will encourage many others to look more deeply into them.

RUTH GAMBLE
June 2019
Manaus, Amazônia, Brazil

Acknowledgments

I WOULD LIKE to thank the people who helped me the most with my initial PhD research: John Powers, David Templeman, and Roger Jackson. I would also like to thank La Trobe University for granting me the time between other projects to write this book, and my family, Jackie and Iona, for putting up with me while I wrote it. The patient teachers who helped me work through the texts and answered questions about them at different times and in different places deserve particular thanks: Gyalwa Karmapa, Orgyen Trinle; Pö Tulku; and Tenzin Ringpapöntsang.

I would also like to thank Casey Kemp of Shambhala Publications and the University of Vienna for her infinite patience as I attempted to finish this work despite a barrage of other commitments and sometimes bizarre obstacles.

The Third Karmapa Rangjung Dorje

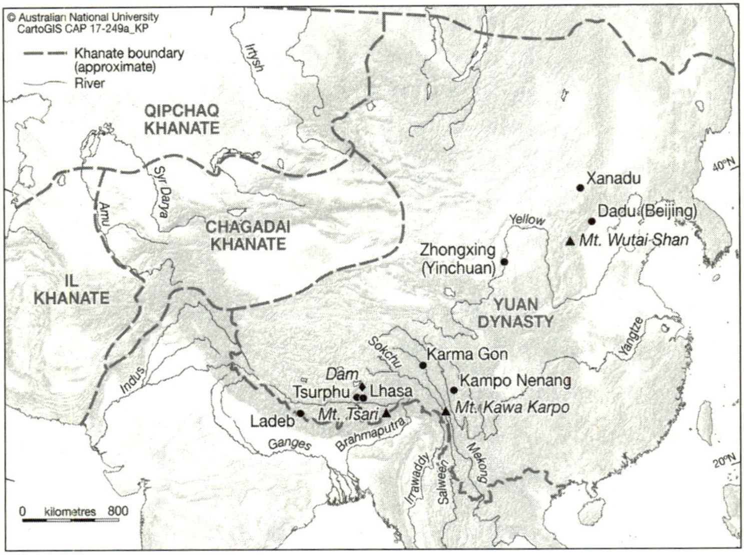
© Australian National University
CartoGIS CAP 17-249a_KP
Khanate boundary (approximate)
River
QIPCHAQ KHANATE
CHAGADAI KHANATE
IL KHANATE
YUAN DYNASTY
Irtysh
Syr Darya
Amu
Indus
Ganges
Brahmaputra
Irrawaddy
Salween
Mekong
Sokchu
Yellow
Yangtze
Xanadu
Dadu (Beijing)
Mt. Wutai Shan
Zhongxing (Yinchuan)
Karma Gon
Kampo Nenang
Mt. Kawa Karpo
Dam
Tsurphu
Lhasa
Ladeb
Mt. Tsari
40°N
20°N
0 kilometres 800

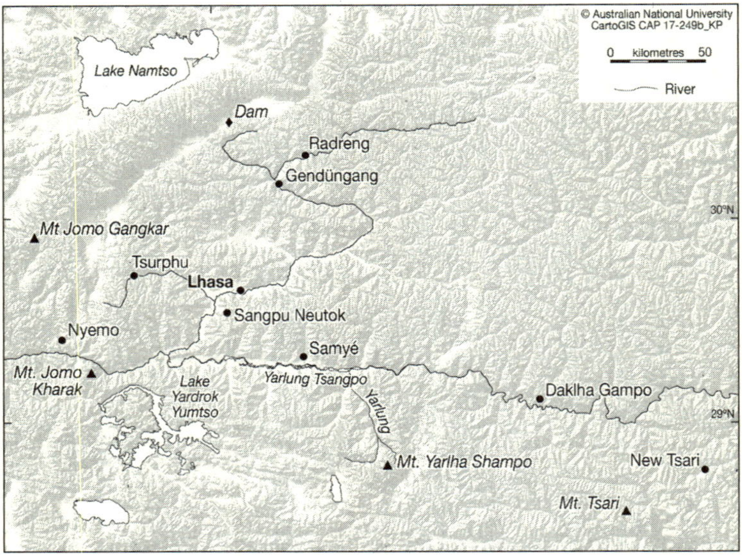
© Australian National University
CartoGIS CAP 17-249b_KP
0 kilometres 50
River
Lake Namtso
Dam
Radreng
Gendüngang
Mt Jomo Gangkar
Tsurphu
Lhasa
Sangpu Neutok
Nyemo
Samyé
Mt. Jomo Kharak
Lake Yardrok Yumtso
Yarlung Tsangpo
Yarlung
Daklha Gampo
Mt. Yarlha Shampo
New Tsari
Mt. Tsari
30°N
29°N

Introduction

Rangjung Dorje's Two Journeys

External appearances are experts in seduction;
[They are] children of our mind, and we are wild in the head.
Preconceptions proliferate and last longer,
And we have few virtuous friends.
The veils and fogs of ignorance grow thicker,
And the cliffs of depravity multiply.[5]

RANGJUNG DORJE, *1334, age 51. Xanadu*

Rangjung Dorje did not like Xanadu.[6] The legendary city, the summer capital of the Mongol Empire's Great Khan, with all its comforts, made him intensely uncomfortable. His writings from his stay there, including the above verse, are full of trepidation.

The tension in his writings from and about Xanadu reflects the paradox of his life there. On the one hand, as his later biographers would repeatedly insist, his invitation to the imperial Mongol court had been a triumph. After starting life as the son of socially disadvantaged potters who lived in the borderlands of the empire in southern Tibet, he was now a guest and teacher of the last Mongol emperor, the Great Khan Toghon Temür (1320–1370, r. 1333–1370). His invitation to the court had, furthermore, reflected his renown as a religious figure. It offered him a chance to teach his dharma to the world's most powerful people, and it would grant him more influence back in Tibet. It was, in other words, a fitting reward for a life of strict personal discipline and hard work.

His stay in the Mongols' summer capital, Xanadu, and their winter capital, Dadu, latterly known as Beijing, also ensured that he was given imperial backing to one of the greatest projects of his life: his effort to be recognized as the third rebirth in the Karmapa reincarnation lineage, to establish this lineage as a continuing tradition, and to develop institutional supports for it.

On the other hand, however, as his songs and autobiographical reflections suggest, neither were places Rangjung Dorje longed to be. Where others saw luxury, he saw treachery and distraction. The capitals were disconnected from—and even an impediment to—the other internal, spiritual journey to which he had dedicated his life. This other journey was the path of mahāmudrā, the journey to awakening. The mahāmudrā path, as Rangjung Dorje describes it in his writing, had two aspects: his efforts to develop the view of mahāmudrā through the practice of tantric yogas, usually in retreat, and his efforts to encourage others to realize mahāmudrā. In pursuit of his personal development, he had spent decades of his life in retreat, preferably in isolated hermitages in eastern and southern Tibet. In these retreats, he focused on breaking down his solid perceptions of the world and on seeing the world as "illusion-like."[7]

To encourage others' development of the mahāmudrā view, he had combined his retreats with teachings and voluminous writings that systemized and made accessible the many teachings on mahāmudrā and related worldviews that he had inherited from his lineage. These were teachings that he considered himself privileged to have received. His efforts to systemize, make assessible, and promote the mahāmudrā are why he is remembered as a master of mahāmudrā, but in some ways this moniker decreases his project's scope. Rangjung Dorje was renowned in his lifetime as a "Lord of Dharma"[8] because his view of the mahāmudrā was expansive enough to accommodate a variety of teachings and approaches to the ultimate truth, the nature of mind.

In his writing, he calls this approach being *chogme*, "sideless" or "impartial."[9] This suggests a precursor to the nineteenth-century Rime, or nonsectarian, approach,[10] but in Rangjung Dorje's writing, this term is used in multiple ways. He uses it to refer to his understanding of ultimate reality; "sidelessness" is beyond a duality that flickers between subject and object. And he uses it in different ways to refer to his more general approach to life. He claims to have been sideless or impartial in his approach to the Buddha's sūtra and tantra traditions and in his approach to other presentations of ultimate truth, particularly those venerated by non-Kagyü traditions in Tibet, such as the Great Completion, or Dzokchen, and the Middle Way, or Madhyamaka. He also advocates for an impartial approach to more mundane aspects of life. "Yogis, mountain hermits like me," he repeatedly states in his songs and stories, should be impartial about the food they eat, the drinks they drink, their clothing, their housing, the weather, their social status, their wealth, their political affiliations, and all other material and social aspects of their lives.

He developed this approach to the material and social spheres of his life as part of what, by all accounts (including his own), was an intense personal discipline. This self-discipline determined his life's trajectory. Rangjung Dorje was not born into a comfortable life, and he did not live in tranquil times. He was born into a poor family living under the dual—and intertwined—threats of war and famine. He only received an education after his teacher Orgyenpa (1229–1309) recognized him as the rebirth of the Second Karmapa, Karma Pakshi (1204–1283), when he was five years old. Even after this, his education and his yoga practice were interrupted by war, the threat of war, lack of food, life-threatening illnesses, and local and imperial politics.

His recognition as a reincarnate and the gift of a religious education also brought with it an array of responsibilities to the various lineages that he inherited. His writings reflect, for example, the seriousness with which he held his monastic vows and his dedication to his fellow monastics.[11] They also outline in some detail the commitments he maintained to the tantric traditions that he was empowered to cultivate. The majority of these were practices propagated by the Kagyü tradition. This tradition was founded in Tibet by the translator Marpa (1012?–1097) after he brought back teachings from the *mahāsiddhas* of India.[12] It was made famous by his student Milarepa (c. 1040–1123), who was renowned for his life story and his songs. The primary practices of the Kagyü were mahāmudrā and those associated with the six dharmas of Nāropā: (1) the yoga of inner heat, (2) the yoga of illusory body, (3) the yoga of clear light, (4) the yoga of dreams, (5) the yoga of the in-between state, and (6) the yoga of the transference of consciousness at the time of death.[13] Nāropā was an Indian mahāsiddha who tradition claims was Marpa's primary teacher.[14] The primary tantric practices associated with this tradition, which were used as the basis for the practice of the six dharmas and the cultivation of mahāmudrā, were those of the Cakrasaṃvara, Vajravārāhī, and Avalokiteśvara tantric cycles.

In line with his commitment to impartiality, however, Rangjung Dorje upheld, cultivated, and encouraged several other practices that were primarily associated with other traditions. He held and promoted lineages associated with the Nyingma tradition, for example, expressing a particular fondness for the Hevajra tantric cycle, the Heart-Essence Treasure tradition,[15] and the Great Completion view and path within it. Furthermore, his devotion to the purported founder of the Nyingma tradition, the "second Buddha" Padmasambhava, is evident throughout his writings. Along with these longstanding connections, Rangjung Dorje also studied with teachers from the Kadam tradition, which had been founded by the Indian scholar and siddha Atiśa (982–1054). At the insistence of his teacher Orgyenpa, he became an adept of the Kālācakra Tantra.

The other lineage to which Rangjung Dorje was devoted was in many ways the most personal and all-consuming of all the traditions he upheld: the Karmapa reincarnation lineage. After being recognized by Orgyenpa as a young child, he inherited what by then was a centuries-long personal history that entwined his story with the lives and responsibilities of both previous Karmapas. The previous two Karmapas, very different characters, had both proved themselves charismatic teachers and successful institution builders.

The man who would latterly become known as the First Karmapa, Düsum Khyenpa (1110–1193), was born into a powerful family in Kham, in eastern Tibet. He developed his reputation as one of the three primary students of the famous monk and yogi Gampopa (1079–1153), who was, in turn, one of Milarepa's most famous students. Düsum Khyenpa was known for several things, primarily for his mastery of yoga, but also for his distinctive black hat and his stories about his past, present, and future lives. It was his purported ability to remember his past lives and speak of his concurrent and future emanations that earned him the moniker Düsum Khyenpa, which means "knower of the three times."[16] Düsum Khyenpa founded three monasteries during his long life: Kampo Nenang in southern Kham, Karma in northern Kham, and late in his life, Tsurpu Monastery in central Tibet, a day's journey from the sacred city of Lhasa.

His successor, the first of the lineage to be known in his lifetime as "the Karmapa," was also born in Kham to another powerful family. When he was in his teens, he was recognized as an emanation of Düsum Khyenpa by Düsum Khyenpa's grandstudent Pomdrakpa (1170–1249), and throughout the rest of his life he promoted his connection with Düsum Khyenpa. It was through his restoration of Düsum Khyenpa's Karma Monastery that he was given the name Karma-pa, the "one from Karma." Later in life he also became known as Karma Pakshi. The second part of this name is a derivation of the

Mongolian word for a religious adept, *bagshi*, and given when he was invited to the court of a young Mongol prince named Qubilai Khan (1215–1294).

Rangjung Dorje's connection with his Karmapa predecessors, these not-quite-others, was complex; throughout his personal writing, he both accepts his identity as their rebirth and adopts a deferential position toward them. His complicated relationship with the two previous Karmapas plays itself out through the many biographical writings he produces, in which he intertwines all three of their lives by using translife narratives while still deferring to them. Despite the complexity of this relationship, readers of his writing are left in little doubt about his commitment to the Karmapa reincarnation lineage. In his writing, he does much to establish the paradigm for a reincarnation lineage. He establishes protocols for the recognition of future Karmapas and goes some way to resolving their complicated relationship with Karma Pakshi's family, who were left in control of his monasteries. He dedicates much ink to justifying the Karmapas' continuing presence in the world, repeatedly arguing through narrative and logic that the purpose of their being is to facilitate the expression and realization of mahāmudrā. He also does much to argue for the conceptual framework of recognized reincarnates; he explains the differences between rebirths, emanations, and manifestations, and clarifies how they can sometimes be the same thing.[17]

Given all these intersecting responsibilities and priorities, Rangjung Dorje's time in the twin capitals of Xanadu and Dadu presented him with a dilemma. It was clear to him and his followers that developing a relationship with the emperor and the court would aid the survival of all the lineages he treasured and grant him influence and power within Tibet. But after training all his life to endure hardship impartially and basing much of his self-worth on his ability to withstand it, how could he endure luxury? For a "mountain yogi like him,"[18] indulgence was more dangerous than deprivation. Like the poem that opens this introduction suggests, he was living in places in which external visions could seduce all but the most mindful of yogis, cause them to lose the path and wander in ignorance, and fall off "the cliffs of depravity."

In the end, Rangjung Dorje determined to leave the capitals by any means necessary, including death and rebirth. He finished telling his life story to his attendant, Könchok Chungne (thirteenth century), set his affairs in order, and, as the narrator of his final hours described it, "left for a pure land,"[19] or died. As his narrators describe it, his determination to continue his inner journey and help others on theirs had proved more important to him than his journey to the center of the Mongol Empire.

Rangjung Dorje's Life and Times

Unlike most life stories, however, Rangjung Dorje's story did not end with his death. His voluminous writings and the Karmapa reincarnation lineage have continued his story for centuries after his life.

It is his writings that provide us with the best access into his world, or at least the version of his world that he wanted to preserve. Compared to many of his contemporaries, and even later Karmapas and other hierarchs, he wrote a lot. Many works are attributed to him, and many of these works use enough similar words, imagery, ideas, and sentence constructions to suggest that they were composed by the same person. What is more, they refer to events and people that lived at the same time as Rangjung Dorje. It would have taken a supernatural effort to fake most of these works, and, given the lack of any evidence to the contrary, we can attribute most of them to the historical personage known as Rangjung Dorje.

In the early 2000s, many of the works attributed to Rangjung Dorje were collated into a new version of his Collected Works, which is by far the most comprehensive collection of his writings.[20] This collection includes twelve volumes of his writing and a further four volumes of commentaries on his works. These volumes include writings on a wide range of topics that were composed throughout his life. The earliest compositions attributed to him insist in their colophons that they were composed when he was five years old. They are not, however, written in the same style as his later works, and it is more than likely that they represent other people's literary renderings of his oral pronouncements. His last compositions are dated to the year he died, a full fifty years later.

During this long period, he wrote in a variety of culturally prescribed genres. But his relationship to these generic forms of his cultural inheritance is playful and sometimes transformative rather than prescribed.

The genres of his writing in which the most details of his life are described are his songs, autobiographies, and the less formal of his letters. He referred to the songs he wrote as *lu*, and those who transcribed these songs used the honorific counterpart to this word, *gur*. These words, *lu* and *gur*, were the simple words used to refer to songs during his time, but after Marpa and Milarepa's lives, the terms were slowly becoming associated with the songs of yogis. Many songs are attributed to Marpa's gurus and to other mahāsiddhas. The songs they sang were most generally in the Indian (perhaps even more specifically eastern Indian) genres of dohā and a specific type of gitī or song called *vajra-gitī*, or vajra songs. From among the singing mahāsiddhas, Rangjung Dorje expressed a particular admiration and connection with Saraha, a semimythical figure to whom three collections of dohā were attributed.[21] Rangjung Dorje composed outlines and commentaries of these texts,[22] but did not compose dohās himself. Instead, he followed the tradition of Milarepa, who had become renowned as a great singer of Tibetan songs about mahāmudrā and his life as a yogi more generally. Milarepa's songs adapted traditional Tibetan folk-song formats to the expression of yogic experience. These Tibetan versions of yogi songs were longer than the Indian songs and tended to include more repetitions, alliteration, and tonal wordplay than their Indian predecessors.

Rangjung Dorje's Collected Works includes two collections of gur, which together consist of 138 songs. A separate manuscript of a song collection of his is also extant, but it does not include any extra songs.[23] These songs map his internal journey through life as he develops his yogic abilities and comes to understand mahāmudrā. In his early songs, he describes his doubts and shortcomings and his determination to fulfill his teachers' wishes. Later, as he enters longer, solo retreats in the mountains, they shift to describing his unmitigated relationship with the world around him and his growing understanding of its illusion-like nature. Eventually, the song collections include his instructions for students and his despair at the political and social corruption he sees around him. Most of the songs also include some reference to retreat; words such as "mountain hermitage"[24] and "isolation"[25] are used just as much as words associated with his yogic practices and standard tantric Buddhist terms such as "guru" and "mahāmudrā."[26]

Many of the songs are transcriptions of live performances at tantric feasts, or *gaṇacakras*.[27] As such, they record the spoken word in a way that is unusual in premodern Tibetan literature. They are followed by colophons that state when, where, and for whom he performed. For those following the arc of his life, these colophons act as something like GPS markers that can be used to pinpoint his location in time and place. As the songs are unpolished and direct, they also offer an alternative perspective to his more polished and otherworldly focused autobiographies.

There are two sets of shorter autobiographies in his Collected Works, both of which are filled out by shorter biographical pieces written by his contemporaries. These works were all written in the genre of Tibetan life-writing called "liberation stories." Their translife nature, however, demanded that this genre be altered to accommodate his multilife identity.[28]

The first of these collections is called *The Liberation Story of the Great Rangjung Dorje*.[29] It is a collection of several shorter texts: (1) *Liberation Story of Rangjung Dorje's Past Lives*,[30] (2) *Liberation Story of the In-Between State*,[31] and (3) a short unnamed section that was not written by him and contains a brief survey of his other present emanations and early visions.[32] This collection of autobiographical and biographical writing covers the time from his death as the Second Karmapa until he composed the first of his songs in retreat near Tsurpu Monastery as a preteen.

The second autobiographical text in the collection is called the *Verse Liberation Story of Rangjung Dorje*.[33] It too contains three parts. Part one is an autobiography he composed at Dechen Teng Hermitage, near Tsurpu Monastery, in 1324, when he was forty-one years old.[34] Part two is an autobiography that he composed (and probably dictated to a scribe) in Dadu in 1339, the year before his death.[35] Part three of this composition was composed after his death by his attendant Künga Özer at the request of a Mongolian minister named Beng-ge.[36]

The autobiographical sections within these compositions connect the external world in which Rangjung Dorje lived to his inner world. They allude to some historical events—particularly natural disasters and skirmishes—but they focus on his inner, intensely visionary experiences. They suggest the life of a hermit who was unhappy in highly populated settings and reluctant to come down from the hills.

The fact that Rangjung Dorje chose to write down all his experiences suggests a need to have his personal journey recognized, however. And the primary reason he gives for seeking this recognition is the establishment of the Karmapa reincarnation lineage. In the pursuit of this recognition, he not only dedicated ink to his own life story but also to retelling and reorganizing the biographies of his lineal predecessors. His rewriting of the early Kagyüpas' stories is a precursor to the Golden Rosary tradition of telling the life stories of lineage members,[37] and his retelling of the Buddha's past-life stories, *Birth Stories of the Teacher*, became his most well-known work in premodern Tibet. *Birth Stories of the Teacher* was carved into wood blocks, and images from it were painted on the walls of large temples.[38]

Not all of Rangjung Dorje's compositions were poetic compositions, autobiographies, or even biographical writings. More than half of the volumes in his Collected Works are filled with his commentarial writings. These commentaries cover an impressive array of topics—from more traditional commentaries on key texts within the Indian Buddhist canon, such as the Five Texts of Maitreya and key tantric texts, to works on astrology, works on extracting essences from plants, and works that describe the performance of various rituals. The other text for which he is most remembered—apart from the *Birth Stories of the Teacher*—is a detailed outline of his worldview, the *Profound Inner Principles*.[39] This work brought together the knowledge Rangjung Dorje had accrued through his education in both the sūtras and the tantras to describe the subtle body's formation, mode of being, and usefulness in yogic practice. Within this work and his other commentaries, he systemized the practices and worldviews of the fledgling Karma Kagyü tradition, creating a system of thought and practice that is still followed today.

Along with this literary systemization of the Karma Kagyü tradition, he also did much to clarify and organize the Karmapa tradition and institution, which, like many of the texts he wrote, survives to this day and provides a living focus around which the lineage coheres. It was not an easy task. When Rangjung Dorje was recognized as Karma Pakshi's rebirth, it was unclear just what that meant and whether the tradition would continue after Rangjung Dorje's lifetime. But by the end of his life, Rangjung Dorje had established a system for the Karmapas' continuance. This system allowed it not only to survive but to thrive and to start to be replicated across the Tibetan Plateau and beyond.

Rangjung Dorje's contribution to the development and spread of reincarnation lineages is difficult to overestimate. He was the first to be recognized as the third in a reincarnation lineage during his lifetime. Until this point, individuals had claimed to be a rebirth or emanation of another being rather than claiming to be part of an ongoing tradition. His synchronic recognition at a young age allowed for the lineage's institutionalization.

But in order to establish the "Black Crown lineage" as an ongoing institution, he had to synthesize several of its disparate precedents. Primary among these was the conceptual dissonance about the linked but separate ideas of emanation and manifestation, on the one hand, and rebirth, on the other. The first two Karmapas had claimed to be both rebirths and manifestations/emanations of other beings in their writing. Rangjung Dorje's guru Orgyenpa had only called him Karma Pakshi's "rebirth."[40] If he was a rebirth of an emanation, did that make him another emanation? Rather than writing a thesis on the nature of reincarnation, he explained their connections through the telling of previous-life stories.

The tradition of remembering and telling the stories of previous lives had a long history within Buddhism. It included some traditions that spoke of past lives and others that developed the idea of multiple manifestations. Some of the oldest Buddhist stories are the *jātaka* tales,[41] which tell the stories of the Buddha's previous lives and which Rangjung Dorje became well known for retelling. The tradition of telling tales of past lives was also enthusiastically pursued by several different Tibetan groups. These groups included the elite students closest to Gampopa, which included Düsum Khyenpa. Perhaps inspired by Gampopa's own reminiscences about his previous life as Candraprabha Kumāra,[42] the person to whom the Buddha entrusted the *King of Samādhi Sūtra*, Gampopa's students seemed to have developed their own tradition of telling past-life tales. As stated earlier, Düsum Khyenpa received his moniker after telling many tales about his past lives and about his present and future emanations. But he was not the only student of Gampopa to receive this moniker. It was also assigned to another of Gampopa's close students, Pakmodrupa Dorje Gyelpo (1110–1170), whose collection of birth stories, like Düsum Khyenpa's collection, is extant.[43]

Another group that was involved in past-life storytelling in the centuries leading up to Rangjung Dorje's life were the Nyingma proponents of the treasure texts. The tradition of the treasure texts involved compositions that were said to have been hidden during the time of the Tibetan Empire (sixth to ninth century), mostly by the students of Padmasambhava, and then rediscovered by these students' reincarnations centuries later.[44] The style of these past-life stories are different than those told by Gampopa's students about their past lives. Their primary purpose was not the proliferation of stories but rather to highlight their memories of lives that linked them with Padmasambhava. Rangjung Dorje saw himself as part of the treasure text movement as well as a Kagyü teacher and claimed to have been a student of Padmasambhava named Gyelwa Chokyang (eighth century).[45]

Along with rebirth stories, stories about reincarnation, emanations, and manifestations also had a long history in Tibet. At some point during the time of the Tibetan Empire, its kings started to be seen as emanations of important bodhisattvas. A century after the empire's fall, during the later propagation of Buddhism in the tenth century, three of Tibet's early kings were reimagined as emanations of bodhisattvas. Songtsen Gampo (seventh century), who unified Tibet, was reimagined as Avalokiteśvara, his great-grandson Trisong Detsen (eighth century) as Mañjuśrī, and their descendant Relpachen (ninth century) as Vajrapāṇi.

The tradition of recognizing three related figures as the emanations of these three bodhisattvas spread and took particular hold in the Kadam tradition. Three of Atiśa's main disciples—Dromtön (1004–1064), Ngok Lekpa Sherap (1059–1109; the founder of Sangpu Neutok Monastery), and Khutön Tsöndru Yungdrung (1011–1075)—were associated with Avalokiteśvara, Mañjuśrī, and Vajrapāṇi, respectively. So too were Dromtön's three main disciples: Zhönnu Gyeltsen (1031–1106) was believed to be an emanation of Avalokiteśvara, Potowa Rinchen Sel (1027–1105) an emanation of Mañjuśrī, and Tsültrim Bar (1038–1103) an emanation of Vajrapāṇi.[46]

The Karmapas, too, became associated with emanation traditions early in their collective history. During his lifetime, Düsum Khyenpa's controversial friend Lama Zhang (1123–1193) claimed that Düsum Khyenpa was an emanation of the future buddha Siṃha, who tradition holds will be the sixth buddha of this age after his teachers Śākyamuni and the fifth buddha, the future buddha Maitreya.[47] This connection was maintained in later Karmapa lineage narratives, but it was not the only emanation lineage associated with the Karmapas. Both the First and Second Karmapas also proclaimed that they had strong connections with the bodhisattva Avalokiteśvara.

In his systemization of the tradition, Rangjung Dorje connected the idea of rebirth and reincarnation by arguing that he and his predecessors were becoming the deities that they practiced, particularly Avalokiteśvara, and, therefore, were developing the ability to manifest in different places. In the meantime, they continued to be reborn.

Not only did he have to coordinate these divergent, prismatic narratives, but he also had to coordinate the disparate lists of other lives provided by the first three Karmapas.[48] Rangjung Dorje's approach to this disparity was inclusive; given the vast expanses of space and time and the numbers of emanations that it was possible for bodhisattvas to create, all of these emanations were possibilities. Nevertheless, it was his list of previous rebirths that were taken up in the later tradition. Perhaps part of the reason for its acceptance was the social and political strategy that was implicit within it. In this list he associates himself with all of Tibet's significant traditions and with all forms of Buddhist life. He is a monk, a lay tantrika, and a yogi. He lives in pure and impure realms. And he has links to Tibetan and Indian royalty, and, importantly, to his major heroes: Buddha, Saraha, and Padmasambhava.

Not only did Rangjung Dorje set up and systemize the narratives and some of the traditions that would come to be associated with the Karmapas' reincarnation lineage, he also repeated the tropes of the name "Karmapa," the wearing of a black hat and the associations with the Karmapas' monasteries that would come to characterize the tradition. Entrenching these associations and their story lines ensured that his successors would continue to be found and that the Karmapas would eventually come to control all of the properties associated with the broader Karma Kagyü lineage. In the process, he coincidently developed a model for reincarnation lineages that could be copied more broadly.

A Life Preserved in Stories and Songs

Rangjung Dorje's texts were preserved and reprinted purposely by his lineal descendants. Their preservation was also aided by Tibet's dry environment and by accidents of history. These texts provide a window into the world in which he lived, and perhaps even—if indeed it is as he appears, and he wrote honestly—into his thoughts about this world. But in approaching these texts and trying to understand his life, we must acknowledge that our view is obscured and fragmentary. Rangjung Dorje lived his life more than seven hunded years ago, and there are not a variety of sources that we can triangulate to create a sense of his life.

To reconstruct his life and times, we have to rely primarily on his preserved writings. Like most of the sources that have been preserved from his time, they exist because he was considered a "great man" (or perhaps "master"). This selected preservation of texts warps our perspective of Tibetan history generally and especially his life and times. These texts must, therefore, be engaged with literarily and historically. They need to be read for their context and form as well as their content. To remember the form of the works is to remember the literary context and conventions according to which they were composed. To remember their context is to acknowledge that Rangjung Dorje lived in a distant time and culture, to respect this fact, and to approach their contents in relation to this world. To merely extract elements from these texts that fit with contemporary paradigms such as political history or philosophical problems ignores the composers' priorities and does the texts and those reading his story a disservice.

Rangjung Dorje lived in a time and place that stood at the intersection of several worlds. He inherited the religious narratives of his lineage, which understood itself to represent an amalgam of cultures that were developed in India and transmitted to Tibet. Along with this Indo-Tibetan perspective, he was brought up to see the world through the local cultures and societies in which he was raised and with a broader Tibetan heritage.

These three traditions promoted common as well as divergent elements. Rangjung Dorje's experience of the world as he recorded it included interactions with many nonhuman spirits, most of which were Tibetan spirits that lived in specific sites, such as Nyenchen Tanglha and Jomo Gangkar, who were both associated with the mountain range to the northwest and west of Tsurpu, and Rongsten Khawa Karpo, who was associated with Khawa Karpo Mountain on the eastern edge of the Tibetan Plateau.

These cultures he inherited were embedded in the landscape and the areas through which he moved, and as he traveled, he reflected on events that had unfolded in these spaces long before his time. Both the spaces themselves and the long-lived gods of the Plateau acted as a way to connect him to these past events.

The past he evokes is understood through Tibet's religious traditions. His writing assumes knowledge of their narratives of the fall of the empire and the "rekindling" of Buddhism in Tibet. This rekindling saw not only the introduction of new tantric traditions from India, including the Kagyü tradition, but also the reformulation of the "old ones," or the Nyingma Buddhist tradition.

As Rangjung Dorje presents it, this idyllic proliferation of various traditions was threatened by the Mongols when they invaded the country in the late 1230s. While they did not colonize the region directly, and while they paid homage to the Tibetans' religious prowess, their rule of the Tibetan Plateau was, ultimately, like the rule of all empires, focused on strategy and extraction. As a back door to central Asia, Tibet was strategically important to them; although this importance was tempered somewhat by its high altitudes and inaccessibility. Tibet was not as rich in easily extractable natural resources and accumulated wealth as many of the other realms they conquered, but Tibet did nurture a knowledge economy that traded in a commodity in which the Mongols were very interested, esoteric powers.

Mongol rule in Tibet (1230s–1368) reorganized its politics and, to a lesser extent, its society, religion, and culture. Although it came close to collapsing several times, the basis of this rule was a relationship between the Mongol Great Khans and the Sakya tradition. The Sakya established preeminence in Tibet after Sakya Paṇḍita

(1182–1251), a religious hierarch and scion of the aristocratic Khön family, traveled to the Mongol prince Köten's (thirteenth century) court in 1246. This relationship was solidified when his nephew Chögyel Pakpa (1235–1280) became the Great Khan Qubilai's guru. Chögyel Pakpa performed the three roles of preceptor to the Mongol court, "Great Lord" of Tibet, and abbot of Sakya,[49] but these roles were later split between various members of the Sakya tradition, usually from the Khön family.

Along with this alignment, Mongol princes and lesser Khans developed and sustained relationships with other Tibetan religious hierarchs. Eventually, these relationships were formalized into a system of thirteen estates in central Tibet, all of which were associated with monasteries, and each of the leaders of these estates could engage with the Mongol court directly. The relative power of these centers changed with the profile of these seats' associated princes and the charisma of their religious adepts. The Mongols collected religious adepts, or bagshis, from all over their empire,[50] and they played a prominent role at the Mongol court. Tibetan bagshis were particularly prized for their abilities in extending life, repelling enemies, and predicting and averting disasters. For a variety of reasons—the prospect of disease, the intricacies and volatility of Mongol politics, attachment to Tibet, or a wish to conduct retreats—many of those who were invited did not go. But those who did were able to accrue power, wealth, and, as Leonard van der Kuijp has shown, many of the cultural and religious treasures for which Tibet became renowned.[51]

Rangjung Dorje's relationship with the Mongol court was both general and specific. The Mongol Empire formed the political backdrop for his life; it fought a war in his home region when he was a child, its indiscriminate rule exaggerated famines and displacement as he was growing up, and it forced him to live the last years of his life at its court. But through his status as Karma Pakshi's rebirth, he was understood to have a complicated personal relationship with some of the most important members of the Mongol court too. Karma Pakshi had fallen out with Qubilai Khan before the latter took Chögyel Pakpa as his guru and became Great Khan in 1260.[52] Rangjung Dorje's relationship with the Mongols was influenced, therefore, by his personal, translife history.

The later versions of Rangjung Dorje's life story miss much of this political context. Rather than context, many of them focus on biographical patterns that reinforce the Karmapa institution. A full survey of all these texts would not be appropriate here,[53] but it is worth noting two texts that diverge from this general paradigmatic tendency that use nonextant sources to create detailed descriptions of his life. The first of these is included within Tsuklak Trengwa's *Feast for Scholars: A Dharma History*.[54] Tsuklak Trengwa (1504–1566) was a renowned scholar who was the regent between the death of the Eighth Karmapa and the ascension of the Ninth. During his lifetime, the Karma Kagyü held the ascendency in central and eastern Tibet by enjoying a close relationship with its Tsang rulers. Tsuklak Trengwa's version of Rangjung Dorje's life presents an attempt to synthesize all available divergent stories about his life and establish the preeminence of the Karmapas more generally. By contrast, the biography of Rangjung Dorje included within the *Rosary of Clearly Reflected Crystal Moons*, which was composed by Situ Paṇchen Chökyi Jungne (1700–1774) and Belo (eighteenth century)[55] takes a much more inclusive approach to his story. It is an extraordinary piece of premodern scholarship that maintains the narrative tensions between its sources and demonstrates well the diversity of approaches to life-writing in the Tibetan tradition.

Part one of the present work draws on Rangjung Dorje's autobiographies and songs, Tsuklak Trengwa's and Situ Paṇchen's biographies, and other sources to continue the tradition of retelling Rangjung Dorje's life story. Like most premodern Tibetan biographies, it tells Rangjung Dorje's story by dedicating sections to his birth, education, retreats, teaching career, and death. Throughout every stage of Rangjung Dorje's life, several themes resound. One is his continued negotiation with his status as a reincarnate and a Karmapa, a negotiation that is made more complicated by his lowly social status prior to his recognition. Another is the backdrop of political, economic, and environmental unrest on the Tibetan Plateau, where people are experiencing war, plagues, and famines. Yet another is his dedication to the development of the mahāmudrā view and his attempts to systemize the teachings he received so that others can access them more easily.

If you read his life story as a singularity, the ending is rather sad. As the dislike he had for Xanadu suggests, he had become increasingly captive to the wishes of its secular rulers. The young monk from a poor background acquired an education and pursued the religious path only to die a virtual prisoner in a faraway land. Contrarily, if you read his life story as one episode in a multilife tale, his death in Xanadu and rebirth in Kongpo is a great escape.

The various parts of Rangjung Dorje's life and works are then re-presented through translations of some of his writings in part two of the book. These writings represent another way that Rangjung Dorje's life has continued past his death in Xanadu. The selection chosen includes samples from several of the genres in which he wrote, with a concentration on his life stories and songs. It does not include any of his ritual texts or extracts from the *Profound Inner Principles,* as tradition dictates that these materials should only be read and engaged with after one has received the proper empowerments from the lineage. Many of these works have already been translated and can be accessed elsewhere.[56] Most of the works included in this text, by contrast, are not readily available to non-specialists. Hopefully, this sample will encourage others to translate more of Rangjung Dorje's Collected Works and thus continue his seven-hundred-year conversation with his readers.

The Biography

CHAPTER 1

Birth

RANGJUNG DORJE'S biographies usually begin with a death. His biological becoming—parents, conception, birth, first years—is given second billing to the interlife journey of consciousness that led to his birth. His memory and articulation of this journey played a crucial role in his recognition as Karma Pakshi's rebirth, and it is, therefore, given particular prominence in almost all retellings of his story.

Many later biographies of reincarnates also highlight the continuity of consciousness between dying gurus and their rebirths, but few focus on the spiritual lineage as much as Rangjung Dorje's story. Equally, few life stories are as dismissive of the protagonist's family lineage as Rangjung Dorje's tale is. Rangjung Dorje was both recognized as Karma Pakshi's rebirth at a young age and born a socially unimportant person. The combination makes for a strange start to his story.

Telling the story of his interlife journey, furthermore, appears to have played a key part in Rangjung Dorje's life. It was not a tale that he told as an adult that was latterly inserted into his story. It was a tale he told and identified with while growing up. His story of his journey between lives has been preserved twice in his writing, in both the *Liberation Story of the In-Between State* and the *Verse Liberation Story*. He also hints at it in his songs.

The extant version of the *Liberation Story of the In-Between State*, a story he claims elsewhere to have dictated to a kindly abbot, does not read like a Rangjung Dorje composition. It has neither the directness nor clarity of expression that is typical of his style, nor does it abide by the same culturally prescribed insistence on spiritual humility that is evident in the *Verse Liberation Story*, his songs, and his letters. It does, however, have some elements in common with a song in his collection that he was said to have composed at a young age.[57] This commonality suggests that perhaps the *Liberation Story of the In-Between State* and this song were scribed and at least partially composed by other people invested in the boy's future.

It is unlikely that these scribes were his parents because, by all accounts, his parents were illiterate. Instead, there appears to have been a community investment in this story. This community investment is also evidenced by the number of times his story was reproduced. It was conserved as an individual text, reproduced in full within omnibus lineage histories, and quoted from extensively elsewhere. The community investment in Rangjung Dorje's recognition is also evidenced by the number of other stories about his childhood that are conserved. Community members told Orgyenpa, his biographer, and later Karma Kagyü biographers stories of his play habits and his parents' antics. These stories are not as prevalent in the retellings of Düsum Khyenpa's and Karma Pakshi's lives.[58] The process of his recognition as a reincarnate spurred the communal remembering of his childhood. The result of this investment is the preservation of more stories about Rangjung Dorje's childhood than most other Tibetan children in premodern history, particularly those from his social class.

Rangjung Dorje is defensive about the inclusion of his interlife and childhood memories in the autobiography he wrote as an adult, the *Verse Liberation Story*.[59] His urge to justify its inclusion may have been caused by its patchy precedents in Tibetan culture and this same culture's insistence on precedents. Parts of the story had clear precedents, but before he told this tale, no other Tibetan had narrated their entire interlife journey from illness, through death, the in-between state, conception, the womb, birth, childhood, and recognition. The exploratory nature of the stories is, furthermore, demonstrated by the way that they do not always add up; the various retellings of this early period of his life sometimes contradict each other and at other times skip over important details. He does not, he claims, expect to be believed, but he still feels he has a duty to note down his memories. He also acknowledges that telling his tale is pushing cultural boundaries.

Although it is easy to see these boundaries as fixed in a society as socially conservative as medieval Tibet, every enactment of social or literary norms also represents a renegotiation with these traditions. As others have noted, there was a symbiosis between the way that life stories were composed in Tibet and the way that lives were lived.[60] If members of an audience held any aspiration to live their lives like the protagonists of the stories to which they listened, they would follow the biographical maps that these stories presented. As a result, when they came to tell their own stories, they would follow a similar pattern. Nevertheless, as no two lives were the same, adjustments had to be made to the socially and religiously prescribed progression. All lives and all life stories represented a negotiation between the person, story forms, and their lived and reading communities.

Rangjung Dorje's status as an outsider and a reincarnate made it necessary for him to negotiate with the traditions he inherited, and he describes this negotiation in his life story, particularly in its early stages. In these parts of his autobiography, he makes claims to traditional authority by relying on biographical tradition. His storytelling repeats, for example, many of the biographical and literary tropes of the first two Karmapas' life stories, and he adheres to and promotes most of the traditions of the broader Kagyü lineage. The setting of these narratives also draws on tradition. His story takes place in a landscape steeped in the cultural, social, political, and religious history of his people. He walks the same paths that Padmasambhava, Milarepa, and other cultural heroes walked. He meets the spirits tamed by Padmasambhava. Even his visions are set within the cultural and religious maps of the Buddhist and Tibetan traditions: Abhidharma cosmography and Vajrayāna mandalas.

As well as following many of these traditions, however, he also quietly subverted them. He had to. He was a fringe dweller claiming to be the rebirth of a religiously and socially highly ranked person. There were precedents within his society for people to rise socially through the ranks of monasteries, armies, and traders, but not in the way he did it. His transformation depended on charisma and on his ability to be believed. His story not only had to be useful, but it also had to contain some innovation and justify this innovation to a skeptical audience. As we shall see, he adopted a multiplicity of strategies to convince them.

Life before Death

In Rangjung Dorje's own version of his life story, he is a bit vague about exactly when Karma Pakshi died.[61] In the *Liberation Story of the In-Between State*, he puts it this way, speaking in the first person.

> In the first month of the Sheep Year [1283], I felt a little uncomfortable in my elements. At that time, I was the one known famously as the Karmapa [Karma Pakshi], and I took this as a sign that I should depart for another pure land [i.e., die].[62]

The date given here, the first month of the Sheep Year, is exactly one year before Rangjung Dorje was born. Tibetan tradition dictates that fetuses spend a year in the womb.[63] This passage describes the process of death, but it does not say how long it took. If it was not instant, it implies that the gap between the two Karmapas was not long enough for the normal processes of rebirth to take place. Later biographers of the Karmapas are either more adamant that there was a year gap between Karma Pakshi's death and Rangjung Dorje's birth or they acknowledge an overlap between their existences and offer various excuses for the overlap.

After Rangjung Dorje's lifetime, the processes for finding a new Karmapa became more expected and established. Most other reincarnation lineages have followed this model. Unless a reincarnation lineage is explicitly associated with an awakened being that produces multiple manifestations, there is a gap of at least a year between their reincarnations. This tradition tends more toward the narratives associated with rebirth than manifestation. The idea of singular, successive rebirths provided nonfamilial institutions like monasteries with a dependable method of intergenerational property transfer; it makes sense, therefore, that these rebirth lineages became more prominent and institutionalized than unpredictable manifestations. But at this stage, when the tradition was in the process of being established, the rules had not quite been settled, and ambiguities around consciousness transferal were still allowed.

The ambiguity over the gap between the Second and Third Karmapas' lives is mirrored in the divergent stories Rangjung Dorje tells (or Rangjung Dorje and the person to whom he narrated the *Liberation Story of the In-Between State* tell) about his consciousness's journey out of Karma Pakshi's body. The *Liberation Story of the In-Between State* says he took a direct route.

> I performed inconceivable magic.[64] I flew into the sky in a rainbow body, traveling upward toward the god realms. On arrival, I was greeted with divine music and saw many

> other inconceivable things, divine parasols and the like. As I watched, bodhisattvas like Maitreya performed awakened deeds. They cultivated immeasurable compassion for beings, trained without respite, and remained in a state in which nothing was generated and nothing stopped.[65]

The Karmapa, this story suggests, had ascended to Tuṣita, the home of Maitreya and all the world's future buddhas. It makes sense—narratively speaking—that this is the heaven to which the Karmapa's consciousness travels between lives. According to the narrative traditions that already existed about the first two Karmapas, they were going to become the future buddha Siṃha, and Tuṣita was the place in which all future buddhas are said to prepare for the final awakening.

Tuṣita is also the departure point for the most well-known and authoritative interlife narrative: the story of Buddha Śākyamuni's descent to earth.[66] This story is outlined in the *Sūtra of This Fortunate Eon*, the sūtra in which the story about Siṃha is told. It is also a sūtra with which Rangjung Dorje repeatedly expressed a particular connection. The *Sūtra of This Fortunate Eon* tells the life stories of "the thousand buddhas of this fortunate era"—including Śākyamuni, Maitreya, and Siṃha—as they prepare for their final lives as "supreme created bodies."[67] In the sūtra, each buddha trains his successor and then passes the leadership of Tuṣita onto them as they descend to earth. Śākyamuni trained there for eons with Kāśyapa, the buddha that came to earth before him, and he then trained Maitreya, who succeeded him.

As Lama Zhang had already linked the Karmapas with Siṃha, whom the *Sūtra of This Fortunate Eon* says will inherit Tuṣita from Maitreya, the Karmapas multibodied narrative has to include an emanation living in Tuṣita and training with Maitreya. After Lama Zhang introduced the idea, Karma Pakshi developed on it. He called the Karmapa emanation living in Tuṣita Lodrö Rinchen, a long-lived god who abides steadfastly at Maitreya's side.[68]

Rather than take the direct route to Tuṣita, the *Verse Liberation Story* suggests that the Karmapa's in-between consciousness took a detour. After it left Karma Pakshi's body at Tsurpu Monastery, it reads, it traveled down the valley to the town of Tölung Partsang, where it entered the body of a recently deceased child.[69] Rangjung Dorje only writes of this event in passing, noting that he told Orgyenpa about it when he was a child. Sending one's consciousness into another's body was famously part of earlier Kagyü teachers' biographical traditions, so later biographers latched onto this story, told it in increasingly more detail, and it became quite well known. The version of the Karmapas' story that was inserted into the *Red Annals*, for example, contains the shortest version of the story.

> When Karma Pakshi's body was about to be cremated, he looked out on all his suffering students in Tsurpu's lands and fell into a swoon of intense compassion. After regaining his senses, he noticed the faultless corpse of a three-year-old child in Tölung Partsang and decided to "enter the residence." After the consciousness entered the corpse, the child opened his eyes and looked around. The dead child's mother was disturbed by her dead child's eye movement and stabbed him in the eyes with a needle. The Karmapa consciousness decided it would not be able to help beings without eyes and left the corpse to look for another. The only corpse he saw was an insect being carried by a bird to a house in the north. When he could not find another corpse, he directed his consciousness to Tuṣita.[70]

Directing consciousness at the moment of death is one of the six dharmas of Nāropā. The most common form of this practice these days is called *powa*.[71] It involves the transference of a dying person's consciousness to a Buddhist pure land, and it can be performed either by a practitioner or by a guru that leads them to their final destination.[72] The liberation stories of early Kagyü yogis, however, tell stories of another form of this yoga that was said to have been lost, the "entrance into a dwelling or town," also called the "entrance into another's body."[73]

The most famous version of this story is found in Marpa's liberation story. In his story, the practice is said to have disappeared from Tibet when its lineage holder, his son Darma Dode, used it to transfer his consciousness into a pigeon after dying and flew away to India. In India, the story continues, he retransferred his consciousness into a sixteen-year-old boy's corpse, and within this reanimated corpse later became known as the siddha Tiphupa ("the pigeon one"). Tiphupa was another teacher of Milarepa's student Rechungpa.[74]

After this, the Kagyü tradition maintained, "entrance into another's body" was no longer practiced in Tibet. There were still folk traditions and taboos in Tibet about zombies or "risen corpses" (*rolang*), but being a risen corpse was, generally speaking, not considered to be a good thing.[75] The reaction of the recently deceased child's mother to his resurrection in Tölung Partsang reflects this tradition. She thought her dead son had turned into a rolang and wanted him to lie back down.

Even though this episode describes an unsuccessful attempt at consciousness transferral, it makes sense that the young Rangjung Dorje's audience would have been excited and encouraged by his description of this event. It was a story that connected with the broader traditions with which they were all familiar, and it evoked a spiritual power that could be transferred from life to life. But it was also only one part of his intriguing and fascinating interlife journey.

After his detour in Tölung Partsang, the next place the in-between consciousness visited was Tuṣita.

A Sojourn in Tuṣita

The *Verse Liberation Story* may only mention the Karmapa consciousness's stay in Tuṣita in passing, but the majority of the *Liberation Story of the In-Between State* is dedicated to it. It describes the consciousness arriving in the sacred realm and spending time with Maitreya and his entourage. But when it develops a routine in this heaven, a group of women appear before him to remind him of his other commitments. These earth-guardian *ḍākinīs* represent the land of Tibet,[76] and they come to convince him to take rebirth in their realm. They state their demands upfront. "Take a human rebirth with time and chances," they say, "protect the Buddha's teachings, parent the six [types] of wanderers, the time has come!"[77]

The Karmapa consciousness thinks that he imagines things, so the earth guardians become more insistent. They will not be dissuaded, they tell him, because they represent the land of Tibet itself. They are connected to him, they tell him, and he has made a commitment to return to their soil. They have come to heaven to make sure he keeps his promises.

> We come from the depths of the human world.
> We are the earth guardians who protect the environment.
> We do not admonish you for our own purposes, human.
> We admonish you on behalf of the six [types] of
> wanderers.[78]

After stating their purpose, they introduce themselves individually. These introductions, offered in order, serve to position each guardian around the Tibetan Plateau, but particularly in its south and center. In presenting themselves, the earth guardians are also creating a sacred geography of Tibet. They then offer Lodrö Rinchen, the Karmapa consciousness, their "life forces."[79] In Tibetan society, the life force is something that is handed down from parents to children. It is linked to the idea of one's *la*,[80] which has no direct correlate in the English language but refers to an individual's own "subtle life essence."[81] A person's *la* is located within and without people. It not only connects individuals with their families but also with the environmental features of the places in which they were born and raised and places such as lakes, mountains, or trees.[82] It represents an individual's connection to kith and kin. The earth guardians' offering of their life force to Rangjung Dorje is meant to intensify the connection between him and the places they represent, creating the causes for him to be reborn back on earth. In many ways, they are embodiments of the Tibetan earth itself, asking him to come back. As earth deities, they are also reminiscent of the Indian goddess Bhūmisparśa, who acted as a witness to the Buddha's awakening under the bodhi tree.

Even though the earth guardians state that they represent the entire "human world," the sites associated with them are clustered around the Latö region in southern Tibet, in which Rangjung Dorje is about to be born. The largest group within them is the "twelve stabilizing goddesses,"[83] whom Padmasambhava tamed and made protectors of Buddhism on the Pelmo Tang Plain in Latö.[84] Another group of them is the five sisters of long life,[85] who are associated with Milarepa and the Gaurishankar mountain range, which is in the same region.

After the twenty-five earth guardians present themselves, they summon another set of celestial beings to convince the in-between consciousness to take rebirth. These are the guardians of the four "hidden lands."[86] As Geoff Childs has noted, during Rangjung Dorje's lifetime, the idea of hidden lands was nascent, but the area in which it was becoming most popular was the kingdom of Mangyul Gungtang, on the other side of Latö from the Pelmo Tang Plain. The presence of the guardians of the hidden lands in this story suggests both a precedent for Mangyul Gungtang's stories of hidden lands and a further geographic connection between this story and southern Tibet.

The relationship that Rangjung Dorje begins with the earth-guardian ḍākinīs in this story continues throughout his entire life. He encounters them in most places that he visits, and they act as his teachers and confidantes. They are also the only females with which he has constant interactions. His mother leaves his story soon after he is born, and the few other women in his tale are referred to in aggregate and in passing. All of Rangjung Dorje's close human relationships are with males.

There are a few superhuman male friends in his story too, and one of the most important of these makes his first appearance in the in-between state. He is the only male deity to do so. This being is Black Coat, an emanation of the tantric deity Mahākāla, who, in Rangjung Dorje's story, is in the process of becoming the Karmapas' personal protector.

The introduction of the hidden land guardians and Black Coat into the *In-Between* narrative brings hints of darkness into a vision that was hitherto brightly colored. Tension mounts between Rangjung Dorje and the earth guardians as the deities intensify the pressure on him to take a human rebirth. Finally, after a few more exchanges, he concedes with several conditions. They have to find him the best "type" of parents and grant him an "inconceivable celestial empowerment" into the "maṇḍala of the sixty-two deities of Cakrasaṃvara."[87] The earth guardians agree to do this and follow the empowerment by offering him songs that grant him with exceptional qualities. Then they direct him to his new body. As the *Liberation Story of the In-Between State* describes this guidance:

> Precious, multicolored rainbow roads appeared. They led me to the place where a human body with free time and favor would be formed. The earth guardians said to me, "The body will be formed in fortunate Mangyul Gungtang. The mother is fortunate, noble Yuchungma, who lives in front of sacred Gang Zhurmo Ridge. The father has a house of clear essence on the fortunate Om Plain, in front of Chewagang Ridge in Tsapu. His house is in the lower valley where three upper valleys meet, Tsa lung pu Valley [literally, "Valley where the channels and energies meet"], in Milarepa's birth region. On the south side of this valley is a clear, dark, red mountain. To the north is a glimmering white mountain.[88]

By following the rainbow roads, the Karmapa consciousness descends from Tuṣita to southern Tibet, to the place he was about to be born in the borderlands between Mangyul Gungtang and Latö. This transition is not merely a descent into the ordinary. It is also laden with symbolism that evokes tantric descriptions of human life.

These descriptions are based upon a schema that presents human bodies as the site of subtle energy networks. After conception, which is created by the mother's red energy and the father's white energy, subtle energies called *lung* travel through networks of channels called *tsa* to create subtle bodies. These subtle bodies underpin human growth and the operation of bodily functions and can be manipulated through yoga to bring about insights to tantric practitioners.

Rangjung Dorje's *Profound Inner Principles* includes one of the most well-known descriptions of the subtle bodies and their processes. In this text, he explains how the mother and father's essences continue to abide in the forming human body at either end of the body's most important channel, the central channel, which sits just in front of the spinal column. The central channel is flanked by two other channels, a white channel on the right through which energy travels downward and a red channel on the left through which it travels upward. These two channels connect at the nostril, and ordinary respiration occurs through them.

The geography of Rangjung Dorje's conception site, the place where "a human body with free time and favor would be formed," evokes this subtle body and links it to an external environment. His father's house of "clear essence" sits on the "fortunate Om Plain"[89] in front of Chewagang Ridge in Tsapu. Tsapu means "the upper part of the Tsa Valley." Two other valleys join the Tsa Valley near its base: the Rön Valley and the Gün Valley. The lower Tsa Valley is, therefore, "the river valley where three upper valleys meet." The choice to call it the Tsa *lung* pu Valley in the *Liberation Story of the In-Between State* suggests a link between the juncture of these three valleys and the juncture of the three energy channels within the body.[90]

Rangjung Dorje's mother, the "fortunate, noble Yuchungma" is positioned "in front of the sacred site Gang Zhurmo," a jagged mountain ridge that sits behind the next valley over from Kyidrong Valley.[91] His parents are, therefore, associated with valleys on either side of the same range. What is more, the site of his birth is also framed by red and white mountains, representing the two essences, red and white, that are necessary for conception.[92]

After delivering him to the site between the red and white mountains, the earth guardians take their leave of Rangjung Dorje. As the *Liberation Story of the In-Between State* tells it, they,

> Created a nine-colored rainbow that became intensely saturated and bright. I watched as they ascended the rainbow,

> then I traveled alone down to a crystal palace with a sky-door, four bright white sides, and a dark base. Rainbows danced around me on all sides.[93]

But as he enters the house through a door on the roof, the colors and mood of the story change abruptly. The *Liberation Story of the In-Between State* suggests that he was so overcome by the change that he fainted.

> And as I gradually came around, all was dark, and I felt a heavy weight. I was whirling in a small space. Even remembering it now, I feel like I am spinning in a small space. My perception gradually became clear again. After this, it was as if I was sometimes tossed by waves, sometimes squashed by mountains, sometimes burned by heat, sometimes frozen by the cold. I was confused. There was no air. It was the suffering of the afflictions, and even now when I think of it, the wind rises in my heart.[94]

He repeats the story in the *Verse Liberation Story*.

> I traveled down a path of myriad, intermingled rainbows that led me to somewhere near Nyenam [another village on the other side of the Pelmo Tang Plain]. There was a crystal palace that had a jeweled staircase. I thought, "I should stay here," and it appeared I would, but—*Kye ma!*—the womb's darkness is a dark family lineage. Karma causes wanderers great suffering. Powerless, I lost consciousness and dwelt in afflictions.[95]

These two descriptions of his time in the womb are extraordinary. They fit with the way the entrance into the womb is described in the

Buddhist tradition, both in India and Tibet. In these descriptions, the in-between consciousness thinks it is entering a house and ends up in a womb, which is usually, unlike many Western and New Age traditions, presented as a space of intense suffering. But these traditional descriptions do not describe the journey to the womb in the first person. Speaking about the experience from this perspective is Rangjung Dorje's innovation.[96]

Birth, Again

The *Liberation Story of the In-Between State* does not continue to Rangjung Dorje's birth. It ends with him in the womb. His story only continues in the *Verse Liberation Story*.

> On the eighth day of the first month of the Monkey Year [1283], as the moon waxed, I was born in accordance with [Karma Pakshi's] prophecy near the sacred, exalted one's [*dam pa*] place. I do not remember the pain of birth, but my faculties were not impaired, and my mind did not waver. When I saw the moon, it made me happy. I could speak, but did not, choosing to remain [as silent as] a jewel.[97]

Like the descriptions of his journey between lives, Rangjung Dorje's description of his birth uses symbolism to pack a lot of information into only a few sentences. One of the clearest uses of these symbols is to create a connection between Milarepa, "the sacred, exalted one," and himself. The *Verse Liberation Story* links his conception to Milarepa, insisting that, as Karma Pakshi, he had seen a vision of "the yogi Milarepa standing in the center of Latö's Pelmo Tang Plain."[98] He held a skull full of nectar in his hand, and he said: "Emanate and perform activities."[99] Both this text and the *Liberation Story of the In-Between State* assert that he was born near Milarepa's home.

This link with Milarepa's homeland is supported by a continuing local tradition in the small valley of Ladeb in this region, which claims that Rangjung Dorje was born there. Ladeb sits at the base of Gang Zhurmo Ridge, which is mentioned in the *Liberation Story of the In-Between State*. This site later became a sacred site associated with the treasure revealer Garwang Dorje (1640–1685) and is right next to the present-day border of China and Nepal.[100] Ladeb is in a side valley of the larger Kyidrong Valley, and it is here that the *Liberation Story of the In-Between State* locates his father and claims Milarepa was born and raised.[101]

The *Verse Liberation Story* also says, however, that Milarepa called him "to near Nyenam," which is on the other side of the Pelmo Tang Plain. And there is another tradition that says Rangjung Dorje was indeed born a few hundred kilometers away from Kyidrong, on the other side of the Pelmo Tang Plain, in the town of Dingri. Both Tsuklak Trengwa and Situ Paṇchen make this claim. In their reading of the source material, the term *dam pa* in Rangjung Dorje's statement that he was born "near the sacred, exalted one's [*dam pa*] place" refers to Pa*dampa* Sangye, an Indian sage who had moved to Dingri centuries earlier and started a religious tradition.[102] Both biographers include a description of his birth on the roof of his maternal aunt's home in Dingri. They say that he, like the Buddha, caused his mother no harm and that as soon as he was born, "he squatted, wiped his face with his hands, and looking at the moon said, 'It is the eighth day of the month.'" This action, they continue, made his maternal aunt very upset, and his parents left Dingri quickly.[103]

There is no possibility with the available evidence to decide which one of these traditions is correct. But what all versions of his story do agree on is that he saw the moon as soon as he was born, and this made him happy. Not only does this represent an auspicious connection with the moon that is repeatedly evoked throughout his life story, the fact that he saw it straight after being born suggests, as his later biographers insist, that he was born outside.

The place of his birth and the lack of certainty about his birthplace both highlight the precariousness of his parents' living arrangements. Despite the auspicious symbolism that those telling his birth story attribute to his viewing of the moon and to his ability to remember the events of his birth and the in-between state, from a mundane perspective, there was little to suggest that this child of a potter would lead the life he was about to lead.

Rather than his familial inheritance, Rangjung Dorje's path to this different life was determined early on by both his precociousness and the willingness of those around him to recognize his abilities and promote them. The records of his childhood are a patchwork of lists of cultural tropes associated with auspicious beings and very ordinary sounding anecdotes. Rangjung Dorje frames this section of his autobiography with a warning that his memories of this time are "dreamlike." The only outright claims he makes are those that would further help his case for recognition. He insists that he was able to read and write at an early age without being taught, just as Karma Pakshi was able to do. He also insists that he could remember his past lives, that he experiences intense visions, and—perhaps more importantly for the path his life would take—that he could articulate his experience of these visions.[104]

The two most important visions he has both occur when he is on pilgrimage with his father, a devotee of the Nyingma tradition. The first of these occurs in the main temple at Dingri, which is dedicated to Padampa Sangye, when he is only four years old. There, the young Rangjung Dorje sees rainbow colors emanating out of Padampa Sangye's statue, and they dissolve into him. After this, he notes, his father begins to tell him about Padampa Sangye's Pacification lineage.

His other vision occurs in front of the Āryavati Zangpo statue in Kyidrong's Pakpa Lhakhang.[105] This statue, which was believed to date back to the time of the Tibetan Empire, inspires the young Rangjung Dorje, such that he "develops a vast happiness at the thought of helping others, which is the sacred compassion that holds all dear."[106]

Along with his ability to articulate his visions, he also becomes well known—just as Düsum Khyenpa had—for his stories about his past lives and, as this chapter has already highlighted, the story of his interlife journey. His autobiography and most of his biographies include an anecdote about the telling of this interlife tale. In the *Verse Liberation Story*, he recalls that "the virtuous scholar Serkhangpa asked me some questions respectfully, and from my reply came the speech that is renowned as the *Liberation Story of the In-Between State*."[107] Several later biographies elaborate on this story and, unusually for the Tibetan biographies of respected Buddhist teachers, they include an anecdote that is less than flattering to his parents. These stories suggest that Rangjung Dorje had already convinced his parents that he was the Karmapa's rebirth, and they were slowly becoming comfortable with this idea. When reading this anecdote, it is important to remember that at this time young children were not regularly recognized as reincarnated teachers in Tibet. In Tsuklak Trengwa's version, the story is told as follows:

> One day, when [Rangjung Dorje's] father felt hungry and thirsty, he told his family they would travel to a nearby village. When they arrived, his parents started enjoying themselves. His father enjoyed himself so much that he got drunk and started telling everyone: "The Karmapa Rinpoche has arrived." This news buzzed around the market, and Rangjung Dorje received so many offerings that they piled up in front of him like a mountain. Everybody there wanted to receive

> his blessing and hear the Dharma. Serkhangpa, who was a great bodhisattva, guru, and spiritual friend of all in Latö, was presiding [over the village] at that time. He asked Rangjung Dorje detailed questions. Rangjung Dorje replied with the *Liberation Story of the In-Between State*. Serkhangpa wrote it down and then bowed at the child's feet.[108]

After receiving such a positive response to their story from Serkhangpa, the family decides to take their claim to the most respected teacher in the area who has a connection with Karma Pakshi, Orgyenpa.

Orgyenpa was one of the most influential and legendary figures of Rangjung Dorje's age. He was a student of the famous guru Götsangpa (1189–1258), who was also from the same region in southern Tibet. Orgyenpa gained his reputation by being one of only a few Tibetans of the Mongol era to travel through the valleys of Kashmir and Swat to the holy lands of India. When he returned, he set up his own retreat center at Bütra near the present-day village of Nyalam, which was then known as Nyenam.[109] After setting up this retreat center, Orgyenpa developed a complex relationship with members of the Sakya-Mongol rulers of Tibet. The Great Lord Künga Zangpo (1220–1280/81) sent troops to raze Bütra and kill all its inhabitants after he heard that Orgyenpa had been spreading rumors about him. After Chögyel Pakpa returned from the Mongol capitals to Tibet, Orgyenpa resumed his former prominence, banished Künga Zangpo, and arranged for a Mongol prince to rebuild Bütra.[110]

Rangjung Dorje's meeting with Orgyenpa was the most pivotal of his life. It is also important more broadly to Tibet's religious, political, and social history. Lucky then that there are several records of it, told from different perspectives. It is recorded in Rangjung Dorje's autobiography, from thirdhand sources in his biographies, and in Orgyenpa's biography.

And while the version of the story being told here will necessarily focus on the impacts that this meeting had on Rangjung Dorje, it is also important to remember how important Orgyenpa's role was in this interaction. If Orgyenpa had not been Rangjung Dorje's local religious hierarch, Tibetan history might have been very different. Orgyenpa was one of only a few revered figures who was invested in the recognition and training of rebirths. His recognition of Rangjung Dorje followed his earlier recognition of Künga Özer as Götsangpa's rebirth and Künden Rema as the rebirth of Götsangpa's consort Drowa Zangmo.[111] He had also made sure that these two young people received comprehensive religious educations. Künga Özer would later become one of Rangjung Dorje's most loved teachers and confidants. Orgyenpa had also been entrusted with the one item that would help Rangjung Dorje's claim to be Karma Pakshi's rebirth more than any other: Karma Pakshi's black hat.

At this stage in the development of the Karmapa reincarnation lineage, Düsum Khyenpa and Karma Pakshi were more connected by their black hat than a common name. Short of attaining the Karmapas' monasteries, possession of the black hat was the one thing that could help establish Rangjung Dorje's status as Karma Pakshi's rebirth. Not only had Karma Pakshi gifted this hat to Orgyenpa before witnesses during Orgyenpa's visit to Tsurpu but he also had, according to Orgyenpa, tasked him with returning it to his rebirth. The story of the meeting between Karma Pakshi and Orgyenpa retold in Orgyenpa's biography not only establishes his credentials for recognizing Karma Pakshi's rebirth but it also tells us quite a bit about Karma Pakshi's idiosyncratic personality. As Orgyenpa's biographer and student, Sönam Özer, recalls,

> When Orgyenpa arrived [at Tsurpu], the great precious Karmapa said, "Ah! Siddha Orgyenpa! You were supposed to

get here three days ago, and you only arrive now? The food [we had for you] has gone bad!"

Orgyenpa replied [jokingly], "I didn't arrive sooner because I am a practitioner of the Drukpa Kagyü's reverse training."[112]

"When you practice reverse training," the Karmapa said, "you are putting shit in your mouth and molasses in your ass!" and many other such gibberish things.

[As the Karmapa talked,] Orgyenpa's attendants stared at the wondrous statues, *stūpas*, and texts in the Karmapa's tent.[113] The Karmapa noticed this and said, "The mahāsiddha Orgyenpa's students' mouths have frozen! What are you staring at? If you want to stare at something, stare at your guru's face!"

Then he took the black, silk hat he was wearing on his own head, placed it on Orgyenpa's head, and told him he would grant him the empowerment of Avalokiteśvara Jinasāgara. He filled up a bowl with barley, stirred it with an iron rod, and placed the bowl on Orgyenpa's head while handing him the iron rod.

Orgyenpa joked again, "Does someone in your lineage wear a black hat?"

Karma Pakshi replied, "I'm a snowy one [white-haired] and unstable.[114] Soon my dependence on my body will be cut. The lineage of black-hat holders will be cut too. But then a black-hatted one will return from sunny Latö . . ."

Later, he said, "We two have been each other's masters so many times. In the future, you will have to guide me. Your disciple [the next Karmapa] will live in the sunny south. For the sake of wanderers, you will have to lead him through the practice of Jinasāgara, the six syllables that are its essence, and the introduction to the three bodies."[115]

This lighthearted anecdote does much to establish the precedents by which subsequent reincarnates would be found. It includes a prediction about Karma Pakshi's rebirth, something that all subsequent Karmapas have been expected to provide. This prediction by Karma Pakshi about his future birth is probably the prophecy to which Rangjung Dorje refers when he says in the *Verse Liberation Story* that he was born "in accordance with prophecy."[116]

By gifting Orgyenpa the black hat so that he can return it, this story also goes at least some way to designating Orgyenpa as the person responsible for finding Karma Pakshi's rebirth and therefore removes this job from Karma Pakshi's family, who would remain the custodians of the Karmapas' monasteries for the next few centuries.

Karma Pakshi's family was well entrenched as the guardians of his legacy, and there was no precedent for the third member of a reincarnation lineage to be recognized. Orgyenpa's recognition of Rangjung Dorje was, in many ways, if not a break from tradition then at least a bending of it. Orgyenpa was not only acknowledging this child's personal attributes, but he had also authorized a continuing rebirth pattern. What is more, he was asserting that the great Karma Pakshi, guru to emperors and head of several monasteries, had been reborn as the son of an itinerant potter. For this to be accepted, the story that legitimized it needed to include all the symbolism and narratives it could muster. With this in mind, it is no doubt significant that Sönam Özer included not only a detailed description of Orgyenpa's visit to Karma Pakshi in his teacher's biography but also a detailed description of Orgyenpa's first interaction with Rangjung Dorje several years later. It reads as follows:

> One morning Orgyenpa got up very early and said, "Last night I dreamt I met the precious Karmapa." Later, a monk named Sungse arrived from Mopuk with an attendant. When he met Orgyenpa, he said, "We arrived last night from

Mukhug[117] at the same time as a potter, his wife, and their son. They think their boy is the Karmapa and want to ask you if he really is. They are staying in a hut at the base of the monastery." Orgyenpa replied, "It could be, but for now we should keep this possibility to ourselves."

An attendant was sent to invite the family to the monastery, and Orgyenpa told his attendants to "Make a high throne: if it is the Karmapa, he will not fear to sit on it." The attendants made a high throne and gathered the community in the temple. They burned incense and greeted each other. When the boy arrived, he made his way through the crowd. Orgyenpa only caught glimpses of him gradually. When the boy eventually came before him, he asked, "I wonder, are you the Karmapa?"

The boy replied, "I am the one known as the Karmapa." Then he raised his right hand, hooked his small sleeve on the arranged throne, and pulled himself up by it. Once up there, he said, "I taught you the Dharma, now you need to teach me. Oh, and in my past life, didn't I give you some things? Didn't I give you my hat?"

Orgyenpa replied, "This is true. It is in my room. Someone get it." An attendant went and retrieved it, and when the [little child who was the] precious Karmapa placed his previous life's hat on his [small] head, everybody laughed.[118]

Rangjung Dorje's life changed forever that day, and so did Tibetan social, religious, and political history. But according to those telling his life story, this was merely the expected destination of his journey between lives.

CHAPTER 2

Education

RANGJUNG DORJE was four or five years old when he arrived at Orgyenpa's Bütra Hermitage. He never returned to his family and did not mention his parents positively in any of his future writings. Instead, he began to refer to Orgyenpa as his "father-guru," and throughout his life he repeats his gratitude for him.

Rangjung Dorje's move to Bütra Hermitage was the beginning of a period of education that lasted until his late teens. It ended when he took final ordination and left central Tibet to travel as a wandering yogi in eastern Tibet. During those years, he was educated in general subjects such as reading, writing, calculation, astrology, and medicine, as well as in the doctrines, philosophies, and practices of several Tibetan Buddhist lineages. The lineage about which he received the most instruction was the Karmapas' sublineage of the Kagyü tradition, but he also received extensive instructions related to the Drukpa, Drikung, and Tropu Kagyü, the Kadam, the Pacification lineage, and the Nyingma's treasure tradition. He developed a particular affection for the Kagyü Mahāmudrā and the Cakrasaṃvara and Avalokiteśvara Tantras. He also expressed great admiration for the Nyingma's Heart-Essence Treasure teachings, the Kadam teachings on the Five Treatises of Maitreya and Mind Training and the Pacification tradition. His writing from this period indicates that he was particularly inspired by and felt a strong connection with certain people from these lineages: the mahāsiddha Saraha, Milarepa, Padmasambhava, and Padampa Sangye.

He spent extended periods in retreat during this time too. He wrote about these periods fondly, but his writing hints at their political and social as well as religious utility. The period of his youth was far from the stablest in Tibet's history. Despite his close relationship with Orgyenpa and his joy at being given an education, Rangjung Dorje had to leave Bütra only a few years after he arrived there and move to Tsurpu Monastery, the Karmapas' primary seat. His move coincided with the outbreak of fighting in southern Tibet, as it became one more theater in a multifronted conflict between rival Mongol rulers. Rangjung Dorje's "return" to Tsurpu Monastery—the return of the Karmapa—is often described as an inevitability in later biographies, but the writings from this time paint a different picture. His time at Tsurpu is difficult; he is not welcomed by all its residents and spends a good deal of his youth in a hillside retreat center behind Tsurpu. Nevertheless, he sticks it out and spends over a decade there. It is only toward the end of his education that he left Tsurpu to attend one of central Tibet's renowned centers of learning, Sangpu Neutok.

These sixteen years of education, and the other life they afforded him, are a direct result of his recognition by Orgyenpa. It is little wonder then that this unorthodox but widely respected character has such a profound influence on the young Rangjung Dorje's life.

Traveling to Tsurpu

The process of educating Karma Pakshi's rebirth and transforming him from a potter's son into "the third yogi to wear the black-hat crown" was well underway by the time that Rangjung Dorje had to leave Bütra for Tsurpu. Soon after he arrived, for example, a monk associate of Orgyenpa, Künden Sherap (twelfth century) of Tropu Monastery, ordained him as a novice monk and gave him Karma Pakshi's secret tantric name: Rangjung Dorje.[119] There is no record of what he was called before this. He never calls himself anything other than Rangjung Dorje in any of his writings. It is almost as if he chose to erase his pre-recognition life.

As he had promised Karma Pakshi, Orgyenpa began by teaching Rangjung Dorje the Jinasāgara form of Avalokiteśvara.[120] But Rangjung Dorje's plans to continue his education in the tantras was cut short by the political problems that engulfed the region and Orgyenpa.

The transcontinental politics that interrupted Rangjung Dorje's childhood in this isolated area on the borders of the Mongol Empire began years before he was born, during Karma Pakshi's life. After Karma Pakshi left Prince Qubilai's camp, he traveled to the court of Qubilai's elder brother, the Great Khan Möngke (1209–1259, r. 1251–1259), in Karakorum on the Mongolian steppe. Following Möngke's death, his two younger brothers, Qubilai and Ariq Böke (1219–1266) fought over the succession. Qubilai eventually won. But not everyone was happy with his victory. In central Asia, the rulers of the Chagadai Khanate were unimpressed. The Chagadai Khanate was ruled by the descendants of Chagadai Khan (1183–1242), the Mongol Empire's founder Chinggis (or Genghis) Khan's (1162–1227) second son. This branch of the Mongol imperial family had been closely allied with Ariq Böke and sheltered his uncle and supporter Qaidu (1185–1241). Their forces lost to Qubilai. This family had also maintained a close relationship with the Drigung Kagyü rulers of Drigung Til Monastery north of Lhasa, who had also been supporters of Ariq Böke.

In the face of the rising Qubilai Khan and Sakya alliance, the Chagadai's ruler Du'a (1282–1307)—backed by Qaidu—and the then Drigung Kagyü heads Tsamche Drakpa Sönam (1238–1286) and Nup Chögo Dorje Yeshe (1223–1293) formed an alliance. These two competitive partnerships between Mongol princes and Tibetan religious figures encouraged regional and sectarian conflicts on the

Plateau. There was resentment about Qubilai's special treatment of the Sayka. The fallout from Qubilai's complicated relationship with Karma Pakshi continued to unfold. And there were tensions within Sakya itself, particularly between the onetime Great Lord Künga Zangpo, who had razed Bütra, and the imperial preceptor and periodic abbot of Sakya, Chögyel Pakpa, who had helped Orgyenpa rebuild it.

Orgyenpa, if his biographers are to be believed, expressed an open disdain for all sides of this conflict. Only a few years after his retreat center had been rebuilt, he was in trouble with the Sakya-Mongol side of the conflict when he whipped Qubilai Khan's emissary Thogmi Temür in public and rejected the summons to Qubilai's court that he carried with him.[121] He was not a fan of the Drigung and Chagadai either. When the Chagadai first attempted to invade southern Tibet in the 1260s, he had arranged for a large ceremony to be conducted on the Pelmo Tang Plain, with the explicit aim to repel their invasion.[122] This history meant that after the Drigung rebelled in 1290 and active hostilities broke out, neither side trusted him.

The Drigung rebellion began when its partisans burned down Jayül Monastery, but with the help of a group that the texts refer to as "the Upper Mongols," which is almost certainly the Chagadai Khanate, it spread across the region.[123] Drigung and their allies fought in central Tibet. The Chagadai dispatched a large force through western Tibet to South Latö. Orgyenpa's biography reports that the people of Latö were overwhelmed and had to surrender, but they refused to offer the Mongols or their allies aid or soldiers.[124] The Sakyas and Mongols were not entirely convinced by Orgyenpa and the Latö people's attempts to remain neutral. When the Drigung and Chagadai were defeated, Aglen, the new Great Lord of Sakya, chased the Drigung abbot to the Kongpo region, near to southern Latö, and he instigated direct Mongol rule of southern Tibet. Orgyenpa's difficult situation at the end of the war may even have been the reason he accepted the next invitation he received from Qubilai Khan and traveled to his court.[125] After Orgyenpa left for the Mongol court, Rangjung Dorje was sent to Tsurpu, both for his protection and to claim something of his reincarnate birthright. None of the sources at the time claim a causal link between these two events, but their timing suggests at least a conditional link between them.

Rangjung Dorje's autobiography glosses over the war and instead adopts a similar narrative to justify his journey to Tsurpu, as he had to account for his rebirth on earth. He claims that his journey to Tsurpu was vindicated and made legitimate by a series of invitations from those people who have the real power and influence in his life and in the world, gurus and guardian deities. The first of these beings to invite Rangjung Dorje to Tsurpu was a Tsurpu-based yogi named Lama Nyenre ("the cotton-clad guru from Nyen"). Lama Nyenre claimed that a vision of Avalokiteśvara told him to visit the rebirth of his teacher, Karma Pakshi in South Latö.[126] While there, he developed a bond with Rangjung Dorje. When trouble broke out in Latö, he invited the boy to Tsurpu.

Next, after the Drigung uprising, Rangjung Dorje experienced two visions of deities telling him to travel to Tsurpu. The first vision was of Black Coat, his and Tsurpu's protector. The second was of the *nāga*[127] king known as Khanak, the Lord of Mantra, who told him forcefully to travel to Tsurpu and said he would protect him on the journey.[128]

Later biographers insist that the first thing he did on his return to the Tölung Valley was to visit the mother of the corpse he had inhabited and give her a *dzo* (a cow and yak crossbreed). When he met her, the biographers insist, he asked her why she had poked him in the eye with a needle. "It was not a needle," she replied, "it was just dirt."[129]

He then continued up the Tölung Valley and arrived at Tsurpu

Monastery. But he did not receive the tumultuous welcome that later Karmapa reincarnates would receive on their return. Lama Nyenre greeted him and claimed to have experienced a vision of him as Saraha, surrounded by all the earlier Kagyü gurus.[130] Another guru, Darma Tönpa, who lived in a hermitage behind Tsurpu called Trashi Sarma, experienced a vision too. In his vision, the entire Kagyü lineage, including Tilopā and Nāropā, manifested to welcome the young boy.[131] But other residents of Tsurpu were less impressed.

Rangjung Dorje does not dwell on others' displeasure in his autobiography,[132] but later biographers provide more details. As Tsuklak Trengwa describes events, there were murmurings and disquiet when Rangjung Dorje arrived, and many did not accept that he was Karma Pakshi's rebirth. To silence his critics,

> Rangjung Dorje walked over to a dry, rocky place and said, "If I am Karma Pakshi, let a spring arise in this place." As he spoke, a spring appeared. Then, he held a half-burnt, twisted stick and said, "If I am Karma Pakshi's rebirth, let this plant, too, be [reborn]." And it occurred just as he said these words.[133]

This spring, the biographers agree, became known as the "siddha spring" and the tree as the "siddha tree." Rangjung Dorje, the story suggests, was creating stories that added to Tsurpu's cultural cache on his first day there. He would continue to create similar stories about the site for the rest of his life.

Unlike later Karmapas, however, he did not take official control of the monastery on his return, nor was he given a position of authority within it. Instead, he seems to have worked out a compromise with Karma Pakshi's family, who retained control of the monastery. They retained control of all three of the Karma Kagyü monasteries—Tsurpu, Karma, and Kampo Nenang—until almost a century later, when the Fifth Karmapa, Dezhin Shekpa (1384–1415), arrived back from the Ming emperor's court in 1407.[134]

Instead of taking charge of Tsurpu, Rangjung Dorje moved into one of the retreat centers on the hill behind the main building, Khyung Dzong, the Garuda Fortress, and spent years studying there under the tutelage of Lama Nyenre and Darma Tönpa. These two monks taught him a combination of esoteric and exoteric religious subjects and secular subjects. The focus of his education was the practices and worldviews of the Karma Kagyü, but he also studied reading, writing, mathematics, poetry, astronomy, and medicine.

Shortly after his arrival, Rangjung Dorje began to experience a series of visions of Black Coat and his consort Remati that confirmed his important relationship with Tsurpu Monastery and the upper Tölung Valley.[135] These two deities presented themselves as manifestations of Tsurpu's sanctity and told him that he was welcome to stay as long as he did not allow himself to be corrupted.[136]

The visions of these deities are relayed in his autobiographies and by later biographies as part of a developing tradition that linked the Karmapa reincarnation lineage (and not just its founder Düsum Khyenpa) with Tsurpu Monastery. This tradition presents a symbiotic relationship between the Karmapas and Tsurpu; they enforce each other's sacredness. Another anecdotal example of this tradition was Rangjung Dorje's insistence that the local earthquake of 1294 was a direct result of his realization of "impartial wisdom."[137] This realization, he explains, was connected to a transformation in his subtle body that led to both a series of intense visions of Black Coat and Remati and to earthquakes as the external sacred site aligned itself with his subtle body. He was ten years old at the time.[138]

There are a series of similar stories in his autobiography and the biographies others wrote about him after his death. Rangjung Dorje did little to change the physical makeup of Tsurpu during his life; his only contribution in this regard was to build Dechen Teng Hermitage in the hills near Tsurpu.[139] But through the stories, songs, and rituals he created about the site, he did much to transform its perception in the community.

Most of his compositions from this first stage of his writing life were songs that he composed while staying at Trashi Sarma and then Khyung Dzong Hermitage. The first twenty songs of his *Collected Songs* were composed in these retreat centers. The first of these songs is mentioned or described in most of his biographies and is translated in full in chapter seven of this book. It describes a vision he had of the mahāsiddha Saraha.[140]

Rangjung Dorje identified closely with this semimythical Indian yogi from a very young age.[141] Within some of his writing, he even hinted that he considered himself Saraha's reincarnation. His commentary on Karma Pakshi's liberation story, for example, says that Karma Pakshi was Saraha's manifestation. Describing Karma Pakshi in this way enabled Rangjung Dorje to make an indirect claim about himself.[142] And in another of his songs, written later in life, he even directed his students to view him as Saraha.[143] Ultimately, however, he stopped short of claiming this past life directly. When he provided a list of his previous incarnations later in his stay at Khyung Dzong, he instead stated that he had only been Saraha's grandstudent Nāgābodhi, the "best student" of Saraha's student Nāgārjuna.[144]

Rangjung Dorje's connection with Saraha was not just biographical; he was also very invested in the mahāsiddha's presentation of ultimate reality. Indeed, his most sustaining interest in Saraha was in his presentation of the mahāmudrā "view." One of the most well-known texts in which he talks about Saraha's view is in the song that opens his *Collected Songs*. This song contains what Rangjung Dorje insists is the essence of Saraha's view but does so within a dream sequence.

The song itself begins with a narrative. Rangjung Dorje travels to meet Saraha in South India. The picture it paints of South India is an incongruous mix of Indian motifs and alpine imagery, but creating the correct imagery is not one of its main aims. Its main components are Saraha's teaching on mahāmudrā and the mahāsiddha's empowerment of Rangjung Dorje through a "sign." Within the Mahāmudrā lineage, signs such as the one Rangjung Dorje describes are understood to be pointing-out instructions that are handed down from guru to student. They are usually given after much preparation to more senior practitioners rather than to twelve-year-old novice monks. Rangjung Dorje's claim to have been given such a sign at such a young age—and from the mahāsiddha Saraha—was a bold statement.

This statement should also be understood in the context of Tibet's religious and political history. At the time Rangjung Dorje made this pronouncement, he was feeding into a long-running controversy over the practice of "pointing-out" instructions. Sakya Paṇḍita had criticized Gampopa for granting pointing-out instructions to those without sufficient tantric empowerments. In making this argument, Sakya Paṇḍita was advocating for a strict, black-letter interpretation of the protocols and precepts outlined in tantric texts.[145] Even at this young age, Rangjung Dorje had received many tantric empowerments. But his claim to have received pointing-out instructions in a dream at this young age was far from a black-letter interpretation of the tantras. What is more, by claiming to have received the sign from Saraha himself and to have understood it, he was presenting himself as Saraha's lineal heir, the twelve-year-old "child of the lineage."

In his writing, Rangjung Dorje presents an acute awareness of the profundity of his claim. It is such a definitive moment in his education that he reflects upon it again in his *Verse Liberation Story*. "Saraha showed me that my own mind was the sacred guru," he says, "and the meaning of his dohā came clearly to my mind."[146]

The content of this first song is all the more striking when we compare it to the rest of the songs that he composed during this period. Most of them were composed at Khyung Dzong, where he appears to have spent much of his time between the ages of seven and seventeen. The contents of these other songs paint a portrait of a child struggling to come to terms with his identity as a reincarnate and to deal with his isolation. They hint at his steely resolve to progress in his studies and to his commitment to his teachers, but none of the rest of them make the same bold claims as those contained within the dream of Saraha. Sometimes, they even suggest that he was a bit mischievous.

There is tension in these writings about his reincarnate identity, but it manifests in different ways. Like many children chosen to perform an important social role, he reflects on his feelings of loneliness and isolation within that role. He often speaks of how much he misses his "father-teacher" Orgyenpa. Lamenting the separation between oneself and one's guru is socially encouraged within Tibetan Buddhist traditions. It is even considered meritorious. The laments Rangjung Dorje wrote during his stay at Tsurpu include many of the same notions and imagery as those found in earlier songs and stories from his lineage. Milarepa's songs about missing Marpa are perhaps the most famous of these.[147] Rangjung Dorje's songs about missing Orgyenpa are written in a similar style. But they are made more poignant because of his young age and difficult situation. Like many young people, for example, he often speaks about his feelings of frustration, uselessness, and not living up to the standards that Orgyenpa, his "father-guru," had set for him. In one song from this period, for example, he laments:

> Father-guru, I have not emulated you,
> But I have not given up on great compassion.
> Mahāmudrā is the greatest meaning, the essence
> Of all past, present, and future buddhas;

I am not entirely familiar with it,
But I have not given up on it; it is the Buddha's intention.
I have not stayed in isolated sites, mountain retreats,
I have not experienced austerities like you,
But I have not forgotten to imagine A HŪMHŪṂ.[148]
I have no expansive understanding
Of the Tathāgata's discourses,
But I have not thrown the sacred Dharma away.[149]

In another song, he expresses a similar sentiment, but this time he includes a few references to his lowly social status.

Alas! How dark it is for a miscreant,
Mountain hermit like me.
Father-guru, wanderers' hero, compassionate one,
Inspire this lazy beggar.
Noble one, from the unseen realm, please inspire me!

It is good for me to stay in this solitude,
This mountain hermitage; but
It would also be good if I weren't
Separated from my loving, compassionate guru.
How dark it will remain if you do not realize this![150]

In another song, he reprimands himself even more directly, beginning with the line, "Stupid, this is just like you!"[151]

During this same period, when he was not berating himself for not living up to Orgyenpa's example and the high expectations of his reincarnate status, he was also engaged, with the help of his supporters, in a series of literary projects that set out the narrative of his multilife journey. These works create a narrative link between his life and the lives of the previous two Karmapas. They include lists of his past lives and give brief descriptions of what happened in them. Later, they would be adopted as the standard set of Karmapa past lives by the Karma Kagyü lineage.[152] He wrote about this list in three different sources:

1. A song composed at Khyung Dzong that is included within his *Collected Songs*
2. The *Liberation Story of Past Lives*, the colophon of which says that it was composed at the request of Darma Tönpa, one of his main supporters at Tsurpu[153]
3. A list within the *Verse Liberation Story*[154]

All three versions of his past-life stories begin with equivocation. The *Liberation Story of Past Lives* and the section that describes his past lives within the *Verse Liberation Story* both begin with a caveat that he does not remember these lives as clearly as he did when he was younger. As he describes the situation in the *Liberation Story of Past Lives*, his memories are "cloudy, obscured, gloomy."[155] But, he goes on to say, he will write them down, before he forgets them even more.

Despite this equivocation, he goes on to give a list of previous rebirths in both texts. Mostly, the two lists agree. The first two names on the list are Indian. The song describes these lifetimes in this way:

Long ago, in India, I was the master scholar,
Ārya Nāgārjuna's best student; Nāgābodhi was my name,
And I trained in all dharmas.

After this, in India again, I was a scholar, a *paṇḍita*;[156]
My expertise in the Three Baskets
And the tantras was unique.

After this, I was Gyelwa Chokyang, a student of the greatest
master,
The renowned Padmasambhava. I became an expert in
Nyingma dharma,
Particularly the Great Completion, so now I know it without
studying it.

After this, I became a paṇḍita again,
And, again, a singular, adroit expert
In all dharmas, completely qualified.

After this, I was the one called Potowa, who was connected
To Kharak Gomchung, and an expert in his dharma.
This person was also a teacher to the great one from Neuzur
[Yeshe Bar].

And again, I was the one called
Śrī Karmapa, who did
Everything he did to help all beings.[157]

The *Liberation Story of Past Lives* and the *Verse Liberation Story* present slightly different lists. Most of the lives are the same, but in these texts, he describes more lives and gives more details about those who are not given names within the song.

The names on the lists are fascinating not just because they are an obvious part of Rangjung Dorje's project to establish himself as Karma Pakshi's rebirth but also for the messages that he sends by choosing these particular names. For a start, none of the people on the list belong to the same lineage. By choosing these names, Rangjung Dorje creates links between himself, the Karmapas more generally, and most of the lineages that were prominent in Tibet during his time. The lists can be read as the beginning of his push for "impartiality" and—given that they emphasize his close connection with many lineages—as an argument for its inevitability.

His choice of Nāgābodhi gives him a connection to the renowned and multifaceted (or perhaps multipersoned) Nāgārjuna, without making a very high claim to have been this important figure himself.[158] Contemporary historians now suggest that the person who Tibetans of Rangjung Dorje's time thought was one historical Indian figure named Nāgārjuna was probably a composite of several figures with the same name. But for Rangjung Dorje, Nāgārjuna was a long-lived Indian siddha who was renowned for his mastery of both philosophy and tantra. He was the founder of the Madhyamaka tradition, but he also composed *In Praise of Dharmadhātu* from the perspective of the Yogācāra school and wrote several tantric commentaries.[159] Within the Mahāmudrā tradition, Nāgārjuna was also understood to be Saraha's primary student. Through claiming to have been Nāgābodhi, Rangjung Dorje was positioning himself as Saraha's grandstudent.[160]

In the *Verse Liberation Story*, Rangjung Dorje names the second person on the song's list, the "Indian paṇḍita," as Kāmadhenu. Kāmadhenu is listed in the lineage of the Hevajra Tantra as a student of Sakarapa, the mahāsiddha that brought this tantra into the world. In Tibet, this tantra was popular in the Sakya and Nyingma traditions and in a lineage that descended from one of Marpa's students, Ngok Lotsāwa.

Gyelwa Chokyang (eighth century) was one of Padmasambhava's closest twenty-five disciples. He was also one of Tibet's first seven monks. By claiming to be Gyelwa Chokyang's future rebirth, Rangjung Dorje connected himself to his great hero Padmasambhava, to Tibet's monastic tradition, and to the Plateau's collective story more generally. This particular claim not only linked Rangjung Dorje to Padmasambhava but it also opened the possibility that he could be a treasure revealer, or *tertön*. Most tertöns claimed a similar link with Padmasambhava. As explained in the introduction, these links underpinned the recovery narratives that legitimized the treasure text tradition. In these narratives, a yogi would claim to have found the text of a practice that Padmasambhava had taught them during the time of the Tibetan Empire and then later hid. Their previous connection with Padmasambhava was then given as the reason they were able to recover the text and empowered them to teach it.

After Gyelwa Chokyang, presumably during Tibet's "era of fragmentation," Rangjung Dorje claims that the Karmapa consciousness returned to India to live another life as a "paṇḍita." Both the *Liberation Story of Past Lives* and the *Verse Liberation Story* name this paṇḍita as Dharmabodhi, a South Indian yogi dedicated to the practice of Avalokiteśvara.[161] The later life stories of Milarepa also include his interaction with a Dharmabodhi. It is possible that they were assumed to be the same person.[162]

Potowa Rinchen Sel is the next person on the list that he mentions. Potowa was a grandstudent of Atiśa, a student of his most famous student Dromtön, and quite well known in Tibet. Potowa was the lineage holder of the Six Basic Texts of Kadam, which included the *jātaka,* or past-life stories, of the Buddha. Potowa was also the abbot of Radreg Monastery, which Rangjung Dorje visited several times. Rangung Dorje was, furthermore, a particular admirer of two other Kadam teachers, Kharak Gomchung (eleventh to twelfth century) and Neuzur Yeshe Bar (1042–1118), whom he also mentions in this song.[163]

The last person in his list was Karma Pakshi, who, during Rangjung Dorje's life, was the person most associated with the name "Karmapa."

The list of previous lives in this song is interesting not only because of the names it does contain but also because of the names it does not contain. Most prominent among those it does not contain is, of course, Düsum Khyenpa. The two other versions of the list do include the monk that latterly became known as the First Karmapa, however, and it could be said that by including Karma Pakshi in this song he was implicitly including Düsum Khyenpa as well.

Apart from the names of previous rebirths that it provides, the song version of the list is also notable in that the mode that it uses to express his insecurity about listing his past lives is humor. The song ends with the following lines:

> Through all these lives, I have studied,
> Reflected, and cultivated. In life after life,
> I put in a great deal of effort, so
> I do not need to make an effort now!
>
> Realized ones who know all dharmas,
> Those of you sitting here, know this!
> If I have made a mistake, bear with me.
> All this may be the truth, or I may be joking.
> Either way, take it as an offering of song to all you assembled here.[164]

Along with insisting that all the work he did in these previous lives now means that he can take it easy in that life, he also walks back the claims he makes in the songs at the end by making a joke of the claims. "This may all be true," he says, "or I may be joking."[165]

This sense of humor is prevalent in most of his songs, and given his status within the Tibetan Buddhist tradition, is often easy to overlook. One of the ways it comes across most obviously is in his playfulness with paradoxes. The most common of these is the idea that, in seeking to describe the mahāmudrā, yogi-poets were seeking to describe the indescribable. Once again, Rangjung Dorje followed Saraha in highlighting this paradox through wordplay and the presentation of incongruent images. Indeed, both poets revel in the idea. "Mountain hermits, yogis like me," Rangjung Dorje says:

> Cultivate simplicity, and yet
> This does not help anything at all.
> Wander the country with no direction and yet
> This does not help expand our perception.
> Collect felt cases for our texts,
> But this does not make reading them more comfortable.[166]

Another trope that he introduces in this initial collection of songs and continues throughout his writing is to question words themselves. In his fifteenth song in the collection, for example, he says:

> They are untrue, illusory, uncreated, so
> What use is this collection of words?[167]

This tendency to switch the audience's focus between the topic about which he is writing and the words he is using to tell his story is very "meta" for a premodern poet, and it can be found throughout much of his writing. In his autobiographies, for example, he will sometimes break the conventionally imposed "fourth wall" between the narrator of the story and his audience by speaking directly to his audience in the middle of a story. Tibetan authors tend to do this at the beginning and end of liberation stories but not in the middle of them.

The songs that Rangjung Dorje wrote during this time not only give us insight into his thinking and personality, their colophons also tell us more mundane information, like where he was living when he wrote them. Through them, we can plot his relative lack of movement during his later youth and teenage years; this is the longest period of his life in which he lived in one place. He stayed at Khyung Dzong for almost twelve years, gaining a prized education and developing a reputation as a young scholar and meditator among those whom he encountered there.

Toward the end of his teens, he started taking excursions from Tsurpu. The first journey that he describes in detail was to Mount Jomo Gangkar. Jomo Gangkar was and is a sacred mountain that could be reached by traveling further up the Tölung Valley. The goddess associated with the mountain is one of the earth guardians that Padmasambhava tamed on the Pelmo Tang Plain and the Karmapa consciousness met in the in-between state.[168] The mountain was home to a sacred cave associated with Padmasambhava, and Düsum Khyenpa had conducted a lengthy retreat there.[169] It was, furthermore, situated between Tsurpu and the Nye Valley, where Orgyenpa's other recognized reincarnate student, Künga Özer, had taken up residence. Rangjung Dorje spent a month in retreat in this cave as a teenager and would return to it to build a Padmasambhava statue later in life.[170]

Soon after finishing this retreat, when Rangjung Dorje was eighteen years old, he traveled down into the Nye Valley to Gendün Gang Monastery. In this monastery, associated with a smaller but elite lineage that was descendant from the Kashmiri scholar Paṇchen Śākyaśrībhadra (1127–1225), Rangjung Dorje was given complete ordination by the abbot Zhönnu Jangchup (1279–ca. 1358). Zhönnu Jangchup then gave him instructions on the monastic discipline described in the Vinaya.[171]

Rangjung Dorje remained a monk for the rest of his life and, if his writings are anything to go by, took his vows very seriously. In his writing, he is scathing about people pretending to be monks when they have partners, occasionally reflects on the difficulties associated with being a monk, and describes the yogic practices he uses to assuage these difficulties.

After receiving his full ordination at eighteen, Rangjung Dorje traveled further from Tsurpu, in the other direction, to the prestigious Sangpu Neutok Monastery. This monastery was famous for its training in the *pramāṇa*, or logic, tradition. Düsum Khyenpa was one of its many well-known alumni. Rangjung Dorje's teacher at Sangpu Neutok was Śākya Zhönnu, the abbot of its lower college. He studied pramāṇa texts and the other foundational texts of the Sūtra Mahāyāna tradition.[172] These included the Five Texts of Maitreya, Nāgārjuna's *Roots of Madhyamaka*, Vasubandhu's *Treasury of Abhidharma* (which is associated with the Hīnayāna in the Tibetan tradition), and Vasubandhu's brother Asaṅga's *Compendium of Abhidharma*.[173]

It is worthwhile noting that after spending most of his second decade studying and meditating on mahāmudrā in Khyung Dzong, Rangjung Dorje still committed to studying all these texts. He was particularly fascinated with Maitreya's Five Treatises, and he wrote several commentaries about them later in life.

After finishing his studies at Sangpu Neutok, he determined that he was ready to leave central Tibet and live as a hermit in the Plateau's less-inhabited and less-governed eastern mountains. Receiving an education like the one he had received was a rare gift in thirteenth-century Tibet, where most people could not read, let alone understand both secular and religious topics. Rangjung Dorje's reincarnate status had given him an opportunity that he would never have otherwise had. But as he rode away from Tsurpu toward the east, it was still unclear in what way he would use this education and what would become of his life.

CHAPTER 3

Retreat

One of Rangjung Dorje's most common descriptions of himself was as a "mountain hermit."[174] When he was not in "mountain hermitages,"[175] he wrote about missing them. When he was in them, he wrote about the joy he felt despite the hardships and the hazards. He may have composed some of his praises for these isolated sites because he felt social pressure to do so; such praise was expected of yogis in his lineage. But this social pressure cannot explain all of his enthusiasm for this lifestyle nor his constant efforts to get back to these sites. Rangjung Dorje clearly loved mountains and retreat.

After leaving Tsurpu Monastery at age nineteen, he spent most of the next decade traveling in eastern and southern Tibet, living in various hermitages. He went first to Karma Monastery in northern Kham, the Karma Kagyü monastery from which Karma Pakshi, and the Karmapas more generally, gained their name. At Karma, like at Tsurpu, he stayed in a hermitage removed from the main monastery. He was only allowed to lead ceremonies for Karma's monks after he had proved himself to its inhabitants. From Karma he traveled south to the third of the Karmapas' monasteries, Kampo Nenang. But his attempts to stay there were even less successful than they had been at Tsurpu and Karma. He was denied entry to the monastery's grounds and, as a result, he left for the sacred mountain of Khawa Karpo. While staying at this mountain, he became its champion, writing guides to it and songs about it.

His writing suggests he planned an extended stay there but was forced to return to central Tibet by the news of Orgyenpa's death. His return to central Tibet, however, did not mean a return to Tsurpu. Instead, he chose to stay with Künga Özer, the person Orgyenpa had recognized as Götsangpa's rebirth, at Nyedo Monastery in the Nye Valley. With Nyedo Monastery as his base, Rangjung Dorje traveled to the local seat of Mongol-sponsored power, Tsel Monastery, south of Lhasa, to attend the installation of its new governor, or *tribön*. He also returned to the Padmasambhava cave at Jomo Gangkar to conduct another retreat.

Soon after this retreat, he left central Tibet for Kongpo in the south. He was on a pilgrimage to its most sacred site, Tsari. From his writing during this time, it is clear that this area had a profound influence on him, and he wanted to stay. After a few years, however, he became ill and had to return to central Tibet, settling back near Tsurpu Monastery.

Rangjung Dorje's writing from this decade away from Tsurpu suggests that he spent much of it living between two worlds: human communities with their attendant social and political pressures, on the one hand, and his visionary retreat world in which he communed with transcendent and local gods and spirits, on the other. He was often forced to interrupt his retreats to manage human-human and human-spirit conflict, and these responsibilities grew with his reputation. His influence in human affairs was directly related to his perceived relationship with the Plateau's nonhuman beings. But as Rangjung Dorje kept telling people through his songs and writing, both spheres were merely the play of illusion, manifestations of mahāmudrā, the ultimate reality he sought to experience.

Journey to Eastern Tibet

Rangjung Dorje's decade-long journey began in the early summer of 1302 when he was nineteen years old. He had only recently returned to Tsurpu Monastery from studying at Sangpu Neutok Monastery, but he decided he no longer wished to stay there and set off for Tibet's east, to the region usually known as Kham. Both Düsum Khyenpa and Karma Pakshi had been born in eastern Tibet, and two of the three Karma Kagyü monasteries were there: Karma Monastery in northern Kham and Kampo Nenang in southern Kham.

As he left central Tibet, Rangjung Dorje encountered one of the Plateau's most powerful people, the Sakya abbot Jamyang Rinchen Gyaltsen (d. 1305), who was on his way to the Mongol capitals to take up the post of imperial preceptor.[176] Although Rangjung Dorje had been brought up by Orgyenpa and others to treat the Sakya-Mongol leadership with suspicion, both Orgyenpa and Rangjung Dorje also seem to have made distinctions between those within the Sakya tradition whom they deemed religious and worthy of veneration and those that were more involved in politics. Rangjung Dorje reported himself to have been very impressed by Jamyang Rinchen Gyaltsen and to have experienced a "pure vision" of "many bodhisattvas" when he met him.[177] He also took his meeting with the elderly Sakya hierarch as a sign that his travels would go well.

As he traveled east, he continued to perform songs for his traveling companions. Their topics changed with his circumstances. Several of the first songs he wrote after leaving Tsurpu were about travel, and from this point on, his songs included more travel metaphors. One of the first of these traveling songs contains the following verse:

> Lucky ones, sitting here,
> If you want to attain awakening quickly,
> Place the bright saddle of clear *bodhicitta*[178]

On the faithful stallion of wisdom,
Use the quick whip of diligence,
Follow the guru who knows liberation's path,
And gallop as far as you can. Now is the time.[179]

In another song from this period, he described his journey to Karma Monastery and Kham more generally as a flight from the entanglements of cyclic existence in the pursuit of uninterrupted insight. In this and other songs, he presents Kham as a borderland, like the borderlands Milarepa acclaimed, and as a space in which he can become a real yogi.

Kye ma! Hear this *dhārmikas*![180]
As the world's dharmas bind, bind—
Now is the time, look at [the] uncreated.
As the distractions of possessions bind, bind—
Now is the time, leave everything.
As wealth and substance bind, bind—
Right now, abandon all commotion.
As food, income, and trade bind, bind—
Right now, experience austerity.
As your relatives and servants bind, bind—
Right now, wander in mountain solitudes.
As house and land bind, bind—
Right now, travel the countryside.
As half truths beguile, beguile—
Right now, look at the final unreality. . . .
[When I do this,] I will be liberated from my bonds.[181]

In this song, as he does in many of the songs he performed at tantric feasts, he starts by admonishing the audience and ends by turning the poem on himself, reflecting that he too needs to act according to the ways he is instructing others to act.

These songs and his descriptions of his stay in Kham speak of a land without Mongols and their Sakya regents, where local rulers have much more control over their affairs. This lack of influence was undoubtedly true, for example, of the area around Karma Monastery, where he lived for the first five years of his stay in Kham.

Karma Pakshi's family members who ran Karma Monastery greeted Rangjung Dorje cordially when he arrived, but as at Tsurpu, he did not end up staying in the monastery's main buildings, preferring instead to move into a nearby retreat hut.[182] As he had at Tsurpu, he moved out of the monastery's buildings quickly. But this time, rather than stay in one of the monastery's outer buildings, he gathered the resources to build his own hermitage, Lha Teng (Divine Heights), in a forest adjacent to the monastery.[183] In this hermitage, the *Verse Liberation Story* suggests, he and a few companions lived in relative isolation, and their presence in the forest caused tensions with the locals. In several of the songs, he praises this hardship as a relief from the social burdens and other distractions of central Tibet and as a chance for he and his fellow retreatants to test themselves. "To train," he said,

> Make a home in isolated solitude,
> Depend on forests and trees,
> Wear clothes of discarded rags,
> Act like your breath has left you,
> Eat food as varied as birds, and
> Be attached to nothing.[184]

While pursuing the life of a hermit, he chose to focus on a different meditation practice than those he had practiced at Tsurpu.

Here, at Lha Teng, he meditated on the Ḍākinīs' Heart-Essence cycle, a treasure text from the Nyingma lineage's Great Completion teachings. During his stay, he recorded a series of breakthroughs in his practice of the Great Completion. He had a vision of Vimalamitra (ca. eighth century), a student of Padmasambhava, whom the tradition held to be closely associated with the treasure tradition. Rangjung Dorje's vision of Vimalamitra led, he described, "to an extremely clear understanding of the Great Completion."[185]

Not all of Rangjung Dorje's experiences in the forest were only internally transformative. One particular event also transformed both his environment and his social standing. After he had lived in the forest for several years, a forest fire broke out that raged around Karma and threatened several local communities. As Tsuklak Trengwa describes it, after the fire broke out, a monk named Zhönnu Bum sought refuge with Rangjung Dorje, and while in his hut he witnessed the young monk using his supernatural powers to quell the natural disaster. As Zhönnu Bum later repeated to whomever would listen, Rangjung Dorje stared down the flames and spoke directly to them, using "words of truth"[186] to subdue the flames, just as he had used words of truth to cause the spring to appear on his arrival at Tsurpu. To the flames, he is recorded as saying:

If I possess altruism as pure as those of old,
If I have accrued the [qualities] of a buddha,
If I am now a lord of the tenth ground,
Then by the power of the truth of my words
May this great conflagration be pacified.

He then reportedly snapped his fingers and made it rain so hard that the rain mixed with the "licking flames that pervaded the sky, causing a mix of dark brown smoke and clouds before the fire went out."[187]

Although he does not describe these events in the same way, in the *Verse Liberation Story*, even Rangjung Dorje notes a marked change in the locals after this event. "It kept raining," he writes, "and water flowed everywhere. This action pacified not only the fire but also the terrified people. They praised me for what I had done."[188]

After the fire, Rangjung Dorje started getting invited to more tantric feasts at Karma Monastery. When he attended, he sang songs and gave discourses on Buddhism. As his reputation grew, so did the crowds at these events. His influence over the local people, however, brought him to the attention of a jealous local ruler, who had, as Situ Paṇchen explained, "used this wealth to accrue dark power."[189] Rangjung Dorje found himself threatened once again, this time from black magic instead of fires. Although not admitting to fear, he did admit, in one of his songs, to being keenly aware of death at this time, referring to himself as "this monk, this young boy, this corpse."[190]

The tensions between Rangjung Dorje and the unnamed local ruler reached a peak one night in 1306. For example, Situ Paṇchen tells the story that while Rangjung Dorje slept,

> This local lord persuaded eight people to begin performing the very wrathful Yama [Lord of Death] practice against Rangjung Dorje. But while they recited it, the sworn enemy of Yama, Mañjuśrī [as Yamāntaka], appeared in their fire with three faces and six arms and began reciting mantras. This vision stopped their recitations and caused the cave in which they were seated to collapse. After this collapse, they all traveled to the other side [i.e., died].

Instead of killing Rangjung Dorje, Situ Paṇchen notes, people around the place had a vision of this event, and he accrued more followers and offerings.[191] Rangjung Dorje himself notes the events in passing, with the obtuse observation that one night, while sleeping, he had a vision of Mañjuśrī appearing as Yamāntaka, with "three faces, six hands, a garland of fire, an expression like a dark cloud, and a voice like thunder." From this vision, he says, "I understood that the obstacles created by the casting of evil spells were being reversed."[192]

Despite, or perhaps because of, his growing influence in the Karma Monastery region, Rangjung Dorje left soon after this event and headed for southern Kham. He was traveling to the last of the Karmapas' three monasteries, Kampo Nenang, near Litang in present-day Sichuan.[193] It was not as long of a journey between these two monasteries as it had been from central Tibet to Karma Monastery, but it took him over a year to get there. As he journeyed south through the steep valleys and mountain passes of Kham, he was stopped repeatedly by requests to either teach or broker peace in internecine conflicts.

On this journey, he reported experiencing repeated visions of the local god Dorje Peltsek, who manifests as a "white man on a white horse [wearing] a white silken coat."[194] He also recalled that the other two Karmapas had encountered this same local deity in southern Kham as they traveled to Kampo Nenang. Even with the help of the deity, however, it appears that he was denied residence at (or perhaps even entry into) Kampo Nenang. There is a gap in the *Verse Liberation Story* at this point; he moves toward Kampo Nenang, and then he appears to leave it. He does not explain what happened. He did not stay there, nor did he ever return to this monastery. It is possible that he did not want to write about what happened, and it is also possible that he did, but later scribes did not copy his descriptions of the events at Kampo Nenang. After all, this happened: he followed Dorje Peltsek further south, to a village called Kolti that was in the middle of a "great fight" that had beset its inhabitants for generations. This fight, Dorje Peltsek told him, had been caused by the region's nonhumans. Rangjung Dorje responded to the situation by using his concentrative abilities to "calm everyone down" until "they did as I said, and I heard them speaking kind words to each other."[195]

One of Rangjung Dorje's songs from the period also dealt with Kolti's "civil strife."[196] But it placed the blame for Kolti's troubles solely on the village's badly behaved humans. It began by situating Kolti amongst the region's steep ravines, "on a small ridge that arose when the earth boiled."[197] The blistering piece of social criticism then continued.

I cannot gauge others' minds in these dark times
When the teachings are declining,
But this is a little of what I have seen.

"Ṣpiritual friends" advertise greatness,
But are swayed by careless laziness.
Obsessed with the taste of meat and beer,
They sink into the mud of wealth and fame.
Doesn't this hurt the teachings?

"Great meditators" advertise meditation,
But they are carried away by materialistic days
And overpowered by slumber each night;
Morning and night, they chase pleasure and food.
Diverted in this way, will their mindstreams be freed?

Power-loving *tāntrikas*[198]
Rely on brave babbling.
Don't those who hurt others
Keep their own mindstreams burning?

Patrons desperate for wealth and fame,
Who do not develop vivid trust;
Don't those who behave badly
Fall to the three lower realms?

My sad mind has encouraged me
To talk in this way.
If no one else listens,
I will tell the empty sky.[199]

After this intervention, Rangjung Dorje traveled further south, into the region around the sacred Mount Khawa Karpo, home of the deity Rongtsen Khawa Karpo (Spirit of the Ravine, Snow White). On this section of his journey, he was still walking in the footsteps of his predecessor, Karma Pakshi. Karma Pakshi had entered the nearby Kaḥtog Monastery as a young man. Kaḥtog Monastery belonged to the "spoken word,"[200] non-treasure-tradition lineage of the Nyingma tradition. Karma Pakshi lived there for many years; he only left it with his teacher Pomdrakpa after a problem, probably a Mongol raid. Later, after Pomdrakpa died, Karma Pakshi went to live at Mount Pungri near Mount Khawa Karpo for eleven years.[201]

For reasons that are not entirely clear, Rangjung Dorje decided to stay at Mount Khawa Karpo rather than Pungri. Later traditions attribute two sacred-site guides to Khawa Karpo to Rangjung Dorje: *Secret Guide to Khawa Karpo* and *Rain of Siddhi, A Site Guide for the Great Sacred Site Khawa Karpo*.[202] But doubts about their authorship are so well established that they were not included within Rangjung Dorje's Collected Works.

Nevertheless, within the works that can be attributed to Rangjung Dorje, he did discuss Khawa Karpo and his stay there. In the *Verse Liberation Story*, he noted that he traveled there after meeting the mountain's god, but he said little else. The only sure clue to his relationship with the mountain is a praise that he wrote to it, which is written in the same style as his other praises to places and contains a colophon that says he wrote it in 1308, at the same time he was traveling in the area. This song suggests that Rangjung Dorje was involved, at least tangentially, in the reimagining of Khawa Karpo as an important sacred site, but it does not necessarily give him the same role in the site's transformation as the later tradition ascribes to him. It begins with a suggestion—repeated in many of his other songs—that these are challenging times for Buddhist practitioners, and they should, therefore, try to stay out of the way, in isolated sites.

> In these dark times, bodhisattvas
> Gaining experience in *siddhi*'s essence[203]
> Should rely on solitude to help these endeavors.
> This claim accords with the sūtras, whose words directly
> praise those
> Who abide in sacred sites like rocky mountains and vast
> borderlands.[204]

After establishing this general principle, the song then links Khawa Karpo to "the twenty-four sites," or *pīṭhas*, that are associated with the *Cakrasaṃvara Tantra*, claiming that one of them, Pretapurī (City of Ghosts),[205] is present there.

> East of the center, of Bodhgayā, is the pīṭha
> The siddhas rely upon, the site from which
> The goddesses who embody desire arise [Devīkoṭṭa].
> In the north is the Kāmarūpa pīṭha.
> Between them is the pīṭha of
> Pretapurī, with all the attributes of a sacred site.
> It is a site for siddhis in dark times; it is difficult
> For all to reach; it is where mother ḍākinīs live . . .[206]

This verse not only aligns Khawa Karpo with Pretapurī but positions it in relation to two other pīṭhas: Devīkoṭṭa, which is said to be at Tsari,[207] to its east and Kāmarūpa to its north.[208] According to the *Cakrasaṃvara Tantra*, these were a series of sacred sites in India that had been associated with the Indian god Śiva and his consort Śakti but were taken over by the male and female forms of Cakrasaṃvara. As the *Cakrasaṃvara Tantra* gained popularity in Tibet, particularly among the Kagyü, these sites were repositioned within the Tibetan cultural sphere. By the time Rangjung Dorje visited Mount Khawa Karpo, the Kagyü had been heavily involved in setting up three sacred Cakrasaṃvara mountains in central and western Tibet that were also understood to be pīṭhas: Tsari as the site of two pīṭhas, Cāritra and Devīkoṭṭa; Lachi as Godāvarī; and Kailash as Himavat. By imagining Khawa Karpo as a pīṭha, Rangjung Dorje was repeating this process of adaptation in Kham.

Later in the poem, he then links this otherworldly tantric schema with local natural phenomena, noting that, around Khawa Karpo,

> Waterfalls crash, yell, and shake through chasms.
> The mountains are just rocks, but they look like
> weapons.
> Terrifying forests are splendid decorations,
> And at their center is a
> Beautiful alpine meadow,
> A Dharma source, exquisitely shaped,
> And graced by a pool.[209]

Later in the poem, Rangjung Dorje also adds elements from the Nyingma tradition to what had been a fundamentally Kagyü landscape by connecting the site with the life story of Vairocana (eighth century).

According to the available historical sources, Vairocana had been an imperial-era translator who—like Rangjung Dorje's claimed previous existence as Gyelwa Chokyang—was one of the first seven monks to take ordination in Tibet. According to the treasure tradition, he had also been one of Padmasambhava's twenty-five close disciples and had been heavily involved in hiding treasure texts for later generations to follow. He was, furthermore, held up by the treasure tradition as one of the most important lineage holders of the Great Completion tradition. Within the treasure-tradition version of his life, there is a story about his being sent into exile in the Tsawarong Ranges, which include Khawa Karpo, where he converted the local king to Buddhism and experienced an intense vision of Padmasambhava.[210] Toward the end of his praise to Khawa Karpo, Rangjung Dorje draws on this story to suggest a connection between the treasure tradition and the mountain.

> It is widely reported that long ago Ācārya Padmasambhava
> And the guru Vairocana visited this site.[211]

When he writes about Khawa Karpo in the *Verse Liberation Story*, Rangjung Dorje suggests that he was going to spend more time in the region teaching and meditating in the sites associated with Karma Pakshi, but an unforeseeable event drew him back to central Tibet. This event was the death of his "father-guru," Orgyenpa. He heard of Orgyenpa's death, he relates, through a vision he experienced at Khawa Karpo. In this vision, he could see Orgyenpa throughout a night and during a sunrise, but as "a sign of (Orgyenpa's) degeneration, he appeared as if reflected in a mirror."[212]

It was too late for Rangjung Dorje to meet with Orgyenpa again, but he determined to fulfill Orgyenpa's wishes by studying the *Kālacakra Tantra* with Künga Özer at Nyedo. So, in 1308, nearly seven years after he had left central Tibet, he returned to the "entangling" region from which he had fled.

His return, he records in his writings, was noted by Nyenchen Tanglha, the god of the mountain range situated north of Tsurpu, and other deities, who greeted him when he crossed the border between Kham and central Tibet. His first stop on his return was Tsurpu, but he did not stay there. He left quickly on a pilgrimage to Lhasa, where he offered a bejeweled parasol to the famous Jowo statue in the central Jokhang Temple and had a vision of "all the buddhas in the ten directions."[213]

From Lhasa, he traveled to Nyedo and based himself at Künga Özer's monastery for the rest of his stay in central Tibet. His friend and fellow reincarnate not only taught him the Kālacakra Tantra but also introduced him to a series of more senior teachers, who gave Rangjung Dorje further instructions on its notoriously difficult contents and other subjects. These teachers were from both the Kagyü and Nyingma traditions. Tsültrim Rinchen and Jñānaśri taught him the Kālacakra Tantra according to his tradition, and Kumārarāja (1266–1343) taught him the Ḍākinīs' Heart-Essence texts from the treasure tradition. Although a Nyingmapa, Kumārarāja had many links with Rangjung Dorje. He studied, for example, with two of Rangung Dorje's main teachers at Tsurpu, Lama Nyenre and Darma. This connection suggests a link not only between Kumārarāja and Tsurpu, but also, inversely, between Tsurpu and the treasure tradition and the practice of diverse traditions within its walls. Kumārarāja had even met Rangjung Dorje as a young boy when he visited Orgyenpa in South Latö.[214]

As he was back in central Tibet, Rangjung Dorje was once again expected to engage in the region's political and social events. The most prominent of the official duties he was forced to perform was to lead the funeral rites of Gawa Pel, the eighth Tsel myriarch, in 1309. Gawa Pel had not had an easy relationship with Orgyenpa.[215] Rangjung Dorje's invitation to conduct these ceremonies suggests that his status in the region had continued to rise and that the Tsel power brokers did not hold his association with Orgyenpa against him. But after these events, Rangjung Dorje described himself as deflated, and he withdrew into retreat. The place he chose for the retreat was, once again, the cave at the base of Jomo Gangkar, at the top of the Nye Valley.[216]

During this retreat, he experienced a vision that would influence the rest of his life. "When I was staying in solitude at Jomo Gangkar," he reported in the *Verse Liberation Story,* "I dreamt I saw all of Kongpo's people aspiring to practice the sacred Dharma. I understood I could help them. And as it turned out, I have helped many of them."[217]

Kongpo is a region in southern Tibet, near the present-day border with the northeastern Indian state of Arunachal Pradesh.[218] The intense relationship Rangjung Dorje developed with Kongpo, its people, and its environment lasted for the rest of his life, and the close relationship between the Karmapas and the people of Kongpo continued for centuries after his death. Kongpo was a Karmapa stronghold until the seventeenth century. In Rangjung Dorje's writing, he expressed his appreciation for it in a variety of ways. He liked it, he said, because the people were kind and supportive, there were many sacred sites, it was home to many isolated but well-watered valleys, and there was less political interference there than elsewhere. The Mongol armies had invaded the area after the 1290 Drigung rebellion, but twenty years later their influence in the region was once again nominal.

After leaving Jomo Gangkar, Rangjung Dorje visited Daklha Gampo Monastery on his way to Kongpo. While in Daklha Gampo Monastery, he experienced a vision of his Kagyü forebear Gampopa, who directed him to travel further into the mountains, to the region's most sacred site, Tsari.[219] By this point, the broader Kagyü lineage and many other people considered Tsari to be Cakrasaṃvara's mind maṇḍala and the site of two of the deity's pīṭhas, Cārita and Devīkoṭṭa.

On his arrival in the region, Rangjung Dorje joined a tantric feast held at Langong Monastery and composed one of his most self-confident and combative songs as a method of introducing himself to his new neighbors. It reads in part:

The Vajra that realizes nonduality [i.e., Rangjung Dorje]
Has a message, a *mālā* (a rosary) of ideas,
For Dharma practitioners in the ten directions:
Don't be distracted, think well, and
Send this message to those who know how to listen.

Others do not look down on me, as
I have worked a long time for peace;
It is the illusory play of helping others
That is known as the greatest patience.
Send this message to the happy;
Tell them Rangjung Dorje sent it.

I have been caught on the nails of passing pain,[220]
But as [the pains] of resting, moving, eating, and sleeping[221]
Are helpfully eliminated by liberation, know that
I am now cleansed of these distracting stains.
Send this message to the diligent;
Tell them Rangjung Dorje sent it . . .

Patrons who amass fame and wealth,
"Upholders of the Vinaya" who've lost their vows,
Teachers who yearn for renown,
"Great meditators" who cultivate stupidity—

Tell them Rangjung Dorje calls them
"Try-hards who don't get results."[222]

His newfound confidence is evident in many of the other songs he composed at Tsari too. But these songs are not all about telling other people off. They also include reflections on his new environment that make connections between his surroundings and his internal experiences. He sang, for example, the following verses:

You won't mind haze outside when ignorant fogs clear.
You won't mind sunsets outside when wisdom's sun rises.[223]
You won't mind torrents outside when preconceptions' rains cease.
You won't mind chasms outside when you realize saṃsāra's cliff.
You won't mind prickly barbs when there are no more hateful thorns.
You won't mind churning rivers when craving's streams dry out.
You won't mind mountains outside when pride's peaks are leveled.
You won't mind flavorless food when you taste samādhi's meal.
You won't mind gloomy gorges when you clear afflictions' jungle ravines.[224]

After spending some time in the high-energy atmosphere of Tsari, Rangjung Dorje joined other groups of yogis and crossed the Ja La (Rainbow Pass) into New Tsari, where he founded a new hermitage. There was less competition for space in New Tsari and less competition between lineages. The songs that he wrote while staying in New Tsari are less combative and more nurturing of the students that had followed him into the mountains. Following the pattern that he established at Mount Khawa Karpo, his songs and other writings about New Tsari set about reimagining it as a sacred site, one in which the yogi's subtle body would receive extra support for its meditations. One of his songs from this time, for example, reads:

> It is tough for people to travel here to this special place, this most sacred site.
> It is here in Jambudvīpa's north, in Tibet, surrounded by vajra-like, rocky mountains;
> And sundry waterfalls cascade from them in all directions.
>
> But it is infused with the bouquet of green trees and flowers.
> Gods, demigods, *kinnaras*,[225] and elemental spirits all make offerings here.
> Externally it appears like a maṇḍala; internally, it is a site of self-arising deities . . .
>
> The body's channels are its branches, as in a forest they branch out,
> It is decorated by its senses, like the forest's fruits and flowers. . . .
>
> In Cakrasaṃvara's actual sacred site, actual innateness is inside, it is our mind.
> When we see this directly, we will see self-arising Tsari.[226]

Despite the hardships of living in New Tsari, Rangjung Dorje did not want to leave. He spoke of living there permanently, building a hermitage for students, and spending the rest of his life in retreat. But something happened. Like at Kampo Nenang, precisely what happened is not entirely clear in his stories and songs. The songs stop for a year and a half. The *Verse Liberation Story* becomes vague.

Later biographers have one explanation for this hole in his story. In Tsewang Gyel's *Lhorong Dharma History*, for example, he says that Rangjung Dorje spent this time in a secret retreat, becoming a treasure revealer. He writes:

> In the Female Water Ox Year [1313], thanks to his relationship with the Guru [Padmasambhava], Rangjung Dorje retrieved the Ḍākinīs' Heart-Essence treasure in Lhodrak. It was written on golden paper. He then spent three months at the confluence of the Lungchu River and one of its tributaries in Tsari, praying intensely to Padmasambhava, before meeting him directly and receiving empowerment and transmission from him.[227]

The Lungchu River runs south through Lhodrak, west of Tsari. It is possible that Rangjung Dorje spent a year in retreat there after living at Tsari. It is also possible that during this retreat on the banks of the Lungchu River in Lhodrak that he developed a special connection with the Ḍākinīs' Heart-Essence cycle of texts. But if he had claimed to have found treasure himself, it is strange for him not to have written anything down about this in his autobiography. Tsewang Gyel acknowledges this and says that Rangjung Dorje purposely did not write about his discovery because it was so secret. But this omission in his work could also be read as evidence for this text's *later* attribution to him. As with many other elements of the treasure tradition, the source of the Ḍākinīs' Heart-Essence texts is shrouded in mystery.

When Rangjung Dorje does begin to write again, he is back in central Tibet, and he is ill. Indeed, he writes of having been ill for quite a while and of worrying if he is going to die. Having made it to the foot of Yarlha Shampo, the mountain god at the head of the historic and sacred Yarlung Valley, he stops to rest, pray, and compose a song. The song he composes contains nothing of the swagger and positivity that infused his Tsari songs. Instead, he reports experiencing intense "obstacles" to his yoga practice and fearing for his life.

> *Kye ma!* Since the beginning of beginningless saṃsāra,
> The power of my generosity has been so weak,
> The force of my morality so feeble that
> I, this beggar, have wandered for all this long time.
> Clouds of noble persons have taught me the pure Dharma,
> And still, I have not destroyed my doubts.[228]

The song's colophon remarks that he sang this song after "he had become very ill" and "thought he might depart to another realm [i.e., die]."[229]

When Rangjung Dorje reflected on this moment years later while writing the *Verse Liberation Story*, he describes it as both a crisis and a moment of transformation. His illness not only gave him pause but it also granted him a vision of the profound interdependence of all phenomena. He vowed to do more to help others. He also said that he learned to depend on others more. He was profoundly indebted to the deity Yarlha Shampo, whom he credited with helping his recovery. Six months later, still ill, he went back into retreat at the bottom of Jomo Gangkar and again credited this mountain deity for further improvements to his health.

Perhaps the most significant evidence of the length of Rangjung Dorje's ill health is, however, that he hardly travels anywhere for the next ten years, preferring to stay in the Tölung and Nye Valleys and dedicate himself to writing and teaching. He may not have been living where he wanted to live during this period, but it proved the most productive of his life. In the next ten years, living in these two valleys, he produced a series of works that are still used and treasured more than seven hundred years after their composition. He also solidified his—and the Karmapas'—reputation across the Plateau and beyond as a writer of substance and a charismatic presence.

CHAPTER 4

Teaching

RANGJUNG DORJE arrived back in the Tölung Valley in 1314 at the age of thirty. He lived in this valley for the next ten years. During these ten years, he composed more texts than at any other period of his life, including his most influential works, the *Profound Inner Principles*, his commentaries on the *Kālācakra Tantra* and astrology, and his most well-known work, the *Birth Stories of the Teacher*. He also wrote the first section of his autobiography here. This period was followed by long retreats in both New Tsari, where he composed an autocommentary on the *Profound Inner Principles*, and Karma Monastery.

Arguably, the texts that he composed during his stay in these three places have become his most enduring legacy. In these works, he took a group of disparate traditions, practices, and compositional forms, and systemized them. His cohesive presentation of reality and how to realize it have served as the fundamental texts of the Karma Kagyü tradition ever since, for over seven hundred years.

His presentation operates on several levels. At its heart is the continuing relationship between gurus and students, which is exemplified through the Karmapa rebirths. He made the Karmapa reincarnation lineage central to the Karma Kagyü lineage and linked their rebirths into a broader sense of an exemplified lineage through the series of biographies and autobiographies he authored.

He then embedded this central relationship—with its associated theme of reincarnated continuity—within a broader presentation of reality, "the way of things."[230] The Buddhist path to awakening was the realization of "the way of things." Rangjung Dorje's descriptions of this *way* were varied, depending on the practices he used to describe it, but all his descriptions contained common characteristics. "The way of things," he argued, is the union of appearances and emptiness; and the union of appearances and emptiness is the nature of mind. Those who wander through cyclic existence, saṃsāra, or get stuck in the cessation of self, nirvāṇa, do so because they have not realized the nature of mind and are enchanted by its appearances or their cessation. They understand this parade of images dualistically; they think there are things, objects, that exist outside, and that they are being perceived inside by a real subject. Through yogic practices, he insisted, we can remove the obstacles to wisdom and experience the nature of mind directly and nondually. He described this nature of mind in one of his most well-known songs, *The Song That Settles the Ground-of-All.*

> It is analogous to a mirror without tarnish,
> On which reflections appear; just like this,
> In the expansive state of unstained mind,
> A variety of awareness flows and perishes.[231]

At different moments in Tibetan Buddhist history, Rangjung Dorje's description of "the way of things" has become a point of much discussion. As his work systemized and clearly defined the parameters of the Karma Kagyü view, many of its followers, including later Karmapas, grappled with his presentation to improve their understanding of reality. His writings on emptiness have also been used, however, within the context of an ongoing, centuries-long Tibetan debate about the difference between and superiority of either "intrinsic emptiness" (*rangtong*, literally "empty of self") and "extrinsic emptiness" (*shentong*, literally "empty of other").[232] Later commentators determined that Rangjung Dorje's approach was an exemplar of the "extrinsic emptiness" view and used it to argue for or against their position. But he did not use either term, and those who suggested he was an advocate for extrinsic emptiness tended to privilege some of his writings over others.

If we position Rangjung Dorje's compositions in their historical context, by contrast, it seems as if he may have been engaged in an entirely other debate. In this debate, he and other members of the broader Kagyü tradition, as well as those members of the Nyingma tradition who practiced and promoted the Great Completion teachings, argued for the primacy of a path based on close, sometimes unconventional interactions between gurus and students. These interactions, they suggested, formed the mainstay of the Buddhist path and allowed for the guru to give direct guidance to the student so that the student may perceive the nature of their mind. The way that the student got to this state depended entirely on the interactions between the guru's wisdom and the student's trust in the teacher. A fully qualified teacher was one with direct insights into the nature of the mind, and a good student appreciated and aspired to develop this quality in themselves.

On the other side of this debate, many teachers of the Sakya tradition, chief among them Sakya Paṇḍita, had argued for very conventional readings of the rules and regulations around tantric practices and the strict adherence to the divisions between the variant Buddhist traditions. They disapproved of those Kagyü practices that they deemed to be "innovations" from the Indian tradition, like those forms of mahāmudrā they deemed to cross boundaries between the tantra and sūtra traditions and the Kagyü reimagining of Indian pīṭhas on the Tibetan Plateau.

The retort from the Kagyüpas, more generally, was to criticize the inflexibility of the Sakya approach.[233] Rangjung Dorje's response combined this criticism with an alternate, argued, and articulated vision of this flexibility. His vision of reality was based on what he understood to be the commonalities between the three teachings that had been most influential in his life: the Mahāmudrā, the Great Perfection, and the Madhyamaka, or Middle Way, the latter of which was often associated with the sūtra tradition. His key insight and contribution in this regard was his conviction that they were all pointing toward the same experience and were, therefore, all valid. If his work does contain the seeds of any later ideas, it is perhaps the nonaligned, or Rime, approach that would be articulated by nineteenth-century adepts six centuries after his life. The term he repeatedly used to describe his approach was "sideless" or "impartial" (*chogme*).[234] His choice to link the abstract sense of this word with a more mundane "sideless" approach to interfamily fights, decisions about where to live, and a general sense of disengagement from ordinary affairs is, furthermore, a notable and insightful element of his teachings.

Another important aspect of his teachings was the links he made between the development of the view and the practice of tantric yoga. Tantric yogas are, he repeatedly stated, the most efficient way to attain clarity about the way things are. To practice tantric yogas, a yogi needed to understand the subtle energies that underpinned appearances and develop the ability to manipulate these energies. To do this, in turn, they needed a very skilled guru, and, if at all possible, conducive external conditions, preferably a sacred site.

Consequently, his writing during this time focused on one of these three interrelated topics: (1) the biographies of teachers, including himself; (2) descriptions of the subtle energies that underpinned our bodily and cosmic realities; and (3) explanations both of "the way of things" and the mistakes unawakened beings make about them.

His approach to these topics reflected the privileged education he received as the recognized rebirth of Karma Pakshi. Their backdrop was the blended Buddhist cosmologies of the Abhidharma and *Kālācakra Tantra*. Within this vast temporal and geographic setting, he crafted both personal stories of lived lives and presented philosophical paradigms. Furthermore, he combined these broader descriptions of reality with more focused instructions for his students. This more personalized approach was primarily based on Nāropā's six dharmas. From within these teachings, he made particular use of the phrase "like an illusion"[235] to describe the way his students should look at their worlds. The ability to experience reality "like an illusion" was not, however, a license for them to behave badly or even wildly. Instead, he insisted that the mahāmudrā vision of the world would most likely be experienced by those who maintained an intense personal discipline.

These instructions reflected his ethos that reality was most easily realized through a combination of rigorous monasticism and yogic practice. His writing suggests that he had early struggles with monasticism but became more comfortable with it as his yogic skills improved. His social world was the heterosocial and strictly ordered world of monks, but his visions were full of all sorts of beings, not just male and female, but human and nonhuman, of this world and beyond.

For most of the middle part of his life, a time in which he systemized the Karma Kagyü tradition, he was based in a large hermitage that he founded near Tsurpu named Dechen Teng. It was located on a hillside, down the Tölung Valley from Tsurpu, and survived for many centuries after Rangjung Dorje's life. Today, no one seems quite sure exactly where it was located. His choice to build this hermitage rather than stay at Tsurpu Monastery demonstrated his still-complicated relationship with that institution; he was not entirely of it, nor was he wholly separated from it. The monastery seemed to enjoy, for example, his growing reputation. He was increasingly asked to preside over rituals at Tsurpu, and it accepted all the donations that he attracted to the region. The monastery even took to sending him to significant social and political events outside the valley as its representative.

As the decade progressed, Rangjung Dorje felt both increasing political pressure to involve himself in local and imperial politics and a growing desire to return to retreat in Kongpo. By then in his forties, he was increasingly torn between these two directions. For a while, retreat won, and he was able to return with better resources to Kongpo. But eventually he was drawn into the powerful centrifugal force of the Mongol emperor's court and forced to leave Kongpo for its capitals.

Composing Texts at Tsurpu

When he first arrived back in the Tölung Valley after over a decade away, Rangjung Dorje went to stay with his teacher Darma at Trashi Sarma Hermitage, where he had first stayed as a child. In some ways, the writing he began there was a continuation of the work he started at Trashi Sarma many years before. When last there, he had composed the *Liberation Story of Past Lives* and the song that listed his previous lives. When he came back, he began to collate, edit, and add to the stories of the Buddha's past lives. He finished this work, which became known as the *Birth Stories of the Teacher*, during his first year back in the valley.[236]

After completing this work, he went into a long retreat on the *Kālacakra Tantra* in which he experienced an intense vision that awakened his interest in astrology. In this vision, he saw that each of the twelve astrological houses were reflections of elements of the subtle body. The vision led him to compose an influential treatise on astrology and create a calendar that has been used by Karma Kagyü followers ever since.[237]

Although these two accomplishments may seem divergent, both the *Birth Stories of the Teacher* and his work on the calendars reflect Rangjung Dorje's lifelong interest in the multiple relationships between time and space, which, given the historical and geographical circumstances of his life, is quite remarkable. As he reflected in his writing, Rangjung Dorje's recognition as Karma Pakshi's rebirth made personal to him the links across time and the vastness of time as a concept. It was an idea he had to grapple with to live with his reincarnate identity. Both of these works, *Birth Stories of the Teacher* and his commentary on the *Kālacakra Tantra*, deal with the concept of time and its vastness in different ways: the *Birth Stories of the Teacher* personalize time, connecting it with lived lives across a grand temporal sweep; the *Kālacakra Tantra* conceptualizes this temporal vastness. Both texts also connect time to places. The lives lived in the *Birth Stories* are embodied lives, lived in specific places. The *Kālacakra Tantra* describes both the passing of time and the space in which this time unfolds.

One of the most interesting ways that Rangjung Dorje's writing articulates the relationship between time and space is with his focus on movement. Even when we are still, he reflects, there is still the movement of energy within and without our bodies. Like the *Birth Stories of the Teacher*, his writings on the *Kālacakra Tantra* also created multiple links between the presence and movement of subtle energies within the body and without it. In these presentations, time and space were described according to the personal experience of them, the cosmic unfolding of them, and—based on the yogic presentations of the body—how these two processes reflect each other.

Rangjung Dorje continued to combine his yoga practice with broader explorations as he first built and then moved into the new hermitage that he called Dechen Teng in 1319. Dechen Teng was named for his grandteacher Götsangpa's retreat in Bütra, which he had visited as a child. Rangjung Dorje built his Dechen Teng down the Tölung Valley from Tsurpu and stayed in it for over a decade. From this site, he was able to attend occasionally to his growing social and political responsibilities as a religious hierarch within Tibetan society and the Mongol polity, but he dedicated most of his time to retreat and writing.

In 1322, three years after moving into Dechen Teng, he composed the *Profound Inner Principles*. The content of the *Profound Inner Principles* was created for followers of the Karma Kagyü lineage who had already been empowered to practice tantric yogas and had already completed preliminary practices. It is important, therefore, to respect the traditions around its use and refer to it in broad rather than specific terms. The chapters of the text outline gradually the "way of being" of the mind in relation to the subtle body. The work takes as its starting point the premise that the nature of the mind, and, therefore, the nature of all beings, is the *sugatagarbha*, the essence of the blissful one, which is to say, the Buddha. It then describes the subtle body's development in utero based on causes and conditions. It explains how the sugatagarbha is immanent within this subtle body, the way to practice yogas that manipulate its energies, the subtle body's connection to the external environment, and how the understanding and practice of yoga will lead to realization. It is remarkable in its detailed exposition of the subtle body, its energies, channels, essences, and cycles. And it links these elements of the body with the aspects of the awakened state—the body, speech, and mind of buddhas.

Elizabeth M. Callahan, a practitioner who worked with Karma Kagyü teachers to understand and translate the *Profound Inner Principles*, writes in her introduction to it that Rangjung Dorje based his presentation on one class of the tantric cycles of texts that were brought from India to Tibet, the Niruttara Tantras, or

Unsurpassed Tantras. These include the *Kālacakra*, *Vajra Garland*, *Hevajra*, *Cakrasaṃvara*, and *Saṃvaroḍaya Tantras*.[238]

Although the *Profound Inner Principles* is primarily focused on the development and use of the subtle body, several chapters within it (chapters one, six, and nine) also outline Rangjung Dorje's understanding of ultimate reality, the nature of mind, and empty appearences. These descriptions of reality fell broadly within the framework of the Vajrayāna in the Tibetan Buddhist tradition. They represented an acceptance of the Madhyamaka, or Middle Way, presentation of reality. But they did it in a slightly different way than his contemporaries, and this made his writing on these subjects of much interest to later Tibetan and Western scholars.

The difference in his approach led many of these later commentators to insist that Rangjung Dorje was an early advocate of "extrinsic emptiness." As already stated, Rangjung Dorje did not use this term in his writing. It was first used by his contemporary and probable student Dölpopa Sherap Gyaltsen (1292–1361) to describe the "way things are" in positive rather than negative terms. Dölpopa insisted that conventional or relative truth was indeed empty of its own nature, but the final truth, the nondual nature of mind, the buddha nature, was only empty of this false conventional nature. It was empty of all else, in other words, but not its own nature. Following Dölpopa, others adopted and adapted the term "extrinsic emptiness" to describe various iterations of a positive presentation of the ultimate reality.

Dölpopa contrasted this positive description of the final reality with another view of it that he called "intrinsic emptiness." Presentations of the final reality as intrinsically empty focused on its lack of an unchanging essence or self; the final reality, they suggest, is the mere lack of this essence or self. It is a negation, not an affirmation by way of a negation.

As the centuries passed, the debate over this philosophical point became entangled with politics and political debates. Dölpopa was associated with the Jonang tradition. Three centuries after his death, this sect was banned by the Tibetan government, which was headed by the then-dominant followers of the Geluk school. The founder of the Geluk school, Tsongkhapa (1357–1419), had spoken adamantly against extrinsic emptiness, and when they banned the Jonang school, the members of the government also decided to ban the extrinsic emptiness presentation of emptiness too. This philosophical censorship lasted for another three centuries until in the nineteenth century, when proponents of the nonsectarian movement, such as Jamgön Kongtrül (1813–1899), began to promote it again. When they did, they claimed anachronistically and perhaps incorrectly that Rangjung Dorje was an early proponent of the tradition.

According to Karl Brunnhölzl, who has analyzed Rangjung Dorje's presentation of reality more than any other modern scholar, the philosophical argument for Rangjung Dorje's inclusion within the "exponents of extrinsic emptiness" category depends on what you mean by "extrinsic emptiness" and which of Rangjung Dorje's texts you are using to exemplify his view.

Brunnhölzl suggests six primary texts that outline Rangjung Dorje's view. Most of these were written during his stay at Dechen Teng or shortly after, in either Karma or Kongpo. They are:

1. *Ornament That Explains Dharma and Dharmadhātu* (1320, Dechen Teng)[239]
2. *Profound Inner Principles,* chapters one, six, and nine (1322, Dechen Teng)[240]
3. *Distinction between Consciousness and Wisdom* (1323, Dechen Teng)[241]
4. *Profound Inner Principles' Autocommentary* (1325, Kongpo)[242]

5. *Commentary on Nāgārjuna's In Praise of Dharmadhātu* (1326 or 1327, Karma)[243]
6. *Pointing Out the Tathāgatagarbha* (date and site of composition unknown)[244]

As Brunnhölzl explains in his analysis of these texts, despite their reputation for advocating extrinsic emptiness, they are "squarely based in both the classical Yogācāra and Madhyamaka systems."[245] The difference in Rangjung Dorje's approach comes down to the fact that he described "the way of things" from a combination of both these traditions and presented them in relation to the presentations of the nature of the mind in the tantras.

Rangjung Dorje's presentation suggested that the "naturally pure mind without any adventitious stains"[246] was equivalent to the buddha nature, which was also known as both the *sugatagarbha* and the *tathāgatagarbha*. Beings did not realize this "way of things," however, and got caught up in dualistic appearances. They thought there was an experiencing person, a subject, who was seeing things out there, objects. Throughout his work, particularly his songs, he describes these mistaken appearances in various ways; they are "birds' footprints in the sky"[247] or "a magician's sleight of hand."[248] In another song, he described beings' dualistic relationship with appearances in this way:

Conceptions[249] are clear and unable to be grasped.
They are like the moon's reflection in the water.
Momentarily impermanent, they are like dew.
Moving yet not apprehended, they are just like a mirage.
Wonderful yet fraudulent, they are like the colors of a
rainbow.
Arising from conditions, they are just like echoes.
Turning out to be insubstantial, they are like a reflection.[250]

The terminology Rangjung Dorje used came from a variety of traditions, depending on the topic about which he was writing. In his stories, songs, and letters, which were not directly linked to any philosophical topic, he combined terminology from various traditions. He used the idea of the two truths and the mere absence of an inherent self from the Madhyamaka, or Middle Way, tradition. And he used terms from the Yogācāra, or Way of the Yogi, tradition, such as the threefold presentation of reality (the imaginary, other-dependent, and ultimate realities), and he described our understanding of reality by way of the eight consciousnesses (the five sense consciousnesses, the mental consciousness, the deluded consciousness, and the basis-of-all consciousness).[251]

He integrated terms and thoughts from the two traditions, presenting them as interconnected and noncontradictory. His was a different approach than those who later analyzed his work because—as Klaus-Dieter Mathes has pointed out[252]—he was less influenced by the "system of tenets" philosophical genre.[253] The whole point of this genre, which came to prominence shortly after Rangjung Dorje's life, was to assign the writings of various teachers to predetermined philosophical categories. This practice then had the flow-on effect of encouraging writers discussing "the way of things" to compose arguments within proscribed categories. Rangjung Dorje paid homage to different systems of thought and wrote on texts within different systems of thought, but he did not write strictly within the latterly imposed doxographic categories, and this confused later analysts.

His point of view was not entirely off the charts either. Brunnhölzl has shown how Rangjung Dorje's presentation closely follows precedents set by early propagators of Buddhism in Tibet—teachers that Rangjung Dorje understood to be closely associated with his hero Padmasambhava—such as Śāntarakṣita (725–788) and his student Kamalaśīla (740–795). These two Indian scholars, who visited

Tibet during the time of the Tibetan Empire, blended Madhyamaka and Yogācāra, leading the doxographers who were trying to classify their approach to call it Madhyamaka-Yogācāra.[254] But Rangjung Dorje does not make a case for this school. His works merely align with it in some instances.

Another significant influence on the development of Rangjung Dorje's work that is less explored in discussions of his view is Saraha. Saraha's influence on Rangjung Dorje's thought might be missed if one only examines his prose writings from this period, but it is everywhere evident in his poetry. During this time, while he was composing prose commentaries, he was also writing a series of songs about Saraha and commentaries to his songs.[255] In these songs, Rangjung Dorje not only evoked the Madhyamaka and Yogācāra perspectives, but he also combined the wisdom of these sūtra traditions with the views of Mahāmudrā. He praised Saraha for his presentation of the view,[256] and he repeatedly wrote about how he saw no contradiction between the presentations of the sūtra traditions and the Mahāmudrā.

He was also one of the most influential advocates for the combining of the Mahāmudrā and Great Completion views during this time. He composed treatises on the Great Completion[257] and included terms and ideas from this tradition within his general writing. Famously, in his *Aspiration for Mahāmudrā*, he wrote:

> The Mahāmudrā is free from mental work.
> The Great Middle Way is free from extremes.
> Since it includes everything, it is the Great Completion.
> May we gain the confidence of realizing all by knowing one.[258]

Rangjung Dorje's view of the ultimate, as he said repeatedly, encompassed multiple presentations without deeming any of them contradictory. He was very much "sideless" or "impartial" when it came to the worth of these various traditions. As he put it in another of his songs:

> Intelligence that knows impartiality
> Actualizes all knowing, all understanding, and
> Destroys all the mind's veils, those internal and external.
> But such intelligence is not expert; it is simply patient.[259]

Rangjung Dorje's advocacy for "sidelessness" stood in contrast to the position the Sakya were advocating. Following the lead of its luminary, Sakya Paṇḍita, they considered some of the Kagyü practices that blended sūtra and tantra traditions, particularly Gampopa's practice of sūtra mahāmudrā, as akin to the Chinese belief of "instant awakening" that was expelled from Tibet after the at-least-semimythical Samye Debate.[260] In many places within Rangjung Dorje's writing, there are veiled and nonveiled jibes at Sakya positions on a variety of topics and on their actions as governors.[261] This pattern suggests that rather than engaging in an anachronistic debate about extrinsic and intrinsic emptiness, Rangjung Dorje's work could be read as an indirect argument against the Sakya position. He, unlike them, was dedicated to finding the common ground between all the different traditions of Tibetan Buddhism—between sūtra and tantra, between Mahāmudrā and the Great Completion, and between the traditional lineages and the treasure traditions.

And it was not just his inclusive attitude to conceptions of the view that brought Rangjung Dorje into conflict with the Sakya polemicists. He was also at odds with them over the repositioning from India into Tibet of the sacred sites described in the *Cakrasaṃvara Tantra*, the pīṭhas. Rangjung Dorje argued for this.[262] Sakya Paṇḍita and other members of the Sakya tradition argued against it.[263]

During this period, Rangjung Dorje developed his long-standing relationships with several important students too. He did not write very much about his students.[264] The only student he mentions by name in his liberation story is the monk who would latterly become known as the First Zhamarpa, Drakpa Sengge (1284–1349).[265] But there are other high-profile students associated with him. These include the scholar Yakde Pachen (1299–1378), the visionary Longchen Rabjampa (1308–1364), and the previously mentioned Dölpopa Sherap Gyaltsen, who established the extrinsic emptiness exposition.[266] The lack of reference to them in his writing makes it difficult to determine how much of an influence he had on them. Even the list of letters and pieces of advice within his Collected Works do not tell us very much about his relationship with his most well-known students.

Toward the end of his stay at Dechen Teng, Rangjung Dorje's attention turned from pondering the extent and nature of the cosmos to his own story, when he composed the first section of the *Verse Liberation Story*. As his time at Dechen Teng drew to a close, he also became more involved with events and projects happening around him, even traveling regularly to events outside the valley. While at Dechen Teng, and as he traveled further around central Tibet, he continued his lifelong habit of engaging with local places, spirits, and gods and of reimagining the way that future generations would understand these places. He wrote several praises to Dechen Teng, for example, describing it as a site in which Indian mythology unfolded within Tibet. It reads in part:

> I wonder at the elephantine king of mountains,
> Mount Meru, the earthly king, on whose crown
> Indra sits proudly, steadying the earth, with
> His ministers arrayed around him.

His ornamental mālā of essential vajras,
These baroque adornments can be seen from all directions,
While the alpine meadows on the mountains' edges are
Decorated by a mantle of assorted flower clusters.

Thick mists are the mountains' white crowns;
They are graced by parasols of peaceful white clouds.
There is a clear spring here that is so clear
The divining Sūrya could use it to see in all directions.

The small mountains, the divine council of Indra's
ministers,
Are decorated with maiden cascades and short-legged trees,
Whose branches move graciously in the breeze.

Flocks and flocks of delightful birds and
Swarms of young bees circle and soar;
I wonder whether [this place] is the
Equal of [Śakra's] pleasure grove?[267]

Along with Dechen, in 1319, he also composed another series of landscaping songs about Mount Jomo Kharak, on the southern bank of the Yarlung Tsangpo River, between the two provinces of central Tibet, Ü and Tsang. Each song describes the mountain from one of the cardinal directions. In contrast to his praise to Dechen Teng, which used many of the images from ornamental Indian poetry, or *kāvya*, his songs about Jomo Kharak emphasized Tibetan imagery. They describe Tibet with ancient terms such as "the heights from which pure rivers descend."[268] And they paint a very localized description of his home. The song written in North Kharak, for example, reads in part:

Up in this group of snowy mountains, this lotus cluster,
We are surrounded by Jambudvīpa's great ocean.
Up here, bright, sweet waterfalls sparkle, refreshing all;
Both those who taste the water and those who imagine it...

Above is the beautiful, pervasive sky
With its delightful star mālā covering all;
I wonder if the wisdom realizing emptiness
Pervades all wanderers in the same way.[269]

During this period, Rangjung Dorje was often involved in rituals that were understood to transform and purify the environment too. His role model for these activities was Padmasambhava, whom he understood to be the original transformer of Tibet's spiritual landscape. While staying at Jomo Gangkar, however, he took his aspiration to emulate Padmasambhava one step further. Instead of praying for Padmasambhava's influence in his rituals, he was convinced that he needed to behave more like him. His change of heart occurred after he had a vision of Padmasambhava while setting up a statue of his hero in the cave at Jomo Gangkar. From this vision, he wrote that he understood "the awakened activity of the scholar of Oḍḍiyāna [Padmasambhava] still needed to be performed in every direction, even in these days."[270]

As his writing reflects, Rangjung Dorje, like most other people in his community, understood himself to exist in an environment in which Padmasambhava had tamed all the problematic spirits and made them honor bound to help Buddhist practitioners, especially yogis like him. Padmasambhava was believed to have tamed the earth guardians in the middle of the Pelmo Tang Plain, for example. Another even more famous story about him describes how he had tamed the spirits in and around Tibet's first monastery,

Samye Monastery, so that it could be built. But here, in the cave at the bottom of Jomo Gangkar, Rangjung Dorje believed himself to have received a clear message from Padmasambhava that this work was not complete; there were still malicious demons out and about on the Plateau.

In the vision, he was even given the location of a place where a spirit was causing trouble; it was further northeast, toward the Chang Tang Plain. A spirit there had begun to transform the locals' behavior and was demanding blood sacrifices and depraved behavior. Tsuklak Trengwa goes into some detail about this behavior. He says that the people were sacrificing everything "from wild yaks to sparrows" to the spirit and creating severe negative consequences for both themselves and the spirit.[271]

Rangjung Dorje set off for the area to right this wrong. When he arrived, the people were misbehaving so badly that he chose not to emulate Padmasambhava's reportedly wrathful approach toward such beings. Instead, he used "the luminosity of Śākyamuni's compassion"[272] to pacify the area. In practice, this meant rather than terrifying the locals into submission, he moved into the village, began to teach them Buddhism, and slowly won them over. At the end of his stay, he and his biographers agree, both the locals and the spirit bowed to him and took vows to help him in this and all future lives.[273]

After his sojourn on the edge of the Chang Tang Plain, Rangjung Dorje became determined to return to Kongpo and engage in long retreats there. He had repeatedly expressed his desire to return to Kongpo through the duration of his stay in central Tibet. Even on the day he founded Dechen Teng Hermitage, he had a visionary dream in which Avalokiteśvara told him to leave for Kongpo. "My luminosity radiates there," the bodhisattva told him, "and it is in accordance with the Karmapa's [Karma Pakshi's] prophecy [that you live there]."[274]

It is unusual for Rangjung Dorje to describe a vision of a deity instructing him to do something and then not do as he was told. Although he does not state it directly, his actions and several other comments in the *Verse Liberation Story* suggest that it took him years to fully recover from the illness he had experienced in Kongpo, and by the time he had, he was enmeshed in the social and political worlds of central Tibet. Eventually, in 1325, over a decade since he first went there, he returned to Kongpo. And this time, shortly after he arrived there, he set up a new hermitage named Nakpu Hermitage, in the Nelungchu Valley, in New Tsari. It, too, lasted for centuries after Rangjung Dorje's death, while Kongpo remained a stronghold of the Karma Kagyü. References to it only stop appearing in the Karmapas' life stories after battles between the Dalai Lama's Ü-based backers and the Karmapas' Tsang-based backers destroyed many Karma Kagyü temples and sent the Tenth Karmapa, Chöying Dorje (1604–1674), into exile.[275]

In creating Nakpu Hermitage, Rangjung Dorje relied on many of the same cultural and social strategies to establish it that he had used to establish pilgrimage routes to Mount Khawa Karpo, Tsurpu Monastery, and his own establishment in the Tölung Valley, Dechen Teng. He described the visions he experienced, sang praises to the site, and "tamed the locals" (humans and nonhumans) by granting them refuge and bodhisattva vows.[276]

He added further to the site's sacred value by using the "exponential increase in wisdom" he experienced there to "compose an autocommentary to the *Profound Inner Principles*."[277] He also linked the region to stories of his heroes, predecessors, and protectors, particularly Padmasambhava, who he claimed had undertaken retreat in the adjacent Kongtrang Valley. What is more, according to his own and others' reports, he followed in Padmasambhava's footsteps in yet another way; he developed a close relationship with the region's female earth guardians, or ḍākinīs. The most detailed narrative about his interactions with the ḍākinīs is recorded in Tsuklak Trengwa's biography of Rangjung Dorje. He quotes a description recorded by a scholar named Tsama Paṇchen who went to visit Rangjung Dorje in New Tsari along with a relatively large entourage. Tsama Paṇchen asked to be introduced to the region's famous ḍākinīs, and Rangjung Dorje agreed but warned them of the ḍākinīs' trickery. Tsuklak Trengwa, relying on Tsama Paṇchen's report of the event, described the encounter.

> It was the dead of winter, and New Tsari was blanketed in snow. Rangjung Dorje, Tsama Paṇchen, and his followers traveled through the region on horseback. After Rangjung Dorje invited the ḍākinīs to come out to meet them, his gaze became like the wind, and his black horse started traveling eastward. Presently, a mist with rainbow colors unfolded itself [around them], and in [the rainbow] they all saw eighteen women singing. They stopped their horses, and [the ḍākinīs] granted them a hand empowerment before telling them to leave. The ḍākinīs then departed. Rangjung Dorje warned them not to let their mind drift in [the ḍākinīs' presence], as he had earlier lost people to them. Even today, he said, they had taken his bodyguard's horse, and he was sure they would return [for more horses and people].[278]

It is worth noting regarding this encounter that it was the visitors, not Rangjung Dorje, who described the ḍākinīs with such foreboding. In his writing about them, both they and their country are much more welcoming and warmer than ominous and scary. Although many stories about ḍākinīs emphasize their otherworldly capriciousness, Rangjung Dorje's stories about them are notable for their ordinary helpfulness. At one time, he notes, a landslide blocked the road, and while he wondered what to do next, he and his companions noticed that "the ḍākinīs, those faithful nonhumans, made a road [for him and his party] out of the [Yarlung] Tsangpo River's sands."[279]

Along with his appreciation for the ḍākinīs, he also writes often of his appreciation for the Nelungchu Valley's environment. One of the poems he wrote there says the following:

> Attain siddhi precisely in
> Solitary places that are bustle-free,
> Like the solitary environs of Tsari and
> Wonderful Nakpu. Then you will be
> Undistracted by worldliness. Lack of distraction is excellent.
>
> In this place, the impartial mountaintops are
> Difficult for ordinary wanderers to pass, and so it is secluded
> From those parts of Dharma that descend into
>   entertainment...
>
> Encircled by a mālā of beautiful snow mountains,
> Is another mālā of rocky mountains, sitting like stūpas.
> The valley below them is filled with forests of trees, and
> Streams of nectar descend from them, as many as you could
>   want.
>
> We sit here in their midst is a beautiful meadow,
> In which there are tasty foods and medicine;
> It is brimming with a multitude of ingredients.[280]

During the same stay, he also wrote descriptions of how to "extract the essence" from some specific plants that grew in the area and likewise noted down ways to live in these regions with minimal access to agricultural products or village luxuries.[281]

In contrast to his earlier cultural landscaping projects, his writings about Nakpu Hermitage are tempered by another tendency in his writing from this period to deconstruct his own literary and cultural processes. In a song he sang for his followers at a meadow in Nelungchu Valley, for example, he writes against the habits of a lifetime to introduce a skeptical attitude toward the idea of a sacred site. Ultimately, he suggests, sacred sites are a mere reference point for understanding the subtle body's processes. Part of this song reads:

When we speak of all the buddhas' pure lands,
The twenty-four sacred sites [and so on], it is not
As if they truly exist out there;
Our bodies, too, contain the channels and *cakras*.[282]
Or, to be specific, at the great, sacred sites
[Within our bodies] those called *ḍākas* and *ḍākinīs*
Abide in the elements and essences.

When we speak of the essence,
We speak of the indivisible hardness[283] which
[Manifests] as hair and fingernails as it descends.
And, likewise, when we speak of the
Twenty-four elements that manifest at these sites,
We speak specifically of the three channels, the hidden
channels:
The left, right, and central bodily channels.

Get the vital point that the myriad interdependencies
Are the indivisible subject and object, method and wisdom.
See saṃsāra and nirvāṇa's nonduality, their nonself;
[See] what the Buddha called "the great sacred site."

Arouse bliss, clarity, and nonconceptual wisdom,
Because the sacred sites of the five hidden channels
Are where the five ḍākinīs live,
And their entity is pure subtle energy...

[To have] the concept of external sacred sites
Is to generate an obsession with places;
This end-of-time vajra yogi destroys
Complicated, external sacred sites.[284]

Soon after he wrote this song, in 1326, political events in central Tibet forced him to leave Kongpo and return there. Rangjung Dorje is obscure about their details, but they have been recorded elsewhere. It appears that he was summoned to the center by Tsurpu's local lord, the Tsel myriarch Künga Dorje—the author of the *Red Annals*—because he needed Rangjung Dorje's help to resolve a dispute between his compatriots and pilgrims visiting Lhasa from Kham.[285] After resolving this conflict, Rangjung Dorje was about to leave for Kongpo again, when the region was consumed by an even bigger fight, this time between the two main houses of the ruling Sakya Monastery.

The tensions at Sakya had begun after the death of Zangpo Pel (1262–1324), its abbot and influential ruler. As the last male heir of Sakya's ruling family, the Khön, Zangpo Pel had been required to produce male heirs. But when he exceeded in this duty by siring eleven sons, Sakya had problems of a different type; there were multiple disagreements over who should succeed him and fulfill the two main administrative roles at Sakya, abbot and lord.

The imperial preceptor, Künga Lodrö Gyeltsen (1299–1327), who was also one of Zangpo Pel's sons but living away from the action in Beijing, sought to resolve the tensions by dividing the monastery into four houses and then selecting four of Zangpo Pel's sons to run them. In the wake of this reform, Namkha Lekpe Gyeltsen (1305–1343), the abbot of Sakya, lost all his power,[286] and Özer Sengge (d. 1329), who was Great Lord of Sakya at that time, took control. This event caused the people from the abbot's house to start fighting with the members of the Great Lord's house. In 1327, rumors began to spread that Mongol troops would be brought in to quell the dispute, and many hierarchs from central Tibet, including Rangjung Dorje, fled to Kham.[287]

Rangjung Dorje arrived at Karma Monastery in the same year. He may have been safe there, but he was also struggling to come to terms with what he had seen on his flight east. It was at this point that he wrote his most poignant, descriptive, and political song. I have provided an extensive analysis of this song elsewhere,[288] so here it will hopefully be enough to quote this song at length. It describes the fighting between the different Sakya houses in the following way:

> Those monks don't behave right.
> Debauchery sustains them, and
> The three Dharma robes don't sit well on them;
> They are just yellow shapes, wearing brocade, carrying the
> sticks
> [They use] to chase away dogs, sons, nephews, and neighbors.
> And still, like dogs, they crave more.
>
> To get what they want, they do things that aren't right;
> The little wealth they have, they use in unjust ways.
> They encourage others to do evil;
> To punish humble dhārmikas,
> They reward lies and other bad behavior.
> They pretend to be Great Ones, but do not behave like them.

Just as it is unseemly for shepherds to kill antelope;
It is also unseemly for these people to drink beer,
Ruin their attention, keep women, and have improper sex.

The emperor does not follow the Dharma,
He is controlled by those who lust and hate.
His lord may be "great" [i.e., the Great Lord of Sakya], but
He is a "great" bandit, a "great" crook.
He brings punishment on truthful people
And fills the land with thieves.
His [followers] destroy temples and stūpas,
Crush and consume their images,
And disrespect Dharma texts.[289]

After criticizing the actions of the monks, the last part of the song goes on to describe the impact of their actions on the land and people they were supposed to be protecting.

Because of this, the gods and spirits
Are shaken, and disease fills the land;
Rain does not fall; there are poor harvests,
And what little that does grow is
Carried away by frosts and hail.

Many are robbed and beaten
By famine's destitution, so they
Cry out, dying on the road.

A few people eat the flesh of others;
A few sell their children for food.
Others, racked with hunger, jump in the river.

Wailing, wailing they don't know night and day;
Their skeletons are barely covered with the skin
That hangs off them: off bones and off heads.
Their [corpses] burn up like vegetation.
Seeing them is like seeing hungry ghosts directly.
Everywhere there is killing, shackling, and beating;
Pus and blood trickle from all the leprous boils and lesions.
Seeing this is like seeing the hell realms directly.
For these people, the road to the four pure continents is
  blocked;
They could easily be taken for animals. They are in human
  bodies
But they experience the sufferings of the lower realms.

Kye ma! Evil times are upon us!
Kye hu! Poor beings!
Don't the bodhisattvas think of them? These destitute
People in these lands of Amdo, Kham, and Tö?
I fear the whole Land of Snows has
Become as unjust as [its rulers].[290]

Rangjung Dorje spent the rest of Özer Sengge's reign at Karma Monastery. Moved by the suffering around him, but unable to move, Rangjung Dorje used his time in this familiar exile to continue his program of textual synthesis, completing commentaries on both Nāgārjuna's *In Praise of Dharmadhātu* and Saraha's *Song Treasury of Dohā*.

His choice to compose these two commentaries at around the same time is telling and further reflects his impartial approach to the various aspects of the tradition he inherited. *In Praise of Dharmadhātu* is often described as a bridge between the sūtra and Mahāmudrā presentations of mind's nature. And Saraha's *Song Trea-*

sury repeatedly downplays the formal aspects of yoga practice in its presentation of mahāmudrā.

During this stay at Karma, Rangjung Dorje lived in the main temple, perhaps because of the fraught state of the region's politics. But he seems, nonetheless, to have kept to himself and his writing during this time. The next public activity he describes himself being involved in only occurred after he left Karma Monastery, on his journey back to central Tibet. This particular activity was quite out of character for him. As he explains in the *Verse Liberation Story*, he interrupted his journey back to central Tibet to become a bridge builder.

> When the first month of the Dragon Year [1328] arrived, I began having many lucid, visionary dreams in which Dharma protectors told me through signs to build a bridge across the Sok River amid the lands of the lay Buddhist Dorje Gyelpo [Vajra King]. I did as they asked, and while we worked on the bridge, neither the nāga king nor his entourage interrupted our work. It meant we were able to achieve our goal.[291]

The Sok River, a tributary of the Gyelmo Ngülchu (Salween) River, was known as a hazardous river that transected a critical trade route.[292] Someone needed to build a bridge across it; the strange thing is that it was Rangjung Dorje, yogi and scholar, who decided to do it. In some ways, it could be seen as an extension of his role as a go-between for humans and spirits, an extension of his spirit-taming exercises, but even he thought that it was out of character. Almost as soon as he had finished the bridge, he reports, he experienced a vision of Avalokiteśvara, who reprimanded him for bridge building and told him to return to retreat and to Kongpo. "If you become distracted by such projects in dark times," Avalokiteśvara warned him in a vision, "obstacles will arise, hordes will invade solitary sites, the Dharma will not proliferate, and many people will become jealous."[293]

After completing the bridge, Rangjung Dorje returned directly to Nakpu Hermitage in Kongpo. He arrived in early 1329 and spent the next three years there. Soon after his arrival, however, a vision reveals to him that he will only be there for a limited time. This vision is not of Avalokiteśvara—who usually tells him to return to Kongpo—but of the bodhisattva Mañjuśrī, who informs him that he will have to travel to the imperial court in Dadu and Xanadu in three years.[294]

Despite this vision, both Rangjung Dorje's *Verse Liberation Story* and his songs described this next stay in Kongpo as productive and peaceful. He established another hermitage in the area, at Lhundrub Teng,[295] and spent much of his time instructing his students there. Initially, he expresses hesitation about taking on the role of guru, reporting frustrations with both himself and his students. In one song, for example, he says,

> I might have developed impartial compassion, but even
> The Buddha's compassion could not protect this lot!
> Their ignorant minds are so densely murky![296]

And, as I have explained elsewhere, he also expressed intense frustration with a group of women that he was teaching during this time; this is the only time in his writing that he is intensely critical of marginalized people.[297] But by the end of his stay in Kongpo, he has embraced his role as a teacher. In one of the last songs he wrote from this period, he reflected on his life's journey in the following way:

> To subdue my pride, I was born the son of a potter,
> But after I die in this life, I will travel to Tuṣita.

My love for wanderers will mean I am present wherever
There are students. I have no other thoughts but to help
others.[298]

But before his journey to Tuṣita, he still had to embark on his longest earthbound journey and to meet an even more demanding group of students. Soon after writing this song, he departed for the Mongol capitals. From this point until the end of his life, he could no longer travel where he wanted or go into retreat as he saw fit; instead, the rest of his life was lived at the behest of the emperor. His return to Kongpo would take some transworldly maneuvering.

CHAPTER 5

Death

IN THE LAST PERIOD of Rangjung Dorje's life, he was gradually forced to leave the mountains and retreat. After departing from Tsari, he traveled not only to central Tibet but also onward to the Mongol capitals: Dadu, in northeastern China, and Xanadu, in southwestern Mongolia.

Many times, and in a variety of ways, he tried to escape his life in the capitals and return to Tibet. His desire to leave created a power play between the last Mongol emperor, Toghon Temür, and the Karmapa that eventually extended over two lifetimes. In many ways, it repeated the tensions that had existed between Karma Pakshi and Toghon Temür's ancestor Qubilai Khan.

Rangjung Dorje had no choice but to come to terms with exile in the capitals. He found ways to occupy himself by teaching and by building temples dedicated to his lineage forebears and to tantric deities. According to his biographers though, eventually, he figured out a way to escape, and in so doing evoke his transmundane power in his contest with the emperor. If Toghon Temür and his advisors did not grant Rangjung Dorje permission to leave the capitals, he would have to leave behind his impermanent body and seek rebirth in the mountains.

Journey to the Mongol Capitals

According to his *Verse Liberation Story*, before the summons from the Mongol emperor arrived, Mañjuśrī appeared to Rangjung Dorje to prepare him for his trip to the capitals. The Mongol Empire was churning through leaders at this point. The ruler who sent Rangjung Dorje his invitation was Tuq Temür (1304–1332). In his short life, he was the Great Khan of the Mongol Empire twice. His first reign lasted from 1328 to 1329. Then his brother Qutughtu (1300–1329; r. 1329) took over for a few months until he was reinstalled in 1329. Tuq Temür then ruled until his death in 1332.

Tuq Temür's summons to Rangjung Dorje has been preserved. As it demonstrates the complicated relationship between the Mongol court and the Tibetans, it is often reproduced in various collections of historical documents.[299] It reads:

> By the blessings of the Three Jewels, [and] in dependence on the glory of great merit, I, the emperor, make this request of Rangjung Dorje. The teachings of the Buddha have spread as far as the northern kings, and the power of their prophetic words has caused a variety of suitable Buddhist Dharma systems to exist [here]. As a consequence of this, even Qubilai Khan respected and relied upon very many spiritual friends. In this place, the popularity of the Buddha's teachings is evident to all.
>
> I also wish to perform excellently [my duty as] an insignificant protector of the teachings. [In this regard,] I have heard much about you. It has been said that you have great learning and that you possess exceptional qualities. I am, therefore, sending you guards and commands [for you to travel to court].
>
> If you offer excuses not to come, then this will disenchant the faithful. The bad-smelling [mental] seeds that would predispose you not to abandon the yogis of your land are faulty; [they] destroy your altruistic desire to help all indiscriminately. [Refusing to come] would be a misdeed that

> does not [accord with] the intention of the teachings. It suggests indifference to the suffering and difficulty of all beings. It is not my intention to cause any harm to the teachings generally, and I will not change [this approach]. I merely ask you as a leader, one who has the intention of helping all beings, to come quickly. If you do come, you will be able to perform teachings as you wish.
>
> This was written on the thirteenth day of the third, spring month in the year of the Sheep [1331].[300]

Unlike his teacher Orgyenpa, Rangjung Dorje did not reject the Mongol summons. He insisted, in the *Verse Liberation Story*, that the reason for his acceptance was his vision of Mañjuśrī rather than the emperor's authority. But there was also intense social pressure for him to make the journey.

At the time when Rangjung Dorje received the summons, central Tibet had endured decades of unrest and famine. Its people had not fared well under Mongol-Sakya rule, and the infighting within the Sakya hierarchy in the 1320s and 1330s had only exacerbated their difficulties. As Turrell Wylie pointed out in an article on Rangjung Dorje's journey to the Mongol courts, Rangjung Dorje's summons was probably an attempt by the Mongol rulers to force a resolution among the Sakya hierarchs.[301] Rangjung Dorje's acquiescence to the request may have been an attempt on his behalf to broker peace amid an internecine conflict.

Not that Rangjung Dorje was in a hurry to get to the courts. For a start, he insisted that before coming he must undertake a rains retreat at Lhundrub Teng. He did not set out until autumn, when he traveled to meet the newly appointed imperial preceptor, Künga Gyeltsen (1310–1365), in Lhasa, and they set off together for the capitals. They had only reached Nakchu, a few hundred kilometers up the China Road from Lhasa, when they were buffeted by a violent storm that Rangjung Dorje described as "a magic show put on for him by Nyenchen Tanglha and other local deities."[302] He took it as a sign that he should not travel, and he returned to Tsurpu Monastery for the winter with his Mongol escort. Künga Gyeltsen continued alone to the Mongol court.

Rangjung Dorje did not travel again until the first day of the second month of the new Tibetan year, at the beginning of another spring. He arrived at the border between Tibet and China months later, having engaged in a teaching tour along the way.

At the border, he experienced another interruption to his journey. This time, he had a foreboding vision that Tuq Temür's health was bad. He performed ceremonies for him in the borderlands and wondered again whether he should return to Tibet.[303] As he pondered this, he had another dream, in which he "heard Dharma protectors proclaiming: 'You will help your students from before, and you will help beings. There will be no obstacles; all your resolutions will be fulfilled.'"[304]

After the dream, he hastened to the capitals. But before he arrived, Tuq Temür died, and a struggle for succession followed. Two of Tuq Temür's nephews, the six-year-old Irinjibal (1326–1332) and the thirteen-year-old Toghon Temür, were both suggested for the throne. When Rangjung Dorje arrived at the palace in Dadu two months after Tuq Temür's death, Irinjibal was about to be enthroned. Rangjung Dorje was presented to him in a grand ceremony at the palace. At the time, according to his biography, he predicted that the young man would not live to be coronated. A year later, both the young emperor and one of his principal backers were dead, and the rival heir, the teenager Toghon Temür, was brought to the capital to ascend the throne.

In Rangjung Dorje's *Verse Liberation Story*, he claims to have had a role in Toghon Temür's coronation ceremony. "On the eighth day of the sixth month of the Bird Year [1333]," he writes, "when

I enthroned the Lord of Men, [I could see] that many worldly protectors had gathered too; they were dancing and gesturing. I took this as a sign that there would be happiness in the empire."[305] Tsuklak Trengwa elaborated substantially on this description. He wrote,

> On the full moon in the first month of the Bird Year [1333], millions of people gathered [in Dadu] at the emperor's invitation. There were so many people that it seemed only a great army could have pushed their way along the road into town. But wherever the precious Dharma noble went, spontaneously, a path appeared before him. Wearing his black hat and chanting OṂ MAṆI PADME HŪṂ, he proceeded smoothly through the crowds.
>
> The emperor was in a big white tent on a golden throne. When he saw Rangjung Dorje from a distance, he left his tent and came to escort him, placing his head at Rangjung Dorje's feet.[306]

This short passage from Tsuklak Trengwa's biography of Rangjung Dorje contains a lot of information, some of which is historically improbable. To begin with, although Dadu was one of the most densely populated cities on the planet at the point, it is highly unlikely that "millions of people" came to Toghun Temür's coronation. The Chinese historical geographer Guanghui Han has estimated that Dadu was home to approximately 418,000 people and another 635,000 in the surrounding region.[307] It is also highly unlikely that Toghun Temür left his tent and placed his head at Rangjung Dorje's feet. If Toghun Temür had behaved like this, it would have been a spectacular breach of protocol that would have been reported elsewhere, and it was not. Indeed, Rangjung Dorje's not-unreasonable claim to have been involved in the coronation is the only historical source we have that he was involved in it at all.

Tsuklak Trengwa's reimagining of the event is historically significant, however, because it shows the importance the Kagyü lineage and Tibetan society placed on Rangjung Dorje's relationship with the Mongol emperor. These interactions, particularly at a ceremony as significant as a coronation, were doing much symbolic work. They lifted Rangjung Dorje's prestige as an individual; the potter's son has traveled far from a life on the edge of the Mongol Empire and the edges of Tibetan society to a position at the center of imperial—or even world—power. It is also an image that reconnects the Third Karmapa, Rangjung Dorje, with the work of the Second Karmapa, Karma Pakshi, who was a guru to Mongol emperors. It is no wonder then that the image of Rangjung Dorje crowning Toghun Temür was reused frequently in Rangjung Dorje's later biographies. Coronations and reincarnates' biographies are, after all, both sites of high symbolism.

Even the high theater and power of the coronation was not enough to convince Rangjung Dorje to stay in the capitals though. Six months after arriving there, he asked the young emperor for permission to leave his court. For a while, there was no answer. As he waited for the emperor's decision, Rangjung Dorje had the first of a long series of visions in which deities he trusted told him to leave the capitals. In this vision, he saw "a hermitage in a fearsome mountainside forest, in which ḍākinīs made offerings to a white man who radiated light. As I watched and listened, the radiant man said, 'Do not stay here, flee to snowy lands. Leaving will help you and others.'"[308]

Rangjung Dorje understood the glowing being to be Avalokiteśvara,[309] once again telling him to leave behind worldly deeds and enter retreat. A short while after this, Rangjung Dorje and the court reached a compromise that he could return to Tibet on the provision that he acquired for the emperor long-life water from Tibet. Long-life water was a highly prized commodity for notoriously short-lived Mongol emperors.[310]

Rangjung Dorje knew that he had to come back to the capitals after attaining the long-life water, so he took his time attaining it. He traveled home via Mount Wutai, a sacred site in northern China dedicated to Mañjuśrī,[311] and then onto the remains of the Tangut court (in what is now Ningxia).[312] The Tangut Empire sat between the Tibetan Plateau and the Mongolian steppe. It had been almost thoroughly destroyed by Mongol forces a century earlier, but the remains of its royal family retained a close connection with the Kagyü tradition and particularly the Karmapas.[313] Rangjung Dorje spent at least several months in Tangut, gave extended teachings to its royal family, and experienced a series of intense visions there.[314] He then continued his travels slowly through Kham,[315] where he once again played peacemaker in a series of disputes, before stopping briefly at Karma Monastery. From Kham, he traveled to Dam in northern central Tibet. There he participated in a religious ceremony and experienced a vision of Nyenchen Tanglha, Jomo Gangkar, and their retinues, "appearing like mists" to welcome him home. But even amid this vision, he notes in the *Verse Liberation Story*, "a voice from the East said, 'Your students here need help,'" and he took this to mean he would have to return to the Mongol court.[316]

After Dam, he continued to Tsurpu Monastery but did not stay there long. The main purpose of his visit was to deposit a good deal of the wealth he had received from the Mongol and Tangut courts. This time, however, he was accorded a great deal more respect than he had been shown as a child. Not only was he asked to stay in the main building, but he was consulted about the choice of the monastery's next abbot; diplomatically, he chose another of Karma Pakshi's relatives.[317]

After Tsurpu, he continued to the site at which he determined he would be able to attain the long-life water, Chimpu Hermitage, in the hills overlooking Samye Monastery. In the *Voice Liberation Story*, he described his stay at Chimpu like this:

> I sought solitude in the Chimpu Hermitage at Samye. I stayed there for six months and experienced many visions of the scholar of Oḍḍiyāna—Padmasambhava—and gatherings of ḍākinīs. I took this as a sign that this scholar and these women would help me. [As I began this retreat,] I saw signs of obstacles. But then came a miraculous display, and [after it] my samādhi became exceedingly peaceful.[318]

Rangjung Dorje does not describe in any detail the process by which he procured the long-life water directly. He also skips over the other activities he performed while back in Tibet. Other sources, for example, suggest that he used some of the funds that he had accrued from the capitals to produce a gold-inked edition of the Buddhist canon.[319] His only mention of this project in the *Verse Liberation Story* reads, "I had all the Buddha's sūtras and the commentaries written out, and when I was consecrating them, countless bodhisattvas appeared to dissolve into them, and I heard a voice proclaiming the Dharma."[320]

This edition of the canon may or may not be the version that later became known as the Tsel edition because it was written or housed at Tsel Monastery, the seat of the Tsel myriarch. If he is referring to the Tsel canon, then Rangjung Dorje's description of having finished it contradicts other sources that say it was finally completed by the young Tsel lord and author of the *Red Annals*, his student Tselpa Künga Dorje, sometime between 1347 and 1351, after Rangjung Dorje's death.[321] Tselpa Künga Dorje does not mention

Rangjung Dorje's contribution to this project in the *Red Annals*. The chronology and relationship between these two writers and their concurrent projects remain unclear and needs more investigation.

As Rangjung Dorje finished his version of the canon, Toghun Temür, or someone from his court, had already sent an envoy to bring him back to the capitals. Rangjung Dorje's protests against his return to the capitals were muffled in the *Verse Liberation Story*. But in his songs from this period and his later stay in the capitals, he is more strident. In these songs, he describes the capitals as the opposite of the sacred sites and hermitages of Tibet. Instead of praising them, he lists their faults and cites the many ways they impede yoga practice. In these descriptions, he produces poetic images of Dada and Xanadu that sit in direct contrast to those found more commonly in both the Chinese and Western poetic traditions. For Rangjung Dorje, Dadu and Xanadu were traps, not paradises. The song he wrote in Xanadu in 1337—which is quoted in the introduction and translated in full in chapter seventeen of this book—reflects this assessment. It reads in part:

> Now you are free from saṃsāra's mud,
> Strike out for nirvāṇa's dry shore.
> Now you have abandoned worldly relatives,
> Rely on sacred, spiritual friends.
> Now you have stopped pointless chatter,
> Recite secret mantras.
> Now you have stopped debauched exertions,
> Exert yourself at *dhyāna*.[322]
> Now you have renounced sweets,
> Rely on samādhi's food.
> Now that you have stopped hankering for towns,
> Wander in mountainous borderlands.

Because when we don't do these things—
External appearances become expert in deception;
Children of the mind, they are crazy in the head.
Preconceptions proliferate and last longer; but
Virtuous friends become increasingly rare.
Ignorant veils and fogs get thicker and
We wander on multiplying cliffs of depravity.
Unwholesome friends lead us
To prison, the three bad destinations,
Where we will wander without end.[323]

The song begins with a plea to his audience and himself not to give up their cultivation of yoga despite their surroundings. In making this plea, it lists unwholesome behaviors that Rangjung Dorje associated with life in large cities; even Tibet's major urban centers could not have been considered cities at that point.

The song pleads with his audience to choose "spiritual friends," Buddhist teachers in other words, over "worldly relatives." Rangjung Dorje, unlike many other Tibetan religious hierarchs and a good percentage of the imperial court, was not part of a large and supportive family group. His outsider status was not as much of a concern within monastic social structures, within which, as a monk, he was considered one of the Buddha's offspring. His plea to focus on spiritual relations is, therefore, a plea for inclusion as well as morality.

Next, he lists further characteristics of city life that he views as detrimental to monastics and yogis: chatter or gossip, debauchery, and sweets. Chatter and gossip, as Rangjung Dorje would come to know all too well, were not just idle nuisances at court, they could get you killed. Rangjung Dorje seems to tire more of the constant intrigues of courtly life than any other of the issues he dealt with there. But this issue was linked to the next issue on his list of problems with cities; according to both his reports and other sources, one of the greatest sources of gossip about monks was their suggested or actual debauchery.[324] His elevation of eating sweet foods to this level of misdeed is also notable. It is a subject that he returned to repeatedly throughout his time in the mountains and the capitals. Eating sweet foods, he suggested, interfered with yogic practice and caused excitement.[325] Sweet food is not usually on the list of things that people find fault with in cities, but it was for Rangjung Dorje.

Although it inverts the order, Rangjung Dorje's negative appraisal of these cities follows a similar process of cultural landscaping to that which he used in other songs to praise sacred sites.[326] The mountains, he had previously declared, were the best place to be. In the mountains, yogis were isolated from the corruption and entertainments of urban centers that were full of politics and distraction. The sacredness of the sites, their visual setting, the medicinal plants, and the animals and spirits that lived there all aided the yogi. Here, he is merely flipping the order and focusing on the decadent center rather than the rarified edges. In cities, one is bombarded by people and politics. The food is harmful, and there is no space for reflection.

His reversal also changes the outcome of the poem; instead of the liberation that one reaches at the end of his other songs, here protagonists that do not leave the city are trapped, imprisoned in the three lower realms.

Along with presenting general overviews in his songs about the dangers of cities, Rangjung Dorje's tells half stories in the *Verse Liberation Story* that hint at episodes in which the mechanics of power in the capitals nearly led to his downfall. They suggest, for example, an episode in which he was forced to appear before a court convened to disrobe all monks because of their alleged corruption. According to Rangjung Dorje, he made representations to the emperor on behalf of the monks and talked the council out of disrobing them all.[327] Another time, he put his own life at risk when he was called to defend his friend, the imperial preceptor Künga Gyeltsen.[328] Another time, he had to defend himself against slander perpetrated by "bad Chinese monks."[329]

Unusually for Rangjung Dorje, and in another inversion of an established literary pattern, he chose to highlight the adverse events he experienced during his stay at Xanadu and Dadu ahead of the positive things he accomplished there. He had been brought to the court to perform the role of a bagshi, and, according to his and other accounts, he performed this role well. It was most probably his acclaimed performance of this role that enabled him to escape and evade the obstacles he encountered while at court. His procurement of the long-life water was the act of a bagshi. But he was particularly venerated at court for his perceived ability to predict when environmental disasters would occur and sometimes even stop them. He was said to have made rain during a drought and to have predicted the 1337 earthquake at Mount Jiming, enabling several of the emperor's family members to escape from it unharmed.[330]

Rangjung Dorje also seemed to get some joy out of using the emperor's resources to build temples. In his *Verse Liberation Story*, for example, he explains in great detail the processes that went into building a large, multiroomed temple in Dadu. The idea for the temple, he explained, came to him in a dream, and thanks to the emperor's acquiescence, he was able to start work on it soon after this. Each room of the temple was dedicated to a different deity with whom he had a special connection. The rooms in the temple were dedicated to the *Cakrasaṃvara Tantra*, to the form of Avalokiteśvara that Orgyenpa had first empowered him to practice, Jinasāgara, to Black Coat and his consort Remati, and to the lineage gurus of the Karma Kagyü. Around the temple's external walls, he then had scenes from the *Birth Stories of the Teacher* painted, along with excerpts from his version of these stories.[331]

The description of the temple at Dadu is the last narrative section in the second part of the *Verse Liberation Story*, which he composed in Beijing in the spring of 1339, a few months before he died.[332] After describing the temple's construction, he wrote a long section that deconstructed his identity as a reincarnate and the relationship between the biographical construction of a person and an actual person. This section of his autobiography also laments that he has not been able to do as much with his life as he had wanted.

At around the same time, Rangjung Dorje wrote the last of his songs. This song offers more closure than the end of his autobiography. Like the first of the songs in the *Collected Songs*, it describes a dream. This time, he does not encounter a hermit like Saraha living in an isolated, faraway place. Instead, he meets Marpa, the householder, living in the middle of a city. The song begins with a relatively lengthy prelude, which describes how his dream meeting with Marpa lasted all night, but in the morning, he only remembered a few pieces of advice. Among these pieces of advice, the part he remembered most clearly was Marpa's instruction for living in the capitals, which he wrote down for posterity. It reads:

> Whatever you think, thinking is an obstacle;
> Transform it into samādhi. Joy will
> Not take long to cultivate, [and] when it
> Frees you from thinking, clarity will arise.
>
> *It* is the nature of innateness; there is no need
> To look for signs and such. [With this view,]
> Whatever and whatever are on your mind,
> Their nature, the nature of this and that,
> Will arise as myriad, jewellike reflections.[333]

The rest of Rangjung Dorje's life story—the last few months of his life, his death, and the journey to his next life—has been told by others. The priority of those who told this part of his tale is twofold. First, they all insist that he chose to die in an attempt to outmaneuver the emperor and the court. And second, they all proclaim that his death was merely the start of his next life. In these ways, they offer a counterpoint to his early liberation stories, which spoke of the Karmapa consciousness's experiences before taking birth as Rangjung Dorje.

The last section of the *Verse Liberation Story* was written by his attendant Künga Özer at the request of the Mongolian minister named Beng-ge. It begins with a prophecy by Rangjung Dorje, which he purportedly delivered in public several years before his death. "In Dadu . . . as the Tiger Year began, he spoke to his childlike students," Künga Özer records:

> Look at my face: I, this yogi, am like a cloud in the sky. It is not certain where I will go. Those who want to pay respect to sacred sites and communities, those few who would delightfully entrust themselves to solitude, should go wherever the Dharma proliferates.[334]

According to Künga Özer, this statement not only suggested that Rangjung Dorje would die soon, but the statement that his students should go "where the Dharma proliferates" was an oblique reference to his desire to be reborn in Kongpo, near Tsari.

Künga Özer also suggests that by making this statement publicly, Rangjung Dorje's choice was warning the emperor and his ministers about his decision to leave the court using any means necessary. But they did not listen.

Later that year, around June, as the court was preparing to leave Dadu for Xanadu, Rangjung Dorje became ill. When he arrived in Xanadu, he "immediately took to his bed."[335] He was able to attend a tantric ceremony in the Cakrasaṃvara Temple a few days later, but he struggled through the procedures and, as Künga Özer describes it, "sat down in the center of this manifested maṇḍala, which had been brought together so very well, and passed into the peace of the *dharmadhātu*."[336] He was fifty-six years old.

The Journey to Birth, Again

For most people, this would be the end of their life story. But for Rangjung Dorje, it was the beginning of a new story, the account of his journey to a new life. This new journey was accompanied by a series of auspicious signs and their accompanying anecdotes.

The first of these occurred fifteen days after his death and gave rise to what became the most famous image of him. That night, one of the palace guards outside Xanadu's gate saw Rangjung Dorje's "complete body and a stūpa on [the face of] the moon."[337] The image stayed for such a long time that they reportedly had enough time to wake Minister Turan Temür so that he could bear witness to their vision.[338] Rangjung Dorje's birth had been connected to the moon, and now his death was too.

The second symbolic event occurred as his body was burned. The contrite emperor, Künga Özer reported, walked at the head of the funeral procession and watched as Rangjung Dorje's corpse produced relics.[339] Most of these relics were said to resemble the tantric deities that he had cultivated throughout his life, Cakrasaṃvara, Vajravārāhī, and Avalokiteśvara.

The third event occurred as these relics were being transported back to Tibet. At that time, across the Plateau at different Karma Kagyü monasteries, numerous people are said to have experienced a vision of Rangjung Dorje. A yogi in Tibet reported visions of him flying in the sky. Another saw him traveling back to Tuṣita. Another saw him traveling south. When his relics were returned, they were interred in stūpas and surrounded by many images of the Buddha.

They added to the growing number of sacred objects associated with the Karmapa lineage.[340]

One of the most evocative of the tales surrounding Rangjung Dorje's death is that of a Mongol mail rider who was returning to the capitals and had not heard of his death. He was convinced that he had met Rangjung Dorje on the grasslands between Xanadu and the Tangut capital. He told whoever would listen that Rangjung Dorje was traveling in a sedan chair with a large entourage, and when he asked him where he was going, the Karmapa told him he was on his way home, to the mountains of southern Tibet.[341]

Rangjung Dorje's reincarnation, Rölpe Dorje (1340–1383), was born in Kongpo a year after Rangjung Dorje's death. The manner of Rangjung Dorje's life and death left little doubt that his rebirth, the next Karmapa, would be found. According to the last section of the *Verse Liberation Story*, his students were already talking about his rebirth as his body was being burned.[342] Unlike Rangjung Dorje, Rölpe Dorje had inherited a clear precedent for his recognition as a child, his education, and his standing as a Karmapa. He was even welcomed back (if not yet endowed with the abbotship) at Tsurpu and Karma Monasteries.

Rölpe Dorje's return and the ongoing Karmapa reincarnation lineage is, in many ways, Rangjung Dorje's most lasting achievement. But it was by no means his only legacy. As Rangjung Dorje explained throughout his life, the development of the Karmapa lineage, tradition, and institution was not purposeful in and of itself. It was developed as a tool through which the Karmapas could work to benefit others by presenting and embodying the mahāmudrā view. Along with Rangjung Dorje's reincarnation and the material objects he had collected for the monasteries—objects that acted as supports for practice and learning for centuries to come—Rangjung Dorje's other significant material legacy was his writing. These texts, some of which will be explored in the second section of this book, provide access to his thought and his world even today. They, too, have been "reincarnated" by the scribes, printers, and editors that have ensured the reproduction or conservation of these thirteenth- and fourteenth-century manuscripts. Through many editions, they have survived until today, when they are available for download across time and space. Like the view that Rangjung Dorje espoused, the impartial form of mahāmudrā he expounded, and the way of life he chose, his legacy is now truly chogme, "sideless," able to be accessed and reengaged with across languages, cultures, lineages, and time zones.

There are still many more conversations that we, their readers, can have with these texts. And the fact that we can now discuss these texts with reincarnations of the Third Karmapa, his teachers, and his students, as part of a living lineage, speaks to the true profundity of Rangjung Dorje's legacy.

The Writings

CHAPTER 6

The Liberation Story of Past Lives and *The Liberation Story of the In-Between State*

These two short liberation stories—or *namthar*—were included in the Collected Works within one larger text, *The Liberation Story of the Great Rangjung Dorje*.[343] They were both written when he was very young and tell the story of how he came to be Rangjung Dorje: the first text dictates his memories of his previous lives, and the second tells the story of his journey between lives, through the in-between state, or *bardo*.

These texts played an important role in establishing Rangjung Dorje's reputation as Karma Pakshi's reincarnation, and they continued to be influential after his life. The list of rebirths that he outlines here, for example, became the standard list of previous reincarnations that are attributed to the Karmapas, despite the fact that they differ from the previous two Karmapas' lists. The only exception to this rule is his claim to have been Marpa, which does not seem to have been taken up by the lineage. Many of the beings he claims to be or to whom he claims to have a connection are historical figures. Others, like Nāgārjuna and Saraha, are semimythical. Within the translation, only historical figures' dates will be given.

His description of this journey between lives is one of only a few such pieces of literature in Tibetan.[344] The majority of its text describes a conversation between the primary Karmapa consciousness—who is said to abide in the Tuṣita Heaven as they train with Maitreya—and a group of female spirits called the earth guardians.[345] The earth guardians represent the world into which Rangjung Dorje will be born. The first five of them present him with the life force of his future body. The remining twenty are guardians of various places across the Tibetan Plateau. Twelve of the twenty external guardians are the famous twelve protectresses, or twelve Tenma goddesses, whom Guru Rinpoche tamed on the Pelmo Tang Plain. Four of them are long-life goddesses associated with the high mountains of his home region in southern Tibet, and the last four are the guardians of the gates to other lands, probably the lands of Nepal, Persia, Mongolia, and the Tangut Kingdom. The purpose of their discussion, it seems, is not only to convince the Karmapa consciousness to be reborn but also to create a link between the Karmapa consciousness and the land of Tibet.

TIME UP UNTIL this point has been inconceivably long, as inconceivable as the time it would take to empty a sesame-seed store were you to remove one sesame seed a year. Ultimately, it is said, there is no transition from life to life. And at this time, Rangjung Dorje, this end-of-time yogi, does not recall the details of former and later times very well: my memory is cloudy, obscured, and gloomy. This is why, with encouragement, I am writing a little of what I do remember. I do remember that I was born many times before in the land of India, and I do remember that I was born repeatedly without control. The doubters will dismiss these memories, but I am offering them here for the few who will believe them.

The Liberation Story of Past Lives

In the main temple of Śrī Kamalaśīla at Nālandā, I was a novice who studied in the presence of two scholars. Their names were Sūryagarbha[346] and the master Akarasiti. Then, I went to another land and met a master there. His name was probably Nāgārjuna.

After that, it seems I was a student of the master Padmasambhava, and I attained the power of Śrī Hayagrīva. This gave me the power to shine forth a variety of emanations, and this in turn meant that I could help wanderers with various types of magic and powers. But I only remember parts of this, and besides, if I say too much about it, who will believe me? This is the time in which the famous Gyelwa Chokyang [early eighth century] of Ngenlam[347] was alive, and my memories are as if I was him.

In the interim, from the naturalness in which nothing is generated, and nothing stops, from the various displays of activity and embodiment, I was also an Indian yogi. This was the time in which Dharmabodhi lived, and it is as if I was him. He was inspired by the past, present, and future buddhas and the eight great mahāsiddhas. He also received blessings from countless yoga lords.

I have a connection with the noble Kamalaśīla.[348] It seems that I was his student and received a few instructions from him. But I should not talk pointlessly.

I also wonder if I was the Kadampa geshe Potowa,[349] and if during that life I knew Kharak Gomchung [eleventh century CE].[350] I believe I have leftover imprints from that time so that these days, as soon as I see Kharak's instructions, I generate an excellent understanding of them in my mindstream. I also think I have a connection with the one known as Nezur Chenpo [d.u.][351] from this time. I also remember a few other [lives and emanations], but if I were to speak of them, no one would believe me; they do not have the capacity to believe me.

Sometimes I also feel that I was none other than the illustrious Düsum Khyenpa, the precious Karmapa. I knew his instructions instinctively; I knew them instinctively and I understood them instinctively.

As well as this, it is as if I was the teacher, the Indian yogi called [Marpa] Chökyi Wangchuk,[352] blessed by Maitrīpa, who, without differentiating between staying or going, displayed many pure visions to his disciples. I think my ability to understand impartiality is a result of that life.

I also knew the instructions of the great Karmapa [Karma Pakshi] merely by hearing them. He is the wanderers' protector, who views them all with great love, and I could see directly the vital points of his instructions on mind and *prāṇa*.

It is for this reason [my connection with the previous Karmapas] that I should retain Düsum Khyenpa's seats. By doing so I can introduce disciples to the three bodies,[353] [leading them] on the paths of ripening and liberation that are characterized by emptiness. It is for this reason that these days I work impartially for beings. By these actions, may all my disciples understand and realize impartially the vital points of mind and prāṇa, thus becoming wise.

The Liberation Story of the In-Between State

In the first month of the Sheep Year [1283], I felt a little uncomfortable in my elements. At that time, I was the one known famously as the Karmapa, and this was a sign that I should depart for another pure land [i.e., die].

I performed inconceivable magic. As a rainbow body, I flew into the sky, traveling upward to the god realms. I was greeted there by the gods performing different types of divine music. I witnessed unimaginable appearances, divine parasols, and the like. I also saw bodhisattvas like Maitreya performing the deeds of awakening. He and his entourage cultivated immeasurable compassion for beings. They trained without rest in a state where nothing was generated and nothing stopped.

While I was there, the twenty-five earth guardians appeared in front of me as a vision and commanded,

> Take a human rebirth with free time and favor!
> Protect the Buddha's teachings!
> Protect the Buddha's teachings!
> Parent the six [types] of wanderers!
> The time has come, *Commit*!

I saw them, but I thought I was experiencing a faulty vision. I started to deconstruct the conceptualization. But these celestial wanderers did not want to wander off. [Eventually] I replied to them:

> You are here, but where did you come from?
> You are here, but when will you leave?
> I don't have parents to make a person with free time and favor.
> I don't have wisdom to protect the Buddha's teachings.
> I don't have the imprints to parent the six types of wanderers.
> Go find another regent to make prophecies about!

They replied:

> We come from the depths of the human world.
> We are earth guardians who protect the environment.

We do not admonish you for our own purposes, human;
We admonish you on behalf of the six types of wanderers.

That is what they said, and then they offered me their life forces.[354] When they offered them, they appeared [in the following groups]:

First, the five exceptional and principal earth guardians [helped form my body]. Dorje Bebma, the descender, moved upward from the secret [place, i.e., genitals].[355] Dorje Barma, blazing, sat at the top of my head. Dorje Topmoche, the strong one, entered my arms and legs. Dorje Tugyälma, powerful, entered my hands. Dorje Tungdrama, the white conch, entered my mouth.[356]

Next came the four primary tamed demonesses: Dakchenmo Dorje Kundrakma, Kangkyi Yumchen Dorje Kuntusang, Penden Lhari Dorje Yamakyong, Drokchen Khordül Dorje Gektso.[357] Then came the four primary Dharma protectors: Tüla Drozangma, Miyo Dorje Langzangma, Trashi Dorje Tseringma, Takzik Dorje Khyunggo.[358] Next came, the four, primary, tamed, harmful spirits: Gangkar Shame Dorje Chen Chikma, Serchen Khadingma Dorje Lungmoche, Kharak Khyungtsün Dorje Pelyum, Mari Rapjam Dorje Drakmogyel.[359] Following them, the primary protectors of the four gates [to other countries arrived]: Satri Dorje Drizangma, Tagasha Dunggi Dorje Moche, Chakso Dorje Topmoche, Ghagha Dorje Reldrima.[360] [These were followed by] the four primary mind changers: Kongtsün Demo Dorje Bökham Kyong, Tsenla Laro Dorje Menchik, Matsün Khukchö Dorje Yarmosil, Yuyi Kenyen Dorje Silema.[361]

[Together they spoke to him.] "If we cannot convince[362] you to take rebirth, we will call on our many companions. Who will we call you may ask? We will call the Dharma protector Bernakchen[363] and the four female, great, principal protectors of the four hidden lands. Even if we cannot convince you, they will—by filling this world [with their presence] from the space of the dancing deities to the underground world of the nāgas."

This is what they said, and as I listened to them speak, that which they evoked happened. Then they said, "Well then, our companions have arrived. Here are the four great women: [at the top] Vajrasatri, below her Dorje Bukyong Litsün, below her Dorje Puchu Menchikma, and below her Dorje Yuchungma.[364] These are the four protectors of hidden lands, and with them is the Dharma protector Bernakchen. From the shadows, they all praise bodies that do not pass into nirvāṇa."

This is what they said. And they stayed in front of me, using these words to admonish me:

Have compassion for the six types of wanderers!
How confused they are, living in saṃsāra!
Do this for wanderers, for beings!

As they spoke and this vision remained, I thought, "I wonder if this is a manifestation of my imprints?" Slowly, this idea faded, and still I did not want to return [to earth]. But the earth guardians did not give up. Again and again they admonished me. This time, I replied to them like this.

Anger makes preconceived self-grasping durable.
The mountain of pride reaches into the sky.
Hearing your words is like being pierced by a chisel;
Your words are rocks, missiles hurled at my meditation.
Why don't I see you disintegrating, cracking, and fading away?
Are the six types of wanderers all happy and healthy?
Of course not! So why do you all, their protectors, look so joyful?

They replied by gathering in the space in front of me. They covered this space, from the dancing deities down to the underground nāgas. And from this space, they held up their hands and made offerings, saying,

Hear this, bodhisattva, son of the gods—
Falling from god realms is an intolerable suffering;
The hostile demigods are befuddled by their suffering;
The suffering of human birth and death is beyond thought;
How great is the suffering of stupid and dumb beasts of
burden;
The suffering of hungry, thirsty ghosts is beyond thought;
And one moment of the hot and cold hells' suffering is so
difficult.

Who will hold up the teachings of the Buddha?
Who will parent the six types of wanderers?
Who will show them the glory of the Buddhas?
Kyi hu! Kyi hu! There is so much suffering!

This is what they said, and as they spoke, we all saw the suffering of beings. I replied to them:

Generally, the pure lands of the Buddha are inconceivable;
Particularly, Jambudvīpa's qualities are said
To include countless spiritual friends
That perform inconceivable Dharma deeds.
Go look for another regent to make prophecies about!
Go look for another to parent the six types of wanderers!
Go protect those practicing the Buddha's teachings!
Earth guardians should show the Buddha's glory!
Those spiritual friends will help the six types of wanderers,
And you should all be happy about that!

The earth guardians replied:

The spiritual friends are all jealous.
The dhārmikas are all competing.
The six wandering types are wild by nature;
And there is no one with the means to help them.
This is why we admonish you, human!

I replied:

I do not have a human body with free time and favor,
And a fully qualified teacher is difficult to find.
The wombs of these dark times are so very defiled,
And helping wanderers of the present and future is hard.
So, I ask you all again, this time with force,
I ask all you earth guardians, Dharma protectors,
To empower me, to integrate with me completely,
To grant me signs and inspiration completely.
Then I will find parents with the correct lineage;
And then I will meet a fully qualified teacher.

In response, the earth-guardian ḍākinīs set up the maṇḍala of the sixty-two deities of Cakrasaṃvara and granted me an inconceivable celestial empowerment. During this empowerment, they set out copious volumes of texts made up of vowels and consonants and spoke the empowerment of the five-gnosis knowledge. They introduced me to the five senses and spoke the empowerment of the perfections' meaning. In the empowerment that [granted] the realization of no-birth, they bestowed verses and eliminated the path of words. They displayed the in-between state, cutting the path of signs; they displayed metaphor, cutting the path of metaphor; and they displayed illusion, cutting the path of illusion. Who would not wish to have this empowerment bestowed upon them? My testament cannot paint its picture properly; but it shines bright for me, it radiates for me, it arises brilliant, lucid, and vivid. At the end, they said, "If you descend, the appearances of saṃsāra and nirvāṇa may not disappear, but the activities of the Buddha will be completed; wanderers will be helped."

Having said this, they empowered and inspired me in inconceivable ways. They concluded with a few auspicious verses, which they spoke with one voice.

Lucid knowledge is
Like an umbrella, a sheltering crown;
Whatever auspiciousness this umbrella has,
May it, sacred and auspicious, flourish here in you, right now!

The golden fish, the gnostic eye, and clarity,
Like the sun and moon, clear away darkness;
Whatever auspiciousness these two eyes have,
May it, sacred and auspicious, prosper here in you, right now!

A melody of bells, *vīṇā*, and flute in symphony,
Is like a praise, a vessel for knowing;
Whatever auspiciousness this melody has,
May it, sacred and auspicious, flourish here in you, right now!

The various smells of sweet incense gathering at the head,
Are like pure faculties, and they, too, clarify;
Whatever auspiciousness this sweet incense has,
May it, sacred and auspicious, flourish here in you, right now!

Ivory[365] conch is as hard as bone,
But it can also become medicinal [like] herbs;
Whatever auspiciousness this ivory conch has,
May it, sacred and auspicious, flourish here in you, right now!

On the tongue, lotus, honey, and
The words of poetry are pleasant;
Whatever auspiciousness this lotus tongue has,
May it, sacred and auspicious, flourish here in you, right now!

This is a precious container, a vase of songs,
The best nectar for satiating hunger and quenching thirst;
Whatever auspiciousness this vase of songs has,
May it, sacred and auspicious, flourish here in you, right now!

Magic hands write letters, and various threads
Create all that is needed and desired;
Whatever auspiciousness these magic hands have,
May it, sacred and auspicious, flourish here in you, right now!

In the mind is an endless knot, thoughts of past and future,
[But] clear knowing does not forget;
Whatever auspiciousness this endless knot of mind has,
May it, sacred and auspicious, flourish here in you, right now!

This body is clothed with a Persian victory banner,[366]
This victory banner does not disappear;
Whatever auspiciousness is in this banner, this body,
May it, sacred and auspicious, flourish here in you, right now!

Wheels on his feet, horses, and myriad possessions
Are the enjoyments of the one who turns the Dharma wheel;
Whatever auspiciousness is in these wheeled feet,
May it, sacred and auspicious, flourish here in you, right now!

This is what they said, along with many other auspicious verses. Then they flew about in front of me, and as they did, precious, multicolored rainbow roads appeared. They led me to the place where a human body with free time and favor would be formed. The earth guardians said to me, "The body will be formed in fortunate Mangyul Gungtang. The mother is fortunate, noble Yuchungma, who lives in front of sacred Gang Zhurmo Ridge. The father has a house of clear essence on the fortunate Om Plain, in front of Chewagang Ridge in Tsapu. His house is in the lower valley where three upper valleys meet, Tsa-lung-pu Valley, in Milarepa's birth region. On the south side of this valley is a clear, dark, red mountain. To the north is a glimmering white mountain. These beings are the undesired bodily frames."

As they explained this process of conception, [the ḍākinīs] created a nine-colored rainbow that became intensely saturated and bright. I watched as they ascended the rainbow, then I traveled alone down to a crystal palace with a sky-door, four bright white sides, and a dark base. Rainbows danced around me on all sides. As soon as I entered the house, waves of passionate blood were aroused and I watched them [the ḍākinīs] flee. Then the nine voices of the nine firmaments spoke as one and said, "Journeying upward from the smallest firmament, you will not be freed. It is difficult to mature karma into the path of liberation."

And as I gradually came around, all was dark, and I felt a heavy weight. I was whirling in a small space. Even remembering it now, I feel like I am spinning in a small space. My perception gradually became clear again. After this, it was as if I was sometimes tossed by waves, sometimes squashed by mountains, sometimes burned by heat, sometimes frozen by cold. I was confused. There was no air. This is the suffering of the afflictions, and even now when I think of it, the wind rises in my heart.

CHAPTER 7

A Dream of Saraha

The *Song about a Dream of Saraha* is the first song in the *Collected Songs of Rangjung Dorje.*[367] Rangjung Dorje wrote it when he was twelve or thirteen (in 1296) and living at Khyung Dzong Hermitage behind Tsurpu Monastery. The song is bookended by a narrative that describes a dream Rangjung Dorje had in which he and a couple of friends traveled to southern India to visit the mahāsiddha Saraha. The song itself, he says, consists of a poetic exchange between Rangjung Dorje and Saraha. Its style is interesting, as fundamentally it is written in the style of a Tibetan song, or *gur*, but it does also contain elements of one of the Indian genres of songs associated with the mahāsiddhas, the dohā genre.

The site at which this poetic exchange occurs is Śrī Dakṣina Parvata, also known as Śrī Sailam, a site in South India which has traditionally been associated with both Saraha and, more prominently, his student Nāgārjuna. It is the same site in which Marpa recounted meeting Saraha in a dream.[368] As Kurtis Schaeffer has pointed out in his extensive study of the Tibetan imagery about Saraha, the song is part of a growing tradition of songs that link Tibetans to the Indian mahāsiddha. Rangjung Dorje's contribution to this tradition is notable for a couple of reasons. First, it is notable because of the young age at which he composed this song about his dream. And secondly, it is noteworthy because within the song, he makes the unusual claim that within this dream Saraha granted him a sign, which is to say he pointed out the nature of his mind to him. In the Mahāmudrā tradition, this makes Rangjung Dorje a direct disciple of Saraha.

OṂ SĀRVA SVASTI SIDDHI HUṂ

One night while I, the yogi Rangjung Dorje, was staying at Trashi Sarma Hermitage, I dreamt that I traveled with two companions to Śrī Dakṣina Parvata Mountain. We were looking for the guru, the Great Brahman [Saraha]. My two friends went to search on the southern side of the mountain. I stayed by myself in a pleasant, wide, open alpine meadow on the mountain's eastern side. I had just made myself comfortable, sitting alone, when masses of flower-snow began to fall. I responded to this by making cairns out of the fallen flowers, and I sat in steady contemplation in their midst. Then a small, sweet voice came down from the sky:

Child of the lineage, hear this!
The guru, the Great Brahman [Saraha],
Is your mind's nature—
It is a grave mistake to look for him elsewhere.

I replied to the voice, saying,

E ma ho! The guru, the Great Brahman, is
My mind's nature, and in this
Maṇḍala where variety has one taste,
There are no seekers and sought;
My two friends still search,

While to me, sitting here alone,
The Great Brahman reveals a sign.[369]
Ah! How wonderful!

This is what I said. And from the sky, in reply, came the voice of the Great Brahman:

E ma ho! This is the guru, the Great Brahman;
I am your mind's nature, and in this
Maṇḍala where variety has one taste,
There are no cultivators, nor things to cultivate.

Hey child! This dohā is beyond speech,
Thought, or expression, so cultivate its advice!
Hey child! Mahāmudrā is the essence of
All past, present, and future buddhas.
Stay uncomplicated!

Hey child! In effortless naturalness,
A state free of extremes,
Realize self-aware wisdom;
Its purpose is to help wanderers.
Don't be distracted; stay balanced!

E ma ho! Mind's nature is simplicity;
It comes from nowhere and has
Nowhere to go, just like a crazy person.[370]

Hey child! Like a river dissolving into the sea,
It has no creation and no cessation,
So stay in mahāmudrā!

This is what he said. And the [flower] cairns I had made, the rocks, and the stone mountain all became the Great Brahman. My mindstream was naturalness: no creation, no cessation, no abiding, no edge, and no falling onto one side. Ah! So vivid! So relaxed! In this state, there was no distinction between waking and sleeping, and it is this joy that I remember as I sing this song.

This is what he said, and great meditators, mountain wanderers, should follow these instructions and experience them, for this song has the blessings of the guru. He said it, it is wonderful, so have no doubt; experience this utmost profundity.

[Rangjung Dorje] said that he met the guru, the Great Brahman, in a dream, and this was his message. [He said he had this dream] in Trashi Sarma, on the tenth day of the eighth month of the year of the Monkey [1296].

CHAPTER 8

A Mālā of Mountain Dharma's Siddhis

Rangjung Dorje wrote this piece when he was thirteen years old and living in the Khyung Dzong Retreat Center behind Tsurpu Monastery. It is an address to mountain hermits, whom he considered to be his cohorts. It is very much like a song from his *Collected Songs*, especially those written during the same period. It was most probably preserved as a separate text because it was more well known than his other songs. The reason for its regard probably had more to do with the efforts to establish Rangjung Dorje's reputation as a reincarnate than its content; this text is not as polished or as substantial as many of his other writings.

What it does show, however, are the earliest forms of some of the illustrations and concepts he used to greater effect later in life. It includes an evocation of the Karma Kagyü lineage, descriptions of mahāmudrā, and the yogas he practiced. It also shows the importance of the environment and particularly the reality and idea of mountains in Rangjung Dorje's worldview. In this work, and throughout his writing, mountains are a synonym for isolation and wilderness; they represent an otherworldly space into which those seeking transformation must travel.[371]

I evoke Vajradhara.

This little instruction was written
For great meditators,
Faithful beings with training.

The *dharmakāya* is as clear as the sky;
It is the best wisdom, the mahāmudrā.
Its essence is the best view.

The always-blissful Tilopā
Was a great mahāmudrā meditator;
With the qualities of a *nirmāṇakāya*,
He was self-made and a mountain wanderer.[372]

The lucky one that followed him
Was the great Jetsün Nāropā;
He realized the spacelike and undivided,
He was a yogi of the highest bliss,
A complete buddha, and a mountain wanderer.

Into this sacred one's presence,
Came an emanation of Lodrö Rinchen;[373]
He opened the door of profound tantra,
Was a supreme expert at instruction,
Was known as Lhodrakpa [Marpa],
And, blessed by wandering in the mountains,
He realized the completely invisible mahāmudrā.

Into this Jetsün's presence,
Came an emanation of Mañjuśrī-Yamāntaka,
Who showed himself to be the greatest of great meditators;

This was Jetsün Milarepa.
Qualified by mountain wandering,
He realized mahāmudrā.

Into this cotton-clad one's presence,
Came an emanation of Candraprabha Kumāra,
Arriving with action and compassion;
This was the guru Dagpo Rinchen [Gampopa].
Qualified by mountain wandering,
He accumulated the ten signs, eight qualities, and the rest.[374]
His activities were inconceivable,
And they arose solely from mountain wandering.

Into this prince's presence,
Came one with great understanding, the Lion's Roar [Düsum Khyenpa].
Perfect at learning, contemplating, and logic,
In Lhodrak's seven sacred sites of siddhi,
He showed how to achieve siddhi without equal.

Into this realized one's presence
Came Drogön Lama Rinchen.
He also found great meaning in mountain wandering.

Into this being's presence,
Came Rinchen Punya Vajra;
He became qualified by mountain wandering,
And realized the final mahāmudrā.

The lucky one who followed him
Was the precious ascetic who escaped [Karma Pakshi].
When he lived on sacred Mount Pungri,

His austerities were unimaginable;
For twelve years he practiced them,
And [he] showed the way to achieve siddhi
In order to ripen the minds of all beings.

Into the presence of this siddha
Came my own guru, [Orgyenpa] Rinchen.
Blessed by the greatest concentration,
He traveled to Oḍḍiyāna and other sacred sites;
He showed how to cultivate, and [he] attained mahāmudrā.

Into the presence of that great being,
Came this end-of-time yogi,[375]
Who is also a qualified mountain wanderer.

To those lucky ones who follow,
To all mountain wanderers, [I say this].

Abandon worldly activities,
Wander sideless in the mountains,
Don't be distracted by bending and stretching,
Abandon all attachment and aversion,
And stay alone, isolated,
In forest hermitages.

Cut away your attachment to food and clothes,[376]
And unattached, alone, wander in the mountains.

Without exception, all of saṃsāra and nirvāṇa
Is the sacred Dharma.
All is mahāmudrā;
Cultivate this greatness.

Without exception, have an attitude of great compassion
Toward the nonhumans, gods, and ghosts
That interrupt mountain wanderers' cultivations.
Cultivate the idea that they are all the guru;
This, I think, is a way to receive inspiration.

When you are staying alone,
You will experience obstacles and qualities arising.
It may be a sign that the mind-prāṇa
In the cakras and secondary channels [has accumulated],
And the five types of buddhas, their pure lands,
And collections of tantric deities are arising;
Or it may seem that obstacles have arisen.
You may seem to shake and be ill;
You may experience powerful displays of magic.

When this seems to be happening,
Use inconceivable dhyāna.
Whatever happens, cultivate the guru
And dauntless compassion.

The profound Dharma instructions explain clearly
How you, a great yogi, should derive qualities,
So that you can expel enemies and ghosts,
And [deal with] obstacles and faults.

All beings who are mountain wanderers—
Those that are ordinary and those who are great—
Stay in great hermitages and
Set out to achieve the greatest siddhis.

Like a lion, the king of snow mountains,
Venerable among his pride,
Mountain wanderers amaze with their
Steadfastness in mountain abodes.

Milarepa and the rest brought together
Mountain landlords and other ghosts,
The malevolent spirits of the high mountains,
Tamed them and made them know.
[Since then, these mountains] have been
Grounds for cultivation and siddhi.

To be on the edge is important,
Especially in places like the great Tsari.
It is one of the twenty-four great places,
Those sites in which ḍākinīs gather.
Even among the 113 sacred sites and the rest,
Tsari is still special.

The twenty-four sites [adapted to] Tibet
Are as follows:
Kāmarūpa is said to be Kampo Nenang;
Near there, the great sites of Pungri,
Rongtsang, and the rest.

The great sacred site of Tsurpu is special too;
In it and other mountain hermitages,
I cultivate alone, and
When I evoke single-pointed admiration,
Inconceivable qualities arise.

When we are alone and cultivating,
Solitary mountain hermitages are pleasant;
But while there, we must [remember] all concepts,
Good and bad, without exception,
Are emptiness, the greatest thing.

We cultivate the union of luminosity and clarity
And generate the perception of great compassion
For all wanderers.

Great beings, sacred beings, perfect their
Qualities by wandering in the mountains.
Even all the buddhas of the three times
Went forth into the mountains;
All the deities, without exception,
Abide in mountain hermitages.
Ḍākinīs and protectors live in mountains too.

The qualities of mountain wandering are these—

Ultimately, that you will realize mahāmudrā;
You will be naturally liberated;
You will leave behind all good and bad signs,
The five poisons, three poisons, and the rest.

But when we live alone,
We must be careful not to make mistakes
Even with the most subtle concepts,
Such as experience, *śamatha* and *vipaśyanā*, and the rest;
Even they are the ultimate mahāmudrā itself.[377]

When we are alone, all we can have
Are mistaken concepts, good and bad,
[Related to] the five cakras and the *nāḍī* focal points.

[When these energies are good,]
We see whiteness and all
The deities and buddhas,
Symbols of concentrated mind-prāṇa,
In the circle of great bliss at the crown of my head.

We see redness and all
Complete enjoyment body's ḍākinīs,
Symbols of concentrated mind-prāṇa,
In the circle of enjoyment at our throat.

We see dreams and reality intertwined
As blue appearances,
Arising as mistaken goodness,
Multiple collections of bodhicitta,
Symbols of concentrated mind-prāṇa,
In the circle of enjoyment at my heart.

We see green itself and all
The collections of tantric deities, without exception,
Symbols of concentrated mind-prāṇa,
In the circle of enjoyment at our belly.

These are the mistaken appearances of goodness;
The negative appearances arise as follows.

Symbols of concentrated delusion arise
In the circle of great bliss at the crown of my head;

And in the other cakras
Prāṇa is reversed.
While this lasts, conceptions arise.

Ignorance amasses like mist on a mountain,
Desire shakes like water,
Anger ignites like flames,
Jealousy is as restless as the wind,
And pride and the rest are also there.

But these are mahāmudrā, too;
Rest evenly within them.
The way to traverse the ten grounds and five paths,
To attain the five eyes, six clear sights, and the rest,
Is to be liberated from these obstacles.
Arousing signs of these attainments one by one
Is the way to complete all attainments.

[Liberation is] the union of luminosity and clarity.
It is mahāmudrā, the essence, the best and final.
It is unconceptualized, ungenerated, uncaused.
It comes from nowhere and has nowhere to go.
It is the great substantiality[378] of all,
Known directly as the union of luminosity and clarity.

Those that make a habit of this
Will see gatherings of ḍākinīs, ḍākas,
And Dharma protectors, again and again.
Their qualities and activities for beings
Will equal the buddhas.

Instructions like this
Come only from me, from Rangjung Dorje,
In the Great Site of Accomplishment, Khyung Dzong.
It arose as experience and I wrote it down;
Lucky ones, do as I have instructed.

This is called *A Mālā of Mountain Dharma's Siddhis*,
And it was written for those who wander in mountains.

Rangjung Dorje spoke these instructions at the isolated site, Tsurpu's Khyung Dzong Hermitage, on the fifteenth day of the sixth month in the year of the Monkey [1296].

CHAPTER 9

The Dancer

From *Birth Stories of the Teacher*

Rangjung Dorje collated and composed *Birth Stories of the Teacher* in 1314 when he was thirty-one years old and staying at Dechen Teng near Tsurpu Monastery.[379] The work consists of a translation of the thirty-four stories contained within Āryaśura's (also known as Aśvaghoṣa) famous Sanskrit text *Garland of Birth Stories* (*Jātakamālā*)[380] and sixty-six stories collected and retold by Rangjung Dorje. Rangjung Dorje's interest in these stories cannot be separated from his wider project to understand his own identity as a recognized reincarnate and to establish translife identities through narration.

This story about a dancer named Jagatī Śrī[381] is not one of the most well-known stories in the collection, but it deserves more attention than it has received for several reasons. Primary among these reasons is that it is a rare—and perhaps unique—instance of the Buddha-to-be represented as a lowborn woman.[382] Rangjung Dorje's decision to include this story within the collection may have been influenced by his own social background and similar stories about outsiders within the life stories of the mahāsiddas. Rangjung Dorje seems to anticipate controversy about the story's inclusion by dedicating as much ink to its justification as he does to tell the story. His defense for its inclusion is made in the traditional way, through recourse to supportive scripture and a reasoned argument about the nature of the Buddha's activities.

His argument for the story's inclusion not only defends Jagatī Śrī's status as a lowborn woman but also her occupation as a dancer. It may seem a trivial and distracting pursuit, he suggests, but the Buddha-to-be uses her form as a young woman to highlight the impermanence of youth and beauty. The Buddha chose the form of a young woman to teach this lesson, Rangjung Dorje suggests, because young women are primarily judged by their fleeting, youthful beauty.

SACRED BEINGS possess skillful means. Even when they do things that may seem to be mere distractions, such as singing and dancing, they can develop beings entirely.

I once heard [a story] like this. It is well known that when the Buddha was a bodhisattva, in one of his lives, he was born into a family of dancers. He lived many lives in ancient times and lived through innumerable forms of existence. The father of the household was an expert dancer, a leader of beings. He was noble, with a clear and prudent mind, wise, stable, and got along with others well. The words he spoke were all excellent. Whenever there were gatherings of people, he danced and made them happy. Astrologers, parents, ascetics, and brahmans all liked him. He followed the order of the world and took people at their word. He was naturally wise, and his mind was clear. The qualities he possessed made him resplendent, and he got along with everybody. He was, indeed, just like a sun maṇḍala.

He had a daughter named Jagatī Śrī. She had developed virtue by interacting with countless Tathāgatas in the past, and now her intention was vast. She had very little attachment, anger, and ignorance.

She was a transcendent human, with the figure and complexion of a god. She was also an extremely skilled singer and dancer. As soon as audiences saw her, they could not take their eyes off her. Her body was splendid. Her complexion was as white as the harvest moon. Her eyes were as blue as blue lotus flowers, wide open, like lotuses were blooming. Her limbs were like lotus roots. Her teeth were straight, like a mālā of white lotuses. Her lips were red and clear, like red flowers. Her nose was high and beautiful, and her eyebrows ornamented her face like two fluttering wings.

With that face, people said she resembled a lotus pond. But Jagatī Śrī intended to use other people's desirous minds to liberate them from desire. When it came to guiding beings' minds, it was as if she had a hook. Draped in precious ornaments, she would move her limbs gracefully. She would raise her voice to sing the melodic song of the kalapingka bird.[383] But her seductive ways were used to encourage others to abandon their [desire]. She would not deceive her brothers. Instead, because of her compassion for beings, she sought to use their attachment to her to destroy their afflictions. Her behavior was impeccable.

Whenever many people gathered together, the dancer's daughter, Jagatī Śrī, would decorate herself with flawless jewelry and sing songs like this.

Like water falling from a mountain, in a moment,
A minute, a few hours, my youth will be gone.
Still, childish beings go crazy for it;
Unaware, the force sways them, and they faint.

Like thick autumn clouds, this beauty is essenceless.
Still, the waterfall of rain that falls from it carries people away.
These people are bound by a being's form, even though
It is impermanent, human, falling, and they can't hold onto it.

Childish beings are like children with a nurse;
Unwise, with weak intellect,
Without knowing it, they can be convinced to go anywhere.

Their minds are permeated by fruitless [thoughts]
About a body that impermanence will desiccate.
It has no merit. Death ends it. Its life is destroyed.

In the discourses of the wise Buddha, he said:
"Youth always, assiduously makes [childish beings] happy;
But the wise do not engage in its merrymaking."

In the discourse of the wise Tathāgata, it says:
"Here is an example of that which is called essenceless;
Youth is, by definition, that which is directly undone by age.
If beings are wise and discerning,
They assume that youth has no self.

Those who are diligently aroused
By that which is desirable but ever-changing
Live in ways that undermine unchanging bliss.

When impermanence and age outlast youth,
Those who have done everything always to stay young
Will live in suffering and constant despondency.

Those experiencing youth
Should not let their strength and effort degrade,
For age will surely snatch their youth away."

With respect to conscientious behavior, the Buddha's teachings say this:
"Beings are captivated by youth;

Kye ma! It betrays their minds and zaps their strength.
Impermanence is strong, it transforms rapidly;
In an instant, youth is gone.

While young, it is difficult to diligently
Evaluate how in an instant changes happen.
Beings grasp at youth, and while they grasp,
Age, death, and release all work diligently
To take them beyond it.
Isn't this how phenomena degenerate?"

And in the teachings of the wise one, the Buddha says:

"If, while you are young, you enter
The path of the Tathāgata's teaching,
You are drinking the nectar of performance.[384]
It is like extinguishing a flame with water;
And by binding Māra in this way, you cut him off."

These are some of the things that have been said. There are many other similar excellent sayings.

Those who enter the three paths and act in accordance with them come to understand that impermanence is empty. They also understand essencelessness directly. Those who behave in this way engage in the performance of a bodhisattva. This behavior is truly marvelous.

However many bodhisattvas there are, this is how they tame beings. These practices are precisely the practices they perform. These are the manifestations of illusion they display. When they create a worldly form, its purpose is to tame beings. They may display one hundred divine bodies that are supreme and ornamented with precious jewelry. But their reason for creating this display is to dry out the swamps of desire. Whether there are six of them or a hundred, their kalapingka-like voices will captivate. Their unsullied speech will resonate, and they will use excellent words.

They transform the desiring into the desireless by [acting] in accordance with desires. They clarify the teachings by clarifying them and [acting] in accordance with the treatises. They illuminate with a splendor that clarifies that which is to be made visible. It is just as if a buddha has come into the world. Anybody who sees or hears them is guided onto the supreme path of liberation. *Kye ho!* Marvelous! How wonderful is their teaching!

The dancer's daughter Jagatī Śrī was just like this. She traveled to the villages, cities, lands, king's palaces, and other places where people were gathered. In these places, she sang and danced. She used these performances to illuminate the Mahāyāna path and to mature and awaken countless beings.

This is one of the ways that sacred beings have the skills to tame wanderers. Their powers are said to be countless. They are also said to pay particular attention to impermanence in their conversations.

This has been story number sixty-six, the story of "The Dancer."

CHAPTER 10

King of the Nāgas

From *Birth Stories of the Teacher*

The birth story titled "King of the Nāgas" is another story that Rangjung Dorje added to the *Birth Stories of the Teacher*.[385] Like the story "The Dancer," it discusses the bodhisattva's use of skillful means. In this story, the Buddha-to-be is not a human; he is a nāga, a serpentine figure that is common within both Indian and Tibetan mythologies. The nāgas are associated with water, skin diseases, and are said to have vast stores of wealth. This story focuses on the way that the Buddha-to-be used the wealth of the nāgas to convince the otherwise-doomed people of Jambudvīpa, our world, to begin to practice the Dharma by bribing them. He sets up a situation where they will practice Dharma as they extract precious gems, therefore creating a habit of practicing Dharma that will transform their avarice.

SACRED BEINGS have many methods for helping wanderers. Their methods are as varied as the intention of those they seek to help, and they apply them appropriately in order to fulfill all their wishes. I have heard a story about this.

In a previous time that was known as an excellent eon, the one who would become the teacher was living in one of Jambudvīpa's lands as the nāga king Vāsuki. This story of one of the Buddha's previous lives is very well known. King Vāsuki was great and performed a variety of activities for a range of other beings.

He was a most potent nāga. This power he had allowed him to bring under his control vast swathes of land and entire oceans, even down to their depths. By the power of his altruism, he was able to be born with this power. His powers were [manifestations of] his compassion, and his body was a manifestation of the wisdom he had [generated]. His head was beautified by a serpentine hood, which was [generated by] his skillful methods. He was surrounded by billowing clouds [generated by] his love. His satiating, lucid expositions [generated] a dragon's roar. His gnosis [generated] a luminous net that emanated from him. His generosity [generated] constant streams of rain. These rains satiated all the wanderers' fields. And he had mastery over all the powerful bodhisattva nāgas. The following describes the way that he taught beings.

This great being, the bodhisattva, abandoned his own interest for the sake of those around him. Signs arose constantly that demonstrated that this was what he was doing. He was known as Jambudvīpa's Vijayāgīrghośa [Melodious Victory].[386]

In the place he lived, the beings born there were poor and destitute because they would not be satiated, even by all the best things. They were stuck in karma, and their behavior defiled them. Having understood that they were all inclined to fall into the lower realms, the Great Being undertook the following in order to stop this from happening. During his time among the nāgas, every evening he would display hundreds of thousands of different precious stones, and then he would proclaim, "Listen up beings! Over here is gold, silver, lapis lazuli, crystal, coral, star stones, water stones, and all sorts of precious stones. They are piled up like treasure. Each of you can take some without any effort. But, when you take them, you will enter into the path of the ten virtues. The method I'm using will lead you to the hearer's vehicle and the vehicle of the solitary realizer. My method is also an entry to the vehicle of the unsurpassable, completely realized Buddha. Whichever one you want to enter, pick your motivation! If you practice in this way, you will generate all this wealth." This method was his way of teaching, and this is what he said.

After he had done this, the poor, desirous, careless, and restive of Jambudvīpa were made conscientious and satisfied. [The Nāga King] asked, "My teaching is a jeweled treasure. Its result is meaningful. How can you all be destitute when you have treasure? *Kye ma!* Beings of Jambudvīpa! These jewels are neither contentious nor quarrelsome. By acquiring them, may you generate the mind of complete awakening. Who will rest [while they acquire jewels], and who will think this is senseless? These gems will be immensely helpful. Enjoy these treasures; they are the jewels of conscientiousness and Dharma. There are hundreds and thousands of treasures more to be won. If you act under the influence of carelessness, strife, and desire, you will not get any enjoyment from your actions. But as long as you perform Dharma, I will keep granting you treasure." This method was the way this great being taught the Dharma to all.

The beings of that place opened their eyes wide with joy and said, "*A la la!*" They shoveled the treasure with open hands, thoroughly enjoying how they could scoop it up. Like the bodhisattva had said, in this way they generated [thoughts of Dharma].

The Great Being continued the same practice for years. He gave until he had given seventy-seven hundred thousand varieties of jewels. He generously gave the teachings to countless, innumerable beings. He led innumerable beings to the three vehicles and definitively to their practice.

In that place, those with desire were desirous. Desire had power over everybody. The bodhisattva prince was free from desire himself, but he found a way to lead other attached beings. He came up with a method, a skillful means that would be praised by other bodhisattvas.

The problem, he decided, was that beings were motivated to help themselves but not to help others. Perhaps beings' desire to help themselves could be used to encourage them to help others? And if they did this as a group, and all their friends and relatives were doing the same thing, they would copy each other and become completely engaged in the practice of helping others. Once they were completely caught up in it, they would develop a firmly established habit of helping others. That would be a good thing. They could help others by helping themselves for eons. By the time they thought of abandoning this habit, their implicit mercy would lead them to see others as a beloved child.

[The irony of the situation occurred to him.] They will not begin this practice [of benefiting others] merely because it grants supreme welfare to themselves and others. *Kye ma!*—beings are strange. Who will realize the nature of saṃsāra naturally [without this intervention]?

This teaching from this tale, then, is that bodhisattvas can begin to tame beings in different ways. This is one of the methods he showed us to use on beings. His aspiration was completely pure and perfected. Through skillful means, sacred beings perfect working for others' benefit, and they do so indefatigably.

It is said that our teacher, the Bhagavān, because of his compassion for all sentient beings, will work without a break until he has completely fulfilled their purpose. This is one of the ways that the Buddha is praised.

Another thing to note in this story is that beings need to be led away from the miserliness that makes them do negative things. Skillful means is one way to ripen the path of awakening within them. They should be employed in this way.

This has been the birth story [known as] "The King of the Nāgas." It is the sixty-eighth story.

CHAPTER 11

A Message to the Entire Kingdom

A Message to the Entire Kingdom is taken from his *Collected Songs*.[387] Rangjung Dorje wrote it when he first arrived in the Tsari area to do retreat in 1312. At that stage he was twenty-nine years old and had been looking forward to coming to Tsari since he was a child. He wrote about how sacred a site it was, for example, in *A Mālā of Mountain Dharma's Siddhis*. Tsari, in southern Tibet, is currently located on the line of control between the Tibetan Autonomous Region and the Indian state of Arunachal Pradesh. It is on the edge of the Plateau, surrounded by several rivers, and the entrance to its southern side is dense jungle. In Rangjung Dorje's time, it was also a borderland and a very isolated site. This isolation seems to have lent to its perceived specialness. It was understood to be the site of a local landlord deity, a place where ḍākinīs gathered, a manifestation of two of the famous twenty-four sacred sites where the drama of the *Cakrasaṃvara Tantra* played out,[388] and, therefore, the maṇḍala of Cakrasaṃvara.[389]

This song, like many of Rangjung Dorje's songs in his song collections, begins with an homage to his teachers and to the nature of mind before it sets out what it wants to say. The body of this song does two main things. First, it sets out the achievements he has had in his yoga practice and the things he still needs to work on, like generosity. Then, it switches into a criticism of others whom he thinks are not living up to their potential or roles. In this way, it contains two of the major themes within Rangjung Dorje's songs: the joy of yoga practice and social criticism.

I honor the sacred,
Noble guru's dharmakāya—
In essence it is *sahaja*,[390] great bliss,
The mind of all buddhas, simplicity.

Please inspire me to realize clearly
The variety of illusory play.

E ma! The amazing, essential meaning!
The Vajra that realizes nonduality [i.e., Rangjung Dorje]
Has a message, a mālā of ideas,
For Dharma practitioners in the ten directions:
Don't be distracted, think well, and
Send this message to those who know how to listen.

I have rid myself of compulsive clinging
To the beginningless impressions of "I";
Now the shackles of my reified thinking are broken,
And I no longer have the pride of fundamental knowledge.[391]
Send this message to those who understand;
Tell them Rangjung Dorje said it.

I have totally abandoned the ignorant house of "I."
I am far from wealth and lust;[392]

I have left lust's residence and
Arrived at the site of great bliss.
Send this message to the passionate;
Tell them Rangjung Dorje sent it.

I have not yet given generously, impartially, but
I have given up my obsession with pleasant things.
I effortlessly collect the Dharma's wealth,
As this collecting is bodhicitta's activity.
Send this message to the avaricious;
Tell them Rangjung Dorje sent it.

Having achieved as the Buddha instructed,
I have lost all intention to attain my own desires.
Pure of the stains of proscribed transgressions,
Mine is certainly the final morality.
Send this message to the monks and nuns;
Tell them Rangjung Dorje sent it.

Others do not look down on me, as
I have worked a long time for peace.
This is the illusory play of helping others
That is known as the greatest patience.
Send this message to the happy;
Tell them Rangjung Dorje sent it.

I have been caught on the nails of passing pain,[393]
But as [the pains] of resting, moving, eating, and sleeping[394]
Are helpfully eliminated by liberation, know that
I am now cleansed of these distracting stains.
Send this message to the diligent;
Tell them Rangjung Dorje sent it.

I am not just wandering around dangerous ravines.
They are blissful, clear, nonconceptual, empty forms
That merge into a direct state, free of conceptions;
This state is the samādhi that destroys saṃsāra's root.
Send this message to the great meditators;
Tell them Rangjung Dorje sent it.

I have not [mastered] the five sciences,[395]
But by listening, I have destroyed external superimpositions.
Now I know all phenomena are interdependent, and
It is this wisdom that clears away mistaken concepts.
Send this message to the scholars;
Tell them Rangjung Dorje sent it.

I have not practiced asceticism,
But I have used the deity's body to purify the aggregates.
What's more, I dissolved this purifier, the conceptual basis,
Into the expanse—uncontaminated, manifested gnosis.
Send this message to the tāntrikas;
Tell them Rangjung Dorje sent it.

I have not been to the all-knowing ground,
But I have no desire for that peaceful, blissful result.
I know saṃsāra's nature, so I have
No hopes, no fears, no dualistic thinking.
Send this message to the bodhisattvas;
Tell them Rangjung Dorje sent it.

Like the Buddha instructed,
I travel everywhere, indiscriminately, destitute.
And my reason for collecting these verses

Is to help beings of this degenerate age.
Send this message to the lucky ones;
Tell them Rangjung Dorje sent it.

Unfortunate, confused beings
Do not understand our teachings;
We show them directly, but they still doubt.
Tell them Rangjung Dorje calls these
People with debauched views
"Destroyers of the freedom lineage."

Patrons who amass fame and wealth,
"Upholders of the Vinaya" who've lost their vows,
Teachers who yearn for renown,
"Great meditators" who cultivate stupidity—
Tell them Rangjung Dorje calls them
"Try-hards who don't get results."

Yogis who doubt,[396]
Tāntrikas without commitments,
Nihilistic "realized ones," and
Important people who commit heinous crimes—
Tell them Rangjung Dorje calls them
"Those who are about to fall to infinite depths."

E ma! This song shows the difference between
The great, good road and the wrong way;
It does not contradict the teachings of the Buddha.
It was sung on the lower slopes of Tsari.
Send its message to everyone, and
Tell them Rangjung Dorje sent it.

A Message to the Entire Kingdom *was inspired by the great siddha, the messenger, Tsangpa Gyare [1161–1211]. Rangjung Dorje sang it at Langong [at Tsari], in the sixth month of the Rat Year [1312].*

CHAPTER 12

Songs of the View, Cultivation, Behavior, and Result

This group of four songs from the *Collected Songs* outlines that which Rangjung Dorje held to be the four elements of mahāmudrā practice: the view, cultivation, behavior, and result.[397] He wrote it when he was a teenager and still staying in Khyung Dzong Hermitage above Tsurpu Monastery. It reads as a combination of a personal pep talk and a teaching. Like many of the songs from this period, it was probably delivered to those who gathered to perform a gaṇacakra, or ritual feast, on a special day. All four songs include word plays and unexpected breaks or twists in their pattern, which are most probably used to entertain his audience.

Within these connected songs, Rangjung Dorje outlines his understanding of the view, cultivation, behavior, and result. His description of the view in the first song mostly follows the standard representations of the Mahāmudrā tradition. Unlike his later writing, which focuses more on pointing to the nature of the mind, this song focuses more on the attitude that one should develop to encounter the view. He tells people to be "sideless" or "impartial" and not to focus too much on concepts. His description of cultivation in the next song links repetition in the song to the repetition that is essential in cultivation. The word translated here as "cultivation" is often translated as "meditation." I have chosen to translate it as "cultivation" while translating Rangjung Dorje's work because his emphasis in using this word is very much in line with the idea—implicit in the Tibetan word *gom*[398]—of creating a habit. It is not enough to see the view, he suggests. Rather, one needs to make a habit of seeing existence from this perspective. The song on behavior talks about how to integrate this habituation of the view into one's life, in and out of meditation. And the song on the result not only speaks of the positive outcomes that result from this practice—including full awakening—but it also provides a recap of the mahāmudrā view.

NAMO RATNA GURU

I go for refuge to the gurus.

This is a little song of the dawning
Appearance of yogic experience.
Lucky ones experience it too!

In sacred Dharma practice,
Do not be attached to country or kin;
Incisively watch your mind.

In the miserable ocean of saṃsāra,
Do not think, "Here is okay";
Homeless, wander the mountains.

When it's time to leave alone [i.e., when you are about to die],
Do not trade trifles, profits, and sundry;
Inertly watch your mind.

Toward the buddhas' infinite intention,
Do not be hypocritical or haughty;
Look at the Dharma impartially.[399]

The moment of death only lasts an instant,
So do not think of many things;
Incisively [re]view the instructions.

Regarding the buddhas' vast intention,
Do not hold onto pride and prejudice;
Unfixated, watch the view.

Truth is in place in the [three] vehicles,
So do not be arrogant or attached;
Impartially envision purity.

The intention of past, present, and future
Buddhas is beyond intellect;
Do not be sidetracked by saṃsāra.

Do not superimpose words
On the wisdom of all past, present, and future
Buddhas' bodies, speech, and minds.

Look at the skylike mahāmudrā.
Do not dissect it with definitions;
Undistracted, stay in your own place.

This has been a song of the view.
Next, is a song of cultivation.

The final intention of all the
Kagyü gurus is cultivation;
Cultivate thinking about this again.

The root of all past, present, and future
Buddhas' sacred Dharma is cultivation;
Cultivate thinking about this again.

In the great, nondual wisdom,
Cultivation does not go from good to bad;
Cultivate cutting through preconceptions again.

If you do not cultivate in this life,
You will regret it when you die;
Cultivate freedom from concerns.

Free from profound pronouncements,
Without using a lot of jargon,
Cultivate cultivating release and attention.

In all the teachings of the Buddha,
There is nothing beyond final cultivation;
Cultivate not being fixated or concerned.

The buddhas' intention
Is the middle way's nature;
Cultivate freedom from the two extremes.

There is no greater comfort, in body or mind,
Than these isolated mountain retreats;
Cultivate the solitude of mountain abodes.

But then again, there is absolutely nothing to cultivate,
These are all half-true mutterings;
Cultivate the state of no cultivation.

All self-grasping preconceptions
Have always been free of concepts;
Cultivate looking right at this.

Keep cultivating until you realize
Mahāmudrā's wisdom is the root
Of all the Buddha's sacred Dharmas.

This has been a song of cultivation.
Next is a song about how yogis behave.[400]

The final behavior of all past, present, and future
Buddhas is to be undistracted;
Be purposefully mindful.

The final behavior of all the gurus,
All the siddhas, is the mahāmudrā;
Stay away from the two extremes.

The root of all the Buddha's
Teachings is not being distracted;
Be purposefully mindful.

The root of all experience,
Sacred Dharma's goal, is recognition;
Implement the profound Dharma.

The vast tracts of the Buddha's intention
Are beyond speech, thought, and expression;
Be purposefully ineffable.

All formulated, sacred dharmas,
All of them, are perishable;
Be purposefully enduring.

In dying you separate from all the world's
Food, wealth, friends, and kin;
Be purposefully inseparable.

The world's translucent gods and demons
Will kill you dead if you depend on them;
Be profound instead.

When you cultivate fused clarity and luminosity,
You see your deity and their entourage;
Be the fusion of clarity and luminosity.

But then again, there is absolutely nothing to be done.
To say "behavior" is inaccurate;
Be purposefully accurate.

In the vast tracts of the buddhas' intention,
There are no subjects, attachments, aversions;
Be free from extremes in your behavior.

This was a song about behavior.
Next is a song about yoga's results.

The final inspiration of the gurus
Is the great bliss of mahāmudrā;
There is no better result.

The forebears' great compassion
Introduces it to their descendants;[401]
There is no better result.

All the greatest, most profound meanings
Are identified as free from extremes;
There is no better result.

In the end, the sacred Dharma is not cultivated
Because it is identified as nondistraction;
There is no better result.

Saṃsāra and nirvāṇa's roots
Are identified as ungraspable;
There is no better result.

Knowing not to place hopes and fears
In the things we do in saṃsāra;
There is no better result.

Knowing all apparent places
Out there are not tangible;
There is no better result.

Knowing that all the heard sounds
Out there are unreal echoes;
There is no better result.

When all forms are naturally apparent emptiness,
And all we see arises as dharmakāya;
There is no better result.

When we are constantly familiar
With the self-liberating, ungraspable view;
There is no better result.

When we know all thoughts of
Things are self-liberating;
There is no better result.

This was a song about results.

Once more—
Practice the sacred Dharma,
Depend on a qualified guru,
Stay in isolated, mountain retreats,
Cultivate the incomparable view.

Once more, this summary is all you need, lucky ones. Experience it. The Dharma noble Rangjung Dorje sang these songs at Khyung Dzong Hermitage.

CHAPTER 13

A Short Praise to Tsurpu Monastery

A Short Praise to Tsurpu Monastery is one of a group of praises to places composed by Rangjung Dorje.[402] He was one of few people to write a series of praises to places in the Tibetan Buddhist tradition. Traditionally, Tibetan religious praises have been written to buddhas, bodhisattvas, gurus, lineages, important statues, and even religious kings. It is more typical in secular and modern poetry to see praises of one's homeland or praises of places of pilgrimage.[403] There are links between Rangjung Dorje's praises to places and the more common Buddhist praises to beings. The praises to beings often set their praise in a landscape associated with the venerated being. Conversely, Rangjung Dorje's praises to places are peopled by venerated beings in order to emphasize their sacredness. But Rangjung Dorje's choice to focus on the places and then set the people within them is unusual.

The places to which Rangjung Dorje wrote praises give clues as to the intent behind these actions. He wrote praises to Tsurpu Monastery and its surrounds, to nearby Dechen Teng Hermitage in the Tölung Valley, and to Mount Khawa Karpo.[404] These praises were, therefore, all associated with two of his three primary sacralization projects. He wrote in the song (*gur* or *lu*) genre rather than the praise (*töpa*)[405] genre about the other main site he was intent on sacralizing, New Tsari.[406]

Unlike his compositions in the song genre, his praises are heavily influenced by the kāvya tradition of Indian courtly poetry that Sakya Paṇḍita had made influential in Tibet.[407] Kāvya is an ornate form of poetry that contains many more figures of speech, metaphors, and references to Indian mythology than other forms of Tibetan literature. Knowledge of this form of poetry was the mark of a sophisticated education in thirteenth- and fourteenth- century Tibet. Rangjung Dorje composed far fewer poems in this form than he did in the song form. These praises to places and the several praises to people and lineages that he wrote are the only works that are written primarily in this style (although there it could be argued that there is some kāvya influence in his *Verse Liberation Story*). His choice to write praises to places associated with his lineage in this style was clearly an attempt to promote them and his own skills.

OṂ SARVA SWASTI SIDDHAM HUṂ

By nature, and in reality, you are the unequaled Dharma noble,
The nirmaṇakāya, the bodily emanation of compassion for
wanderers.

In complete accordance with the perfected intention of
Düsum Khyenpa and the Dharma noble Rinchen [Gampopa],
I will write down a few praises for this great,
Solitary sacred site, this Tsurpu.

This solitary, pleasant region is called the colorful [Tsur] upper
valley [pu].
As Prince Candraprabha Kumāra prophesied,

It is a land with sites of especially great attainment.
It has a backdrop of hills [shaped like] stūpas,
In which birds, carnivores, and herbivores all sing
Melodies, dance, and play artfully [together].

Sometimes, this land looks like heaven—
An assortment of flowers bloom in the meadows;
Utpala flowers decorate the grasslands;
There are shang-shang flowers
And an inconceivable variety of other perfumed blooms.
Along with flowers, there is
An inconceivable variety of medicinal plants,
Each one imbued with its own scent.
These medicinal plants are cultivated by
An inconceivable gathering of streams;
The streams in this sacred site
Quench the thirst of all wanderers, humans, and nonhumans;
Their waters are so refreshing they
Take away your breath as well as your thirst, creating
contentment.

And there is more—
The great mountains around the valley
Contain incredible, naturally formed shapes of gods and letters.
In the mountains, special green vegetables grow
That breathe life into beings.
In their foothills, at their base,
Are tens of thousands of trees.
The trees' wood generates great fires and great warmth;
It relieves the suffering of cold,
The freezing torments of unclothed animals.

All these medicinal plants, flowers, streams, and the rest
Provide a home for herbivores, birds, and even carnivores;
They are all so happy that they aren't afraid of each other.

If you travel up the valley a little further from here,
There is a meadow that looks like a golden maṇḍala.
It is a solitary site, a land of delights, a divine abode,
Where you will be in the presence of the Snow King.

The mountain at the back is sacred Gyalwa Ri;
From it clear, fragrant streams descend
That quench thirsts and nurture a variety of beings,
Humans, and other wanderers too.

On full-moon and no-moon days,
On the eighth and third of each month, and all other special days,
Canopies of rainbows appear in the sky above
This greatest of great sacred sites,
And flower-rain falls from the same sky.

In the center of all this is Tsurpu Monastery,
Arranged like flowers in the meadow.
How radiant it is! How vivid it shines!
Illustrious, colorful, high valley,
You are the greatest of sacred sites. Wondrous Tsurpu, I bow to you.

This praise to Tsurpu was written by Rangjung Dorje.

CHAPTER 14

The Song That Settles the Ground-of-All

The Song That Settles the Ground-of-All is a short song that says a lot. Because it is characteristic of his view on the nature of mind, it is considered one of Rangjung Dorje's most important compositions and has been translated several times.[408] Rangjung Dorje's presentation of the nature of mind, which he held to be synonymous with the ultimate truth, has been very influential within the Karma Kagyü tradition and beyond. To this day, however, not all commentators agree on what his position was.

These discussions about his position have been influenced by the broader debate about the validity and compatibility of the two views of emptiness that I discussed in chapter four—and which have been discussed in much more detail elsewhere[409]—intrinsic emptiness (*rangtong*) and extrinsic emptiness (*shentong*). Among those arguing for and against the validity of extrinsic emptiness—and its compatibility with intrinsic emptiness—it was considered important to ascertain Rangjung Dorje's position on these topics. The arguments about whether Rangjung Dorje was a *shentongpa* (i.e., one who holds to extrinsic emptiness) or not seem to depend on the definition of this term and how the assessor approaches the topic. From a historical perspective, there is little argument. The term *shentong* does not appear in Rangjung Dorje's writing, and he does not refer to himself as one who holds this view. To call him a shentongpa is anachronistic. Doxographically, however, the arguments for and against his inclusion within this category are less clear. From this definitional perspective, it could be argued that Rangjung Dorje held the characteristics of a shentongpa, and it could be held that he did not. It depends on how the author defines shentong. Some of his statements could be counted—and have been counted by such luminaries as Karma Trinlepa (1456–1539) and Jamgön Kongtrül Lodrö Taye (1813–1899)—as advocations of the extrinsic emptiness position. But his views do not align with all presentations of shentong.

As explained in chapter four, the basic difference between intrinsic and extrinsic emptiness is as follows. Intrinsic emptiness is the mere negation of a phenomena's intrinsic emptiness: there is no essence in any phenomena. It does not exist. Extrinsic emptiness, by contrast, is the "not this" of emptiness. Emptiness is said to be no thing that can be articulated. Some advocates of extrinsic existence are strident about the implications of this argument. Dölpopa Sherap Gyaltsen, who is purported to have been Rangjung Dorje's student, argued, for example, that extrinsic emptiness meant that the ultimate existed in some way.[410] There is nothing in Rangjung Dorje's writing that suggests that he held the same view. Rather, his writing suggests that he held that the ultimate is beyond duality and therefore could not be articulated.

As I also argued in chapter four, situating Rangjung Dorje's arguments in their historical context suggests that his position on emptiness was formed within an entirely different argument from the intrinsic and extrinsic emptiness argument. During his lifetime, there was an ongoing polemic between the Kagyü and the ruling Sakya tradition about the appropriateness and utility of combining the teachings of different forms of Buddhism. The Sakya school held that it was inappropriate. Rangjung Dorje and many other Kagyüpas held that it was appropriate. Rangjung Dorje went even further than most adherents of the Kagyü, presenting a "sideless" view that combined three major traditions: the Great Middle Way (which was similar to the Yogācāra-Madhyamaka tradition and based on his reading of Maitreya's Five Works), Mahāmudrā, and the Great Completion.[411]

What is it that Rangjung Dorje says in this particular song that speaks to his position on emptiness? There are several parts of the song that are of interest in this regard. First, the song's topic, the "ground-of-all" (*künzhi*) is of interest. Rangjung Dorje uses this term as a way to describe the ultimate truth; "ground-of-all" functions, in other words, as a synonym for the *dharmakāya*, *dharmatā*, or the "nature of phenomena,"[412] and the "nature of the mind." His usage is somewhat idiosyncratic. The term *ground-of-all* sounds like the term *ground-of-all consciousness* (*künzhi namshe*; *ālayavijñāna*). The term *ground-of-all consciousness* is used within the Yogācāra tradition to refer to the storehouse consciousness in which the imprints and potentials for continued existence in saṃsāra are stored. Rangjung Dorje is not talking about this consciousness. Instead, he is referring to the nature of that consciousness, which has the same nature as all phenomena. He uses the term *ground-of-all* to highlight his view that all of the world's experiences, whether they be in saṃsāra or nirvāṇa, have the same nature, the ultimate nature, the nature of the mind.

NAMO GURU

Illuminator of my own mind as dharmakāya,
Greatest of gurus, I invoke you.

Those seated here, hear these words,
Realize their purpose, then arouse their experience.
The ground-of-all is the base of both saṃsāra and nirvāṇa;
When you do not realize it, you are in saṃsāra,
When you realize it, it is the Tathāgata's mind.
This is an expression of the ground-of-all's nature.

It is analogous to a mirror without tarnish,
On which reflections appear; just like this,
In the expansive state of unstained mind,
A variety of awareness flows and perishes.

[Even] the duality that grasps at place and sense of place,
Is the flow of appearance in your own expanse.
Saṃsāra and nirvāṇa are not two, but one entity;
Not realizing this is a mistake, realizing it causes liberation.

But there is no realizing and realizer;
Holding their duality is the base of saṃsāra.
Seeing their essential lack of duality
Manifests the Buddha's essence directly.

This is *The Song That Settles the Ground-of-All.*
It was sung at a solitary site.
Through clearing the veils to the ground-of-all,
May you realize your own unstained mind!

This song was sung by the Dharma noble Rangjung Dorje for the great meditator Darma[413] *and his entourage at Tölung Gyaldo,*[414] *in the ninth month of the Sheep Year [1319] as the moon waxed.*

CHAPTER 15

Rangjung Dorje's Recipes for Taking the Essence

This is a collection of three short texts in which Rangjung Dorje instructs yogis on how to "take the essence" out of herbs. These practices have two purposes. They enable yogis to live for longer on limited supplies, and they are supposed to be a clarifying practice on their own. These practices include a variety of substances that can be found around mountain retreat centers and others that have to be carried into the site. The texts read like medical texts in some parts and speak to both Rangjung Dorje's knowledge of traditional medicines and the crossover in knowledge sets between yogis and traditional doctors.

Given the number of famines that were experienced during the thirteenth century and early fourteenth century in Tibet, it is also interesting to note that the colophon to this collection states that these practices "liberate from famine."

Extracting the Essence of Solomon's Seal

I pay homage to the sacred guru. The *amrita* [nectar] called Solomon's seal [*Polygonatum*][415] grows along the edges of the mountains, near cultivated fields.[416] Its roots are like a curved horn of a sheep.

Its stalks are purple; its leaves are fine. Its flowers are dark red and grow in bundles. The taste [of its fruit] is sweet and strong.

In past times, Rahu stole the pot in which the lake of mild was churned. Vajrapāṇi's weapon, a wheel, cut his throat, and from it flowed drops of amrita. When they hit the earth, these drops became Solomon's seal. They are also called the plants of suchness.

I will explain the way to eat them. It is best to collect them in autumn and spring. When boiling them, a fluid will ooze out of them. When this is dry, add a measure equal to a fifth of its volume of incense and crush it into powder. Use it to make a warm broth.

When you want to make beer, make the portions as above. Add yeast and lay it to rest well. And keep it going by adding water and separating the water [from the base].

When you want to make tea, boil the leaves and place it into the brew. To get rid of the strong aroma of the tea, beat it until it is fine, then boil. Use whatever hot rocks you have around.

This is the best way to eat. You will not be able to eat anything else continually and reliably. It increases physical strength and longevity. It expels kidney disease and cold stomach [rheumatism], and it has still other qualities.

Rangjung Dorje practices extracting the essence of the amrita Solomon's seal. Lucky ones, you should experience it too.

Extracting the Essence of Early Purple Orchid

I pay homage to the sacred guru. I'm about to give you instructions on how to extract the essence of early purple orchid [*Orchis mascula*].[417] This includes an explanation of discerning which ones they are, the way to eat them, and their benefits for dispelling health obstacles. The name of the plant [in Tibetan] is "powerful hand." In past times, because the gods and demigods were fighting, a demigod shot an arrow at a god's arm, and blood fell from it. It created a handful of blood [that created this plant]. That is why this practice is called extracting the essence of "powerful hand."

This plant is famous within the sciences of life. In these, it is described well as white, with blue-green leaves and stems. Two or three [types] of it are bad, blackened, and thin.

The way to eat this plant is this. At the right time, dig in irrigation ditches and in the places where nomad tents are pitched. [Remove them from the earth] by hitting it. This is excellent for stopping poison. Wash it well in water and pound it into fine powder. Mix it well with incense and refine it.

Then, when you are going to extract the essence, warm it so that the gruel rises to an appropriate temperature. Adding a little stock to it is good too. When you eat the food, concentrate on the three syllables to transform it into nectar. Practice having the pride of the deity.

So that no other beings will obstruct this [practice], hang the powerful one up for a few days on its side, and when discharge emerges from it, use ginger with it. The benefits of this are inconceivable. It is particularly helpful for developing strength and putting on weight. You do not need to mix it with any other grown food. I have written this so you will realize its purpose, which is to extract the essence and avoid hunger. Rangjung Dorje practices this. Lucky ones, you should all attain the siddhi of taking the essence.

Extracting the Essence of a Lustrous Plant

Taking the essence of a lustrous plant is an experience for the fortunate.[418] This [text] will show you its sign, the way to eat it, how to clear obstacles, and its benefits. First, it is asserted that there are three types of this plant: those with white, yellow, and blue [flowers]. These plants are tasty[419] and are all found in fields in which dew forms.[420]

[Second,] this is the way to eat it. Pulverize [the plant] when it is well dried. Separate it into sections that you can eat in three sessions. Mix it together with good honey, put it in apricot oil, and make little balls. When it is time to eat it, do not eat any of it fried. Eat it as gruel. If you have milk, beer, or bone broth, it works very well with them. If you do not have them, the substance does not become faulty.

I will now explain the way to eat it. [Reciting] the [Sanskrit] letters from *A* to *Ba* seven times will clear eye sickness. When [this practice] is combined with the [keeping of] the four root precepts,[421] it improves the complexion and the body, increasing the taker's life span. If it is taken with the golden-colored gooseberry,[422] without penetrating the flesh of any being,[423] and while practicing Vairocana,[424] it will defeat leprosy. If taken with horse[425] bone, it will increase fleet-footedness. If it is taken with sesame oil, it increases well-being. If it is taken with meat broth, it increases strength. If it is taken with the three heats, one will warm the four types of cold.

The extent of these combinations' [benefits] is this. If the king were to be offered these substances in combination when the drumbeats,[426] in sulphur with honey three times, it would benefit even the king himself. But if he were not to combine them, it would not be wrong either.

The impact of medicine depends on the times it is taken. This is the dose for mountain [people's] stomachs.

[Third,] I will now explain how to purify obstacles. For wind, perform nutritional *kunye* massage.[427] Mountain raspberries[428] are especially good to give for old bones. If phlegm arises, give pomegranate,[429] or give ginger and coriander seed. If there is nausea, give green leafy vegetables. If there is bile,[430] give broadleaf plantain[431] with rice soup or, alternatively, give larkspur.[432] If there is a worm, give garlic [or leek] and turnips.

[Section on geomancy.] If a white pond has collected, raise a flag.[433] If there is saline water in the north, it is harmful to drink. If there is a type of hawk on the river or lake bank that is flesh colored, give gooseberries.[434] When you are hungry, who eats the sky? This has been the way to remove obstacles.

Fourth, I will show the benefits [of this practice]. If I were to expand on the benefits of this practice, my explanation would be inconceivable. In brief then, here are its benefits. It would have pacified the illnesses and negativity of those who have died. It makes eyes and concentration clear. It gets rid of white hair and wrinkles. It grants fleet-footedness and strength. It is superior to all the world's dedications. Its other benefits are inconceivable.

Before you eat it, be certain to transform it. In particular, recite this and cultivate this practice when you are going to eat. Cultivate the idea that you are your personal deity, that the guru is at the crown of your head, and that there is a HŪṂ in this space. Imagine that as wisdom amrita descends into you, your body and mind become full of bliss.

Receive the blessings of the three substances, fire, air, and seed syllables as other [texts] instruct. This is a secret instruction. There are many forms of taking the essence with honey. This is the concentration that is like the essence. And Rangjung Dorje wrote it.

If mountain hermits practice these extractions, they will eliminate the mind that holds the idea of a self. There is nothing greater than this. They will also be liberated from famine. This is the great kindness of Rangjung Dorje.

CHAPTER 16

Aspiration for Mahāmudrā, the Definitive Meaning

The *Aspiration for Mahāmudrā* is one of Rangjung Dorje's most famous compositions.[435] It is the subject of several commentaries, including the well-known composition by the Eighth Tai Situ, also known as Situ Paṇchen, Chökyi Jungne (1700–1774), *Teachings of the Supreme Siddhas*.[436] It is also regularly chanted in Karma Kagyü monasteries, homes, and at other gatherings. The work contains many of the same themes as his other poetic compositions. It begins with his paying his respects to his gurus and meditational deities. It then gives an overview of the practice of mahāmudrā, encouraging those reading and speaking it to aspire to buddhahood for the benefit of all beings, work through the ground, path, and result of mahāmudrā, and achieve its final state of awakening. It is focused on mahāmudrā. But Rangjung Dorje asks his followers to approach it in an open way, that it represents the same ultimate truth as other presentations such as Madhyamaka and the Great Completion. It is possible that it has resonated so much with the followers of the tradition because of its directness and inclusion. In this aspiration, Rangjung Dorje asks all those reading or reciting his poem to aspire to awakening.

NAMO GURU

Gurus, *yidams*, maṇḍala deities,
Buddhas of the ten directions and three times, and your children,
Love us and send waves of inspiration
So that we will fulfill my aspirations as intended.

Our own and immeasurable sentient beings'
Pure thoughts and deeds are snow-mountain sources;
May their streams, collected virtue, descend unpolluted through the three realms
And join the ocean of the Buddha's four bodies.

For as long as it takes to achieve this,
From life to life, in the succession of our lives,
May no one even speak the words "misdeed" or "suffering,"
And may we enjoy the ocean of happiness and virtue.

May we have free time and opportunity, trust, enthusiasm, and wisdom.
May we rely on good teachers, extract the essence of their advice,
And achieve results as we are instructed, without obstacles.
May we enjoy the sacred Dharma in all my successive lives.

Learning scripture and reason liberates us from the veil of ignorance.
Contemplating advice destroys the fog of doubts.
The clear light of cultivation clarifies the way things are.
May the appearances of the three wisdoms increase.

The ground means the two truths free from the extremes of
realism and nihilism.
The best path is the two accumulations, free from exaggeration
and denial.
Its result is the two purposes, freed from the extremes of
existence and extinction.
May we encounter this unmistaken, certain Dharma.

Purification's ground is the mind itself, unified clarity and
emptiness.
The mahāmudrā's great vajra yoga is the purifier;
The stains of adventitious mistakes are that which is to be
purified.
May they be purified directly in the stainless dharmakāya.

A confident view undermines exaggeration in the ground.
Cultivation's point is to guard against distraction from the view.
The best behavior develops agility in all cultivation's principles.
May we have confidence in the view, cultivation, and behavior.

All phenomena are the mind's magical illusions.
The mind is . . . there is no mind; the mind's nature is empty.
It is empty and unstoppable, so everything appears.
May our excellent analysis destroy the roots in the ground.

We mistake our projections—existents we don't experience—
for objects.
Ignorance makes us mistake self-awareness for self.
Clinging to duality, we wander in the vastness of becoming.
May the spreading roots of ignorance be destroyed.

Even buddhas do not see that which does not exist;
But these nonexistents are the basis of saṃsāra and nirvāṇa.
This is not a contradiction. It is the middle path's unity.
May we realize the mind's dharmatā, free from extremes.

Nothing can indicate that "it is this";
Nothing can refute that "it is not this."
The unconstructed dharmatā is beyond intellect;
May we be certain it is authentic reality's limit.

Not realizing this is cycling in saṃsāra's ocean;
Realizing this is buddhahood, nothing else.
This is everything; there is nothing else.
May we know the underlying basis of all, dharmatā.

As appearance is mind and emptiness is also mind,
Then realization is mind and mistakes are in mind.
As arising is mind and cessation is also mind,
May we destroy all exaggerations within my mind.

Uncorrupted by the cultivation of intellectual effort,
Unaroused by the winds of ordinary business,
Knowing how to settle in unconstructed simplicity,
May we be skilled at and protective of our experience of mind's
principle.

When the waves of subtle and gross conceptions subside,
The placid stream of mind naturally comes to rest.
May our ocean of calm abiding be stable and calm and
Free from the silt of turbid drowsiness and lethargy.

When we look again and again at invisible mind,
We see unseen meaning vividly, just as it is.
By destroying doubts about whether it is or is not,
May we know our own nature unmistakably.

Looking at objects . . . there are no objects. We see mind.
Looking at mind . . . there is no mind. We see natural emptiness.
Looking at both naturally liberates clinging to duality.
May we realize the clear-light mind as it is.

The mahāmudrā is free from mental work;
The Great Middle Way is free from extremes.
Since it includes everything, it is the Great Completion;
May we gain the confidence of realizing all by knowing one.

Free from obsession, great bliss never ceases;
Without ascribed attributes, clear light is unobscured.
Beyond intellect, without concepts, there is spontaneity.
May our effortless experiences never cease.

Grasping at the experience of goodness is liberated on the spot.
Mistaken, negative concepts are naturally purified in the
expanse.
Ordinary mind neither adopts nor discards, adds or removes.
May we realize dharmatā's truth, simplicity.

The nature of beings is always buddhas, but
Not realizing it they wander in saṃsāra.
These beings' suffering is boundless;
May unbearable compassion for them arise in our continuums.

When there is love—the unstoppable expression of which is
Unbearable compassion—the empty essence arises starkly.
May I never deviate from the best path, the path of union.
Cultivate it continually, all day and all night.

Through the power of cultivation comes insight, clairvoyance,
The maturing of beings, the intense cleansing of buddhafields,
And our aspirations to attain Buddha's Dharma are fulfilled.
May we attain the buddhahood that finishes completion,
    maturing, and cleansing.

Through the power of the compassion and the pure virtue
Of the buddhas of the ten directions and their children,
May my and all beings' aspirations
Be accomplished, just as we wish.

Karmapa Rangjung Dorje wrote this Aspiration for Mahāmudrā, the Definitive Meaning.

CHAPTER 17

In Xanadu

This is the second to last song within the *Collected Songs of Rangjung Dorje*, and he wrote it when he was far from home, in the Mongol summer capital, Xanadu.[437] Like many of his other songs, it combines reflections on yoga practice and a life lived in contemplation with social criticism. This song is also notable because of its subject, the legendary Xanadu. Not only does it present a very different take on the city than Samuel Taylor Coleridge's orientalist poem "Kubla Khan," it also represents one of the few premodern Tibetan poems about city life.

NAMO GURU

I honor the gurus.

In these dark times for the Buddha's teachings,
Those beings who trust are rare,
Those who teach the sacred Dharma precisely are few,
And in every hundred people, only a few make an effort at Dharma.

In dark times like these,
To benefit both yourself and others,
Followers of the Buddha [should hear this]—

Now you are free from saṃsāra's mud,
Strike out for nirvāṇa's dry shore.
Now you have abandoned worldly relatives,
Rely on sacred, spiritual friends.
Now you have stopped pointless chatter,
Recite secret mantras.
Now you have stopped debauched exertions,
Exert yourself at dhyāna.
Now you have renounced sweets,
Rely on samādhi's food.
Now that you have stopped hankering for towns,
Wander in mountainous borderlands.

Because when we don't do these things—
External appearances become expert in deception;
Children of the mind, they are crazy in the head.
Preconceptions proliferate and last longer; but
Virtuous friends become increasingly rare.
Ignorant veils and fogs get thicker, and
We wander on multiplying cliffs of depravity.
Unwholesome friends lead us
To prison, the three bad destinations,
Where we will wander without end.

This is why now is the time to strive. He said this in the fifth month of the Ox Year (1337) in Xanadu.

Notes

1. Rang byung rdo rje, *Mgur rnam*, 7.7–8.3, and Rang byung rdo rje, *Mgur 'bum*, vol. *ca*, 189.6–190.3.
2. *mgur.*
3. *glu.*
4. *rnam thar.*
5. Rang byung rdo rje, *Mgur rnam*, 202.2–203.2, and Rang byung rdo rje, *Mgur 'bum*, 414.3–415.1.
6. To generate some consistency in transliterations, all Tibetan language proper names in this book are written following the Tibetan and Himalayan Library's phonetic program: http://www.thlib.org/cgi-bin/thl/lbow/phonetics.pl?sep_join=%20. And most dates are taken from the Treasury of Lives website: https://treasuryoflives.org/.
7. *sgyu ma lta bu.*
8. *chos rje.*
9. *phyogs med.*
10. *ris med.*
11. I outline this relationship in some detail in my previous book. See Gamble, *Reincarnation in Tibetan Buddhism*, 54–58.
12. The *mahāsiddhas* (Tib. *sgrub thob chen po*) were Indian tantric adepts who were either the lineage predessesors or composers of many of the tantric traditions practiced in Tibet. Traditionally, there are said to have been eighty-four of them, whose life stories were recorded in the *Lives of the Eighty-Four Siddhas* (Skt. *Caturaśīti-siddha-pravtti*), which is attributed to Abhayadatta and translated into Tibetan by Smon grub shes rab (*Grub thob brgyad bcu tsa bzhi'i lo rgyus*). The most literal translation of this work is James B. Robson's *Buddha's Lions: The Lives of the Eighty-Four Siddhas* (Berkeley: Dharma Publishing, 1979).

13. *na ro chos drug*. For an emic analysis of this tradition, see Kragh, "Prolegomenon to the Six Doctrines of Nā ro pa: Authority and Tradition," 131–78.
14. Ronald Davidson questions Marpa's relationship with Nāropā and suggests he studied instead with Nāropā's student Maitrīpa. Davidson, *Tibetan Renaissance*, 143–45.
15. *snying thig gter ma*.
16. For more details on this, see Gamble, *Reincarnation in Tibetan Buddhism*, 32–38.
17. I discuss all three terms—rebirth (*yang srid*), emanation (*rnam 'phrul*), and manifestation (*'phrul ba*)—in *Reincarnation in Tibetan Buddhism*, 64–75.
18. *bdag dang 'dra ri khrod pa*.
19. Rang byung rdo rje, *Rang byung rdo rje'i rnam thar tshigs bcad ma,* vol. *nga*, 412. Hereafter, this text title will be abbreviated to *Tshigs bcad ma*. Unless otherwise stated, Rang byung rdo rje's texts cited in these notes are from *Rang byung rdo rje'i gsung 'bum* [Rangjung Dorje's Collected Works], 2006.
20. Rang byung rdo rje, 412.
21. Kurtis Schaeffer and Lara Braistein have both translated, researched, and written histories of different parts of the collection of texts attributed to Saraha. See *Adamantine Songs (Vajragīti): Study, Translation, and Tibetan Citical Edition*, trans. Lara Braistein (New York: Columbia University Press, 2015) and Schaeffer, *Dreaming the Great Brahmin*, 2005.
22. *Phyag rgya chen po gang gA ma'i gzhung gi sa bcad* [Outline of the texts of the *Ganga Mahāmudrā*], vol. *a*, 159–60; *Phyag rgya chen po gang gA ma'i 'grel ba* [Commentary on the *Ganga Mahāmudrā*], vol. *a*, 161–75; *Rgyal po do ha'i sab cad* [Outline of the *King Dohā*], vol. *a*, 177–80; *Bstun mo do ha'i sab cad* [Outline of the *Queen Dohā*], vol. *a*, 180–85; *Do ha mdzod kyi bsdud don bcad la ldeb* [Condensation of the meaning of the *Dohā-Kośa*], vol. *a*, 185–91.
23. Rang byung rdo rje, *Mgur 'bum*, vol. *ca*, 185–297; and Rang byung rdo rje, *Gsung 'gur* [*sic*] *thor bu*, vol. *ca*, 359–416.
24. *ri khrod*.
25. *dben pa*.
26. In Tibetan the guru is called lama (*bla ma*), and *mahāmudrā* is called chak gya chen mo (*phyag rgya chen mo* or *phyag chen*).
27. *tshogs 'khor*.
28. *rnam thar*. These texts are not designated by the usual term for autobiography in Tibetan, *rang rnam* (one's own liberation story; *rang gi rnam*

thar, or *rang rnam* for short) by their compilers, and Rangjung Dorje does not refer to them as *rang rnam* within the text either.

29. Rang byung rdo rje, *Dpal chen Rang byung rdo rje'i rnam thar*, vol. *nga*, 353–76. Hereafter referred to as *Dpal chen rnam thar*.
30. Rang byung rdo rje, *Sngar pa'i skye bor rnam thar*, vol. *nga*, 353–58.
31. Rang byung rdo rje, *Bar de'i* [*sic*] *rnam par thar pa*, vol. *nga*, 358–74. Some scholars suggest that the *Liberation Story of the In-Between State* was missing, as it is not listed individually in Rangjung Dorje's Gsung 'bum. See, for example, Manson, "Introduction to the Life of Karma Pakshi," 44–45; Seegers, "Lord of the Teachings," 39, 48, 72, 79–81; and Berounský, "Entering Dead Bodies and the Miraculous Power of the Kings, Part 2," 25. It is, however, included within this larger text and translated in full in the second section of this book.
32. Rang byung rdo rje, *Dpal chen rnam thar*, 367–73.
33. Rang byung rdo rje, *Tshigs bcad ma*, 374–414.
34. Rang byung rdo rje, 376–402.
35. Rang byung rdo rje, 402–12.
36. Rang byung rdo rje, 412–14.
37. E. Gene Smith wrote an informative summary about this literary genre. See Smith, *Among Tibetan Texts*, 39–52.
38. Rang byung rdo rje, *Ston pa'i skyes rabs*, vol. *kha*, 1–666.
39. Rang byung rdo rje, *Zab mo nang don gyi gzhung*, vol. *ja*, 308–60.
40. See note 17. The terms "rebirth" (*yang srid*), "emanation" (*rnam'phrul*), and "manifestation" (*'phrul ba*) were used more commonly and almost interchangeably during Rangjung Dorje's time than the latterly more widely used term *tulku* (*sprul sku*), which came to be used to designate reincarnates after Rangjung Dorje's death. Gamble, *Reincarnation in Tibetan Buddhism*, 5–6, 67–68.
41. *skyes rabs*.
42. Zla ba gzhon nu.
43. These two collections can be found in the following: Rdo rje rgyal po, "'Gro mgon phag mo gru pa'i skyes rabs kyi skor la chos tshan lnga," 33–72, and Rwa Lo tsā ba, "Chos rje Dus gsum khyen pa'i skyes rabs rin po che ser gling le'u bco brgyad pa" [Eighteen chapters (from the) *Golden Isle: The Precious Birth Stories of the Dharma Noble Düsum Khyenpa*), 247–80.
44. Janet Gyatso outlines the role of biography in the treasure tradition in her book *Apparitions of the Self: The Secret Autobiographies of a Tibetan Visionary*.

45. Daniel Hirshberg's research on Nyang ral nyi ma 'od zer (1124–1192) shows how this treasure revealer not only remembered and recorded his past life during the time of the empire but produced a list of concatenating rebirths in between that life and what was his current life. See Hirshberg, *Remembering the Lotus-Born*, 55–84.
46. van der Kuijp, "The Dalai Lamas and the Origins of Reincarnate Lamas," 24. Rangjung Dorje claims to have been Potowa Rinchen Sel but ignores his association with Mañjuśrī. Rang byung rdo rje, *Mgur rnam*, 23–24; Rang byung rdo rje, *Mgur 'bum*, vol. *ca*, 203–4.
47. The names of future buddhas are given in the *Āryabhadrakalpikasūtra* (*'Phags pa bskal pa bzang po'i mdo*). Within the Lhasa edition of the Kangyur, the list of future buddhas is given on folio 154b.1 of this text.
48. Manson, "Elastic Time, Magical Memories."
49. There were different kinds of preceptor. Qubilai appointed Chögyel Pakpa "national preceptor" (Ch. *guoshi*, 國師) in 1260. In 1270, he was appointed "imperial preceptor" (Ch. *dishi*, 帝师). He was only briefly the Great Lord (*dpon chen*) of Tibet and abbot (*mkhan po*) of Sakya Monastery when he returned to Tibet for a few years.
50. Thomas Allsen gives an overview of the roles of these religious hierarchs in *Culture and Conquest in Mongol Eurasia*.
51. van der Kuijp, "The Kālacakra and the Patronage of Tibetan Buddhism by the Mongol Imperial Family," 32.
52. Manson, "Introduction to the Life of Karma Pakshi," 37–38. See also Richardson, "The Karma-Pa Sect: A Historical Note," 340.
53. I have outlined these texts in the appendix to Gamble, *Reincarnation in Tibetan Buddhism*, 273–78.
54. Gtsug lag phreng ba, *Chos 'byung mkas pa'i dga' ston* [*Feast for scholars*], 345–402. Hereafter this text is abbreviated to *Mkas pa'i dga' ston*.
55. Si tu paṇ chen chos kyi byung gnas and 'Be lo tshe dban kun khyab, *Bka' brgyud gser 'phreng rnam thar zla ba chu shel gyi 'phreng ba*, 345–452. Hereafter this text is abbreviated to *Zla ba chu shel*.
56. Apart from the translations that have been mentioned already, Karl Brunnhölzl has published several books on Rangjung Dorje's work that contain translations. These include: *The Center of the Sunlit Sky: Madhyamaka in the Kagyü Tradition*; *In Praise of Dharmadhātu: Nāgārjuna and the Third Karmapa, Rangjung Dorje*; and *Luminous Heart: The Third Karmapa on Consciousness, Wisdom, and Buddha Nature*.

57. Rang byung rdo rje, *Mgur rnam*, 170–71, and Rang byung rdo rje, *Mgur 'bum*, vol. *ca*, 388–90. Its colophon states, "This is what the Dharma noble Rangjung Dorje said at five years old [1288]."
58. Rwa Lo tsā ba, *Ser gling*, 37–38; Tshe dbang rgyal, *Lho rong chos 'byung*, 235. This skip in narrative is also described in Manson, "Life of Karma Pakshi," 31.
59. Rang byung rdo rje, *Sngar pa'i skye bor rnam thar*, 354–58, and *Sngar pa'i skye bor rnam thar*, 375–76, 399–402. As Berounský notes, this remains only one of two complete tales of a journey between lives in Tibetan literature. He writes: "Only one other representative of similar genre is known to me. It is a description of the reincarnation of the Fifth Dalai Lama into the Sixth . . . and again in this much later text the need for proofs of the veridicality of the new Dalai Lama becomes apparent." Berounský, *Entering Dead Bodies, Part 1*, 8.
60. For example, see Quintman, *The Yogin and the Madman*, 5–12, and Yamamoto, *Vision and Violence*, 105–8.
61. Most biographies of Karma Pakshi say he died "on the third day of the ninth month of the Female Water Sheep Year [1283]." Manson gives an overview of those biographers that do not give these dates. They include: Tshe dbang rgyal, *Lho rong chos 'byung*, 238; Kun dga' rdo rje, *Deb ther dmar po*, 94; and 'Gos Lo tsā ba gzhon nu dpal, *Deb ther sngon po*, 37a. See Manson, "Introduction to the Life of Karma Pakshi," 44. I thank Charles Manson for sending me these references.
62. Rang byung rdo rje, *Bar de'i rnam par thar pa*, 358.
63. Rangjung Dorje, by contrast, notes in the *Profound Inner Principles* that gestation takes around nine months, which is closer to the 40 weeks that contemporary science suggests. See: Rang byung rdo rje, *Zab mo nang gi don*, 314–16. I thank Charles Manson for pointing this out to me.
64. The Tibetan reads: *chos 'phrul bsam gyis mi khyab pa byung*.
65. Rang byung rdo rje, *Bar de'i rnam par thar pa*, 358.
66. This has also been acknowledged by Berounský. See "Entering Dead Bodies, Part 1," 30, and "Entering Dead Bodies, Part 2," 7. See also Seegers, "Lord of the Teachings," 53, 80n226, 83n241, and 112–13.
67. Skt. *paramanirmāṇa-kāya*. Tib. *mchog gi sprul sku*.
68. Karma Pak shi, *Grub chen karma pakshi'i bka' 'bum*, 11, and Rang byung rdo rje, *Bar de'i rnam par thar pa*, 366–67.
69. Rang byung rdo rje, *Bar de'i rnam par thar pa*, 377.

70. Kun dga' rdo rje, *Deb ther dmar po*, 95.
71. Tib.*'pho ba* or *'chi 'pho*. Skt. *saṃkrānti*.
72. Roberts, *Mahāmudrā and Related Instructions*, 9.
73. "Entrance into a dwelling or town" is *grong 'jug* in Tibetan and *purapraveśa* in Sanskrit. "Entrance into another's body" is *phar gzugs 'jug* in Tibetan and *parakāyapraveśana* in Sanskrit. Berounský gives a list of seven stories that include an "entrance into another body" account. See "Entering Dead Bodies, Part 1," 10–13.
74. This story was included in Tsangnyon Heruka's version of Marpa's liberation story. See Gtsang smyon He ru ka, *Sgra bsgyur Mar pa lo tsa'i rnam par thar pa mthong ba don yod*, 222–25.
75. Several scholars have discussed this phenomenon. See, for example, Zivkovic, *Death and Reincarnation in Tibetan Buddhism*, 24.
76. *zhing skyong 'gro ma*. For more details about the earth guardians, see chapter six of this volume.
77. Rang byung rdo rje, *Bar de'i rnam par thar pa*, 359.
78. Rang byung rdo rje, 359.
79. *srog snying*.
80. *bla*.
81. Barbara Gerke has investigated the *la* (*bla*) in Tibetan culture and medicine. See Gerke, "Engaging the Subtle Body," 195.
82. Gerke, 200–201.
83. *brtan ma bcu gnyis*.
84. For a description of the "twelve locality spirits," see de Nebesky-Wojkowitz, *Oracles and Demons of Tibet*, 181–98.
85. *tshe ring ma ched lnga*.
86. Childs, "Refuge and Revitalization," 126–58.
87. Rang byung rdo rje, *Bar de'i rnam par thar pa*, 363.
88. Rang byung rdo rje, 365–66. The translation of the last two lines follows Gtsug lag phreng ba, *Mkas pa'i dga' ston*, 922–23, which reads: *lho ri dmar smug mdangs gsal ba. byang ri dkar po'i mdog ldan na*. Rang byung rdo rje, *Bar de'i rnam par thar pa*, 366, by contrast, reads: *lho ri smug la dmar ba'i mdangs chags pa. byang ri dkar la dmar ba'i mdangs dang ldan pa*. The scribal errors in the latter text turn red and white into two types of pink.
89. This refers to a Tibetan place name, 'Om lung, not the Indic syllable *oṃ*.
90. Rangjung Dorje adjusts that name of the valley in Tibetan so it means "channel" (*rtsa*) instead of "grass" (*rtswa*).

91. Ehrhard, *Die Statue und der Tempel des Arya Va-ti bzang-po*, 122, 289, and 438–40.
92. Berounský, "Entering Dead Bodies, Part 1," 28.
93. Rang byung rdo rje, *Bar de'i rnam par thar pa*, 366.
94. Rang byung rdo rje, 366.
95. Rang byung rdo rje, *Tshigs bcad ma*, 378.
96. Despite its adherence to tradition, one part of Rangjung Dorje's description proved particularly problematic for his later biographers: the moment where he loses consciousness. This is a sign that he was not completely awakened. For more details on this, see Gamble, *Reincarnation in Tibetan Buddhism,* 150–52.
97. Rang byung rdo rje, *Tshigs bcad ma*, 379.
98. Pelmo Tang Plain (Dpal mo thang) lies between Shishapang Mountain (Shi sha spang) and Pelkhu Tso Lake (Pal khu). It is also the site at which Padmasambhava subdued the twelve stabilizing ḍākinīs.
99. Rang byung rdo rje, *Tshigs bcad ma*, 375.
100. Ehrhard, *Buddhism in Tibet & the Himalayas*, 323.
101. Rang byung rdo rje, *Tshigs bcad ma*, 366.
102. Gtsug lag phreng ba, *Mkas pa'i dga' ston*, 924, and Si tu paṇ chen, *Zla ba chu shel*, 356.
103. Gtsug lag phreng ba, *Mkas pa'i dga' ston*, 924.
104. Kun dga' rdo rje. *Deb ther dmar po*, 2 and 96; Gtsug lag phreng ba, *Mkas pa'i dga' ston*, 927; Si tu paṇ chen, *Zla ba chu shel*, 356.
105. This vision is discussed in Peter Aufschaiter's pre-1959 survey of the area. See "Land and Places of Milarepa," 175–89. It is also described in Ehrhard, *Die Statue und der Tempel*. The Āryavati Zangpo statue is now housed in the Dalai Lama's compound in Dharamsala, India.
106. Rang byung rdo rje, *Tshigs bcad ma*, 379–80. Later authors highlight the connection between the Avalokiteśvara and the Karmapas' statues as Avalokiteśvara emanations. Gtsug lag phreng ba, *Mkas pa'i dga' ston*, 926; and Si tu paṇ chen, *Zla ba chu shel*, 358.
107. Rang byung rdo rje, *Tshigs bcad ma*, 380.
108. Gtsug lag phreng ba, *Mkas pa'i dga' ston*, 925.
109. Brenda Li has completed a thorough study of Orgyenpa's life. See "A Critical Study of the Life of the 13th-century Tibetan Monk U rgyan pa Rin chen dpal Based on His Biographies." But this is someone whose story wants more investigation and retellings.

110. Bsod nams 'od zer, *O rgyan pa'i rnam thar*, 185; Vitali, "Grub chen U rgyan pa and the Mongols of China," 45.
111. Gamble, *Reincarnation in Tibetan Buddhism*, 80–83.
112. *zlog sgom*.
113. A *stūpa* (Tib. *mchod rten*, literally "base for offering") is a mound-like structure that houses sacred objects. Its architecture is highly symbolic and as the Tibetan term for it suggests, it acts as a focus for devotional acts.
114. The text says: *gya ba gangs pa'i gyu ba byas*. My guess is that Karma Pakshi is calling himself "the snowy one" on account of his age.
115. Bsod nams 'od zer, *O rgyan pa'i rnam thar*, 197–200.
116. Rang byung rdo rje, *Tshigs bcad ma*, 379.
117. I cannot locate Mopuk (Mo phug) or Mukhug (Mu khug) in Latö (Lho stod).
118. Bsod nams 'od zer, *O rgyan pa'i rnam thar*, 248–49.
119. Rang byung rdo rje, *Tshigs bcad ma*, 381; Tshe dbang rgyal, *Lho rong chos 'byung*, 239; Kun dga' rdo rje, *Deb ther dmar po*, 96; 'Gos Lo tsā ba, *Deb ther sngon po*, 38a; Gtsug lag phreng ba, *Mkas pa'i dga' ston*, 928; and Si tu paṇ chen, *Zla ba chu shel*, 360. Tsewang Gyal and Kunga Dorje say he was given the name Rangjung Dorje at this ordination ceremony. Tsuklak Trengwa and Situ Paṇchen say Orgyenpa gave it to him.
120. Rang byung rdo rje, *Tshigs bcad ma*, 381.
121. Bsod nams 'od zer, *O rgyan pa'i rnam thar*, 225; and Vitali, "U rgyan pa and the Mongols," 46n37 and 47.
122. Li, "U rgyan pa's Biographies," 95–96.
123. 'Gos Lo tsā ba, *Deb ther sngon po*, vol. *ca*, 27b; and Li, "U rgyan pa's Biographies," 96. For more information on the Chagadai, see Amitai and Morgan, *The Mongol Empire and Its Legacy*.
124. Li, "U rgyan pa's Biographies," 86.
125. Li, "U rgyan pa's Biographies," 96; Vitali, "U rgyan pa and the Mongols," 48–49.
126. Rang byung rdo rje, *Tshigs bcad ma*, 381–82; Kun dga' rdo rje, *Deb ther dmar po*, 98; Gtsug lag phreng ba, *Mkas pa'i dga' ston*, 928; and Si tu paṇ chen, *Zla ba chu shel*, 360.
127. *Nāga* (Tibetan *klu*) are snake-like or dragon-like spirits that are said to rule the underworld. They are associated with still, clean water, are said to possess many jewels and sharp intelligence, and need to be propiti-

ated before journeys across bodies of water or the building of structures around bodies of water.

128. Khanak (Mkha' nag) is the seventh of eight nāga kings often seated around Vajrapāṇi.

129. Kun dga' rdo rje, *Deb ther dmar po*, 98; Gtsug lag phreng ba, *Mkas pa'i dga' ston*, 928; and Si tu paṇ chen, *Zla ba chu shel*, 361.

130. Rang byung rdo rje, *Tshigs bcad ma*, 382; Kun dga' rdo rje, *Deb ther dmar po*, 96; 'Gos Lo tsā ba, *Deb ther sngon po*, 38a; Gtsug lag phreng ba, *Mkas pa'i dga' ston*, 928; and Si tu paṇ chen, *Zla ba chu shel*, 361.

131. Rang byung rdo rje, *Tshigs bcad ma*, 382.

132. Rang byung rdo rje, 382.

133. Gtsug lag phreng ba, *Mkas pa'i dga' ston*, 928.

134. For a list of Tsurpu's (Mtshur phu) abbots up until the fifteenth century, see 'Gos Lo tsā ba, *Deb ther sngon po*, 51b.

135. Remati is also known as Palden Lhamo (Dpal ldan lha mo, i.e., Glorious Goddess). She is sometimes presented as the leader of the twelve Tenma goddesses (Brtan ma bcu gnyi).

136. Rang byung rdo rje, *Tshigs bcad ma*, 383.

137. Rang byung rdo rje, 383; Kun dga' rdo rje, *Deb ther dmar po*, 98; Gtsug lag phreng ba, *Mkas pa'i dga' ston*, 929; and Si tu paṇ chen, *Zla ba chu shel*, 362.

138. Rang byung rdo rje, *Tshigs bcad ma*, 383; Kun dga' rdo rje, *Deb ther dmar po*, 97; Gtsug lag phreng ba, *Mkas pa'i dga' ston*, 929; and Si tu paṇ chen, *Zla ba chu shel*, 362. See also, Rang byung rdo rje, *Mgur rnam*, 2–29; and Rang byung rdo rje, *Mgur 'bum*, vol. *ca*, 186–208.

139. Rang byung rdo rje, *Tshigs bcad ma*, 403; Kun dga' rdo rje, *Deb ther dmar po*, 100; 'Gos Lo tsā ba, *Deb ther sngon po*, 39a; Gtsug lag phreng ba, *Mkas pa'i dga' ston*, 932; and Si tu paṇ chen, *Zla ba chu shel*, 374.

140. Rang byung rdo rje, *Mgur rnam*, 3.3; Rang byung rdo rje, *Mgur 'bum*, vol. *ca*, 186.1. This song's dream performance is mentioned at the end of the survey of visions that follows the *Bar de'i rnam thar,* 372–73, and in Rang byung rdo rje, *Tshigs bcad ma*, 383.6. It is also mentioned in Gtsug lag phreng ba, *Mkas pa'i dga' ston*, 929, and Si tu paṇ chen, *Zla ba chu shel*, 362. Kurtis Schaeffer has translated and analyzed the song in *Dreaming the Great Brahmin,* 41–42.

141. Schaeffer discusses Saraha's semimythical status in detail in *Dreaming the Great Brahmin*.

142. Rangjung Dorje does this in the commentary that he embeds in the retelling of Karma Pakshi's liberation story. See Rang byung rdo rje, *Bla ma rin po che'i rnam par thar pa'o*, 276–77.
143. Rang byung rdo rje, *Mgur rnam*, 179–181; Rang byung rdo rje, *Mgur 'bum*, vol. *ca*, 396–97.
144. This will be discussed in more detail later in this chapter. Rang byung rdo rje, *Mgur rnam*, 23–24; and Rang byung rdo rje, *Mgur 'bum*, vol. *ca*, 203–4.
145. I discuss this controversy in more detail in chapter four.
146. Rang byung rdo rje, *Tshigs bcad ma*, 383.
147. Tsangnyon Heruka's version of Milarepa's life story contains a narrative about him missing Marpa. See Gtsang smyon He ru ka, *Mi la ras pa'i rnam mgur*, 196.
148. These syllables are used in inner heat yoga practice, *tummo* (*gtum mo*), one of the six dharmas of Nāropā.
149. Rang byung rdo rje, *Mgur rnam*, 7–8; Rang byung rdo rje, *Mgur 'bum*, vol. *ca*, 189–90.
150. Rang byung rdo rje, *Mgur rnam*, 17–18; Rang byung rdo rje, *Mgur 'bum*, vol. *ca*, 198–99.
151. Rang byung rdo rje, *Mgur rnam*, 19–20; Rang byung rdo rje, *Mgur 'bum*, vol. *ca*, 200–201.
152. This is the list that is given, for example, at the start of Düsum Khyenpa's life story. See 'Gos Lo tsā ba, *Deb ther sngon po,* 31a–31b. Düsum Khyenpa's biographies contains his remembrances of an entirely different set of lives.
153. The song can be found in Rang byung rdo rje, *Mgur rnam*, 23.1–24.4, and Rang byung rdo rje, *Mgur 'bum*, vol. *ca*, 203.3–204.3. The *Liberation Story of Past Lives* can be found in Rang byung rdo rje, *Dpal chen rnam thar,* 354–58.
154. Rang byung rdo rje, *Tshigs bcad ma*, 376–77.
155. Rang byung rdo rje, *Dpal chen rnam thar,* 355.
156. The Sanskrit term *paṇḍita* (sometimes translated as *mkhas pa* in Tibetan and sometimes transliterated as *paṇ ḍi ta*) was used to refer to scholars with a specialist education in the five sciences (for information on the five sciences, see note 395). In more contemporary usage, it is used to describe venerated people or members of certain Brahman castes. It is the source of the English word "pundit."
157. Rang byung rdo rje, *Mgur rnam*, 23–24; Rang byung rdo rje, *Mgur 'bum*, vol. *ca*, 203–4.

158. All three sources list the first person on the list, but they describe them differently. This verse calls him Nāgābodhi (Klu'i byang chub). The *Sngar skye rnam thar* gives him no name. The *Tshigs bcad ma* calls him Prajñālaṃkāra (Shes rab rgyan). For more details on the differences between the early Karmapas' variant past-life claims, see Manson, "Elastic Time, Magical Memories."

159. Modern scholars dispute the idea that it was the same Nāgārjuna who composed works in accordance with these three schools. They attribute the works of "Nāgārjuna" to at least two, and sometimes three, different people. See: Christian Lindtner, *Nāgārjuniana: Studies in the Writings and Philosophy of Nāgārjuna.*

160. Si tu paṇ chen, *Zla ba chu shel*, 26–27.

161. Rang byung rdo rje, *Dpal chen rnam thar*, 356; Rang byung rdo rje, *Tshigs bcad ma*, 376–77.

162. The *Skye rnam thar* also mentions another life between these two, in which he was a student of "the noble Kamalaśīla, 356–57. The *Tshigs bcad ma* (378) does not include this life. By contrast, it says he "performed deeds in an eastern city," which suggests an intermediary life in China.

163. 'Gos Lo tsā ba, *Deb ther sngon po*, vol. *ca*, 13a. Neuzur (Sne'u zur) is one of Potowa's disciples.

164. Rang byung rdo rje, *Mgur rnam*, 24; Rang byung rdo rje, *Mgur 'bum*, vol. *ca*, 204.

165. Rang byung rdo rje, *Mgur rnam*, 24; Rang byung rdo rje, *Mgur 'bum*, vol. *ca*, 204. The last line reads: *mad kyang ku re byis pa lags*. This suggests two readings that pivot on a play between two words: *mad* (*pa*) means "truth," and *med*, an existential negating particle, means "there is not." Both of these syllables are pronounced "mé." This means that, when spoken, the last line could mean, "(All) this may be the truth, or I may be joking" or "These didn't happen, I am just joking."

166. Rang byung rdo rje, *Mgur rnam*, 7–8; Rang byung rdo rje, *Mgur 'bum*, vol. *ca*, 189–90.

167. Rang byung rdo rje, *Mgur rnam*, 22; Rang byung rdo rje, *Mgur 'bum*, vol. *ca*, 202.

168. Rang byung rdo rje, *Bar de'i rnam par thar pa*, 387; Gtsug lag phreng ba, *Mkas pa'i dga' ston*, 929; and Si tu paṇ chen, *Zla ba chu shel*, 365.

169. Gzhon nu byang chub, "Re'u mig brga rtsa brgyad," 88; Rgwa Lo tsā ba, *Ser gling*, 41.

170. Rang byung rdo rje, *Bar de'i rnam par thar pa*, 368 and 381; Tshe dbang rgyal, *Lho rong chos 'byung*, 238–39; Kun dga' rdo rje, *Deb ther dmar po*, 96; Gtsug lag phreng ba, *Mkas pa'i dga' ston*, 928; and Si tu paṇ chen, *Zla ba chu shel*, 360.

171. Rangjung Dorje was ordained by the abbot of Gendün Gang (Dge 'dun sgang), Zhönnu Jangchup. Zhönnu Jangchup is named as the third in list of Gendün Gang's abbots. 'Gos Lo tsā ba, *Deb ther sngon po*, vol. *pha*, 5b; Rang byung rdo rje, *Bar de'i rnam par thar pa*, 387; Tshe dbang rgyal, *Lho rong chos 'byung*, 239; Kun dga' rdo rje, *Deb ther dmar po*, 96; 'Gos Lo tsā ba, *Deb ther sngon po*, 38a; Gtsug lag phreng ba, *Mkas pa'i dga' ston*, 928; Si tu paṇ chen, *Zla ba chu shel*, 360. Elena Pakhoutova describes a thangka (*thang kha*) that records this ordination. See "A Wondrous Great Accomplishment: A Painting of an Event." For a short discussion of Gendün Gang Monastery's ordination lineage, see van der Kuijp, "On the *Lives* of Sakyasribhadra," 604n19.

172. For a survey of this monastery and its succession, see van der Kuijp, "The Monastery of Gsang-phu Ne'u-thog and its Abbatial Succession from ca. 1073 to 1250," 103–27. Düsum Khyenpa's stay is noted in Rwa Lo tsā ba, *Ser gling*, 38; Rang byung rdo rje, *Tshigs bcad ma*, 387; and 'Gos Lo tsā ba, *Deb ther sngon po*, 38b.

173. Maitreya's Five Texts (Byams chos sde lnga); Nāgārjuna's *Roots of Madhyamaka* (Skt. *Mūlamadhyamakakārikā*; Tib. *Dbu ma rtsa ba shes rab*); Vasubandhu's *Treasury of Abhidharma* (Skt. *Abhidharmakośa*; Tib. *Chos mngon pa'i mdzod*); Asaṅga's *Compendium of Abhidharma* (Skt. *Abhidharmasamuccaya*; Tib. *Chos mngon pa'i kun btus*).

174. *ri phrod pa*.

175. *ri phrod*.

176. Rang byung rdo rje, *Tshigs bcad ma*, 388; Kun dga' rdo rje, *Deb ther dmar po*, 98; and Si tu paṇ chen, *Zla ba chu shel*, 365.

177. Rang byung rdo rje, *Tshigs bcad ma*, 388.

178. The term *bodhicitta* (Tib. *byang chub kyi sems*) means "mind of awakening" and is usually defined as the mind that seeks awakening for the benefit of all beings.

179. Rang byung rdo rje, *Mgur rnam*, 36.5–7; and Rang byung rdo rje, *Mgur 'bum*, vol. *ca*, 213.2–4.

180. *Dhārmikas* (Tib. *chos pa*). This term refers to those who are defined by their practice of dharma.

181. Rang byung rdo rje, *Mgur rnam*, 32–33; and Rang byung rdo rje, *Mgur 'bum*, vol. *ca*, 208–9.
182. Despite later commentaries to the contrary (Gtsug lag phreng ba, *Mkas pa'i dga' ston*, 930; and Si tu paṇ chen, *Zla ba chu shel*, 365), there is no suggestion in Rangjung Dorje's writing that he took control of Karma Monastery.
183. This site is spelled several ways: Lha stengs, Lha stangs, and Lha steng.
184. Rang byung rdo rje, *Mgur rnam*, 48.4–6; and Rang byung rdo rje, *Mgur 'bum*, vol. *ca*, 222.6.
185. Rang byung rdo rje, *Tshigs bcad ma*, 388.
186. *tshigs bden*.
187. Gtsug lag phreng ba, *Mkas pa'i dga' ston*, 931. The same story is told in Si tu paṇ chen, *Zla ba chu shel*, 366.
188. Rang byung rdo rje, *Tshigs bcad ma*, 389.
189. Si tu paṇ chen, *Zla ba chu shel*, 366.
190. Rang byung rdo rje, *Mgur rnam*, 47.5; and Rang byung rdo rje, *Mgur 'bum*, 222.2.
191. Si tu paṇ chen, *Zla ba chu shel*, 367.
192. Rang byung rdo rje, *Tshigs bcad ma*, 389.
193. Kampo Nénang Monastery (Kam po gnas nang) still exists. Since the seventeenth century, it has been a Geluk monastery aligned with the large monastery in nearby Litang (Li thang).
194. Rang byung rdo rje, *Tshigs bcad ma*, 390.
195. Rang byung rdo rje, 390.
196. Rang byung rdo rje, *Mgur rnam*, 56.4–5; and Rang byung rdo rje, *Mgur 'bum*, vol. *ca*, 229.2.
197. Rang byung rdo rje, *Tshigs bcad ma,* 389 and 390. Here the text describes his adventures at Khawa Karpo (Kha ba dkar po) before those at Kampo Nénang (Kam po gnas nang) and Kolti (Kol ti). The songs' colophons suggest he traveled first to Kampo Nénang, then to Kolti, and then on to Khawa Karpo. Rang byung rdo rje, *Mgur rnam*, 54–56; and Rang byung rdo rje, *Mgur 'bum*, vol. *ca*, 226–29; Rang byung rdo rje, *Kha ba dkar po'i bstod pa*, 49–53. No village in the region is called Kolti today, but several have similar names, including Gongziding and Gongpo.
198. Like *dharmika,* the term *tantrika* (Tib. *sngags* pa) refers to those who are defined by their practice of tantra.
199. Rang byung rdo rje, *Mgur rnam*, 55.1–56.3; Rang byung rdo rje, *Mgur*

'*bum*, vol. *ca*, 226.1–229.1. The colophon reads: "Rangjung Dorje wrote this song while he was negotiating an end to civil strife, on the twenty-eighth day of the twelfth month of the Sheep Year [1307], at Kolti Temple."

200. *bka' ma*.
201. Manson, "Life of Karma Pakshi," 34–35.
202. *Kha ba dkar po'i gsang yig* and *Gnas mchog kha ba dkar po'i bsang yig dngos grub char 'bebs*. For these guides, see Rin chen rdo rje and Tshe ring chos 'phel, *Gnas chen kha ba dkar po'i bsang mchod dang gnas yig*, 8–9 and 1–7. Part of the reason for the lack of clarity about these works is the competing claims on the site by two sanctification processes: one by branches of Kaḥtok Monastery and the other associated with the Second and Third Karmapas. The history is further tangled by Karma Pakshi's close association with Kaḥtok Monastery and the possibility that he wrote about this site using the name Rangjung Dorje.
203. The term *siddhi* (Tib. *grub* or *dngos grub*) refers to accomplishments attained through Buddhist practice.
204. Rang byung rdo rje, *Gsung 'bum,* vol. *ca*, 49.
205. There is a tradition of associating this site with an area in western Tibet near Khyung lung Monastery, which lies about seventy-five kilometers west of Mount Kailash. Matthieu Ricard, *The Life of Shabkar*, 346n64.
206. Rang byung rdo rje, *Gsung 'bum,* vol. *ca*, 49–50.
207. For more on this site, see Huber, "Where Exactly Are Cāritra, Devikoṭa and Himavat," 121–64.
208. Kāmarūpa was a kingdom in Assam that lasted between 350 CE and 1140 CE. The area continued to be called this for centuries after the kingdom's demise. A goddess named Kāmarūpa is worshipped at the main temple at Guwahati, Assam.
209. Rang byung rdo rje, *Gsung 'bum,* vol. *ca*, 50.
210. Nyingpo, *The Great Image*, 145–92.
211. Rang byung rdo rje, *Gsung 'bum,* vol. *ca*, 51.
212. Rang byung rdo rje, 96–98.
213. Rang byung rdo rje, *Tshigs bcad ma*, 390.
214. Ron Garry, "Kumārarāja," *Treasury of Lives* (2007).
215. Si tu paṇ chen, *Zla ba chu shel*, 372.
216. Rang byung rdo rje, *Tshigs bcad ma*, 393; Kun dga' rdo rje, *Deb ther dmar po*, 99; and Si tu paṇ chen, *Zla ba chu shel*, 372.
217. Rang byung rdo rje, *Tshigs bcad ma*, 393.

218. The area designated as "Kong po" is designated slightly differently throughout Tibetan history. When Rangjung Dorje uses this name, he is referring to the area south of the Yarlung Tsangpo River (Yar glung gtsang po) past Daklha Gampo (Dwags lha sgam po).
219. Rang byung rdo rje, *Tshigs bcad ma*, 393; Kun dga' rdo rje, *Deb ther dmar po*, 99; and Si tu paṇ chen, *Zla ba chu shel*, 372.
220. This translation follows the *Mgur 'bum*, which uses the word *gzer ma*, "nail," in place of the *Mgur rnam*'s *zer*, "to be said" or "rays (of light)."
221. The text reads: *spyod lam rnam bzhi*, "the four aspects of performance," which indicates resting, moving, eating, and sleeping.
222. Rang byung rdo rje, *Mgur rnam*, 62.3–63.1; Rang byung rdo rje, *Mgur 'bum*, vol. *ca*, 233.1–235.4.
223. This translation follows the *Mgur 'bum*, as the *Mgur rnam* states *nub kyang bgod*, which would mean "you will not establish" or "you will not laugh at" and seems to be a scribal error.
224. Rang byung rdo rje, *Mgur rnam*, 70.3–7; Rang byung rdo rje, *Mgur 'bum*, vol. *ca*, 242.1–243.1.
225. *Kinnaras* (*ci*, also *shang shang*) are half-human, half-bird celestial musicians.
226. Rang byung rdo rje, *Mgur rnam*, 69.6; Rang byung rdo rje, *Mgur 'bum*, vol. *ca*, 239.6.
227. Tshe dbang rgyal, *Lho rong chos 'byung*, 240.
228. Rang byung rdo rje, *Mgur rnam*, 154.2–3; Rang byung rdo rje, *Mgur 'bum*, vol. *ca*, 376.3–4.
229. Rang byung rdo rje, *Mgur rnam*, 154.3; Rang byung rdo rje, *Mgur 'bum*, vol. *ca*, 376.4.
230. *gnas lugs*.
231. Rang byung rdo rje, *Mgur rnam*, 97–98; Rang byung rdo rje, *Mgur 'bum*, vol. *ca*, 262–63. This song is translated in chapter fourteen of this book. It has also been translated elsewhere. See, for example, Brunnhölzl, *Luminous Heart*, 201. Brunnhölzl translates the title as "A Song on the *Ālaya*." See also Kurtis Schaeffer, "The Enlightened Heart of Buddhahood," 174; and Klaus-Dieter Mathes, *A Direct Path to the Buddha Within*, 63.
232. *rang stong* and *gzhan stong*.
233. Brunnhölzl, *Luminous Heart*, 121–165.
234. *phyogs med*.
235. *rgyu ma lta ba*.
236. Rangjung Dorje's location when he completed this work is noted in the

colophon to one of his songs. Rang byung rdo rje, *Mgur rnam*, 91–92; and *Rang byung rdo rje'i'gur thor bu,* 257. It reads: "He sung this when he had finished composing the *Ston pa'i skyes rabs* in Trashi Sarma (Bkra shis gsar ma), on the fifth day of the second month of the Tiger Year [1314]."

237. This vision is described in Rang byung rdo rje, *Mgur rnam*, 394. Several small works included within Rangjung Dorje's Gsung 'bum deal with astrology. See vol. *a*, 579–616.
238. Callahan, "Introduction," 71–102.
239. Rang byung rdo rje, *Chos dang chos nyid rnam par 'byed pa'i bstan bcos kyi rnam par bshad pa'i rgyan*, vol. *cha*, 488–613.
240. Rang byung rdo rje, *Zab mo nang don gyi gzhung*, vol. *ja*, 308–60.
241. Rang byung rdo rje, *Rnam shes dang ye shes bstan pa'i bstan bcos*, vol. *ja*, 269–76.
242. Rang byung rdo rje, *Zab mo nang don gyi 'grel pa*, vol. *ja*, 361–634.
243. Rang byung rdo rje, *Dbu mo chos dbyings bstod pa'i rnam par bshad pa*, vol. *ja*, 1–125.
244. Rang byung rdo rje, *De bzhin gshegs pa'i snying po bstan pa'i bstan bcos*, vol. *ja*, 282–90.
245. Brunnhölzl, *In Praise of Dharmadhātu*, 160.
246. Brunnhölzl, *Luminous Heart*, 87.
247. Rang byung rdo rje, *Mgur rnam*, 56–58; Rang byung rdo rje, *Mgur 'bum*, vol. *ca*, 229–31.
248. Rang byung rdo rje, *Mgur rnam*, 94–95; Rang byung rdo rje, *Mgur 'bum*, vol. *ca*, 260. *Song of Concealed Knowledge about Places and Mind.*
249. This follows the *Mgur 'bum*. The *Mgur rnam* reads *rtogs pa*.
250. Rang byung rdo rje, *Mgur rnam*, 112–14; Rang byung rdo rje, *Mgur 'bum*, vol. *ca*, 273–76.
251. The three natures (Skt. *trilakṣana* or *trisvabhāva*; Tib. *mtshan nyid gsum* or *rang bzhin gsum*) are: the imaginary (Skt. *parikalpita*; Tib. *kun btags*), dependent (Skt. *paratantra*; Tib. *gzhan dbang*), and ultimate realities (Skt. *parinispanna*; Tib. *yongs grub*). Sonam Thakchöe has written a good overview of them in "Reification and Nihilism: The Three-Nature Theory and Its Implications," 72–110. The eight consciousnesses (Skt. *aṣṭa vijñānakāyāḥ*; Tib. *Rnam shes tshogs brgyad*) are the five sense consciousnesses, the mental consciousness (Skt. *manovijñāna*; Tib. *yid kyi rnam shes*), the deluded consciousness (Skt. *kliṣṭamanovijñāna*; Tib. *nyon yid rnam shes*), and the

basis-of-all consciousness (Skt. *ālāyavijñāna*; Tib. *kun gzhi rnam shes*). For more details, see Waldron, *The Buddhist Unconscious,* part one.

252. Mathes, *A Direct Path to the Buddha Within*, 51–74.
253. *sgrub mtha'*. Jeffrey Hopkins speaks briefly about the precursors and development of this tradition in "The Tibetan Genre of Doxography: Structuring a Worldview," 170–217.
254. David Seyfort Ruegg, *The Literature of the Madhyamaka School of Philosophy in India*, 87–99.
255. Rang byung rdo rje, *Phyag rgya chen po gangA ma'i gzhung gi sab cad* [An outline of the texts of the *Ganga Mahāmudrā*], vol. *a*, 159–160; Rang byung rdo rje, *Phyag rgya chen po gangA ma'i 'grel pa* [A commentary on the *Ganga Mahāmudrā*], 161–75; Rang byung rdo rje, *Rgyal po do ha'i sa bcad* [An outline of the *King Dohā*], 177–80; Rang byung rdo rje, *Btsun mo do ha'i sa bcad* [An outline of the *Queen Dohā*], 180–185; Rang byung rdo rje, *Do ha mdzod kyi bsdud don bcad* [A condensation of the meaning of the *Dohā-Kośa*], 185–91; Rang byung rdo rje, *Do ha mdzod kyi glu yi don gsal bar byed pa'i tshig gi rgyan dri ma med pa'i sgom me ldeb* [A stainless lamp that ornaments the words of the *Dohā-Kośa*, making their meaning clear], 193–264.
256. Rang byung rdo rje, *Mgur rnam*, 6; and Rang byung rdo rje, *Mgur 'bum*, vol. *ca*, 186.
257. Rang byung rdo rje, *Rdzogs chen po'i snying thig spros bcas kyi dbang lce btsun* [An elaboration on great completion: the empowerment of venerable tongues], 341–55. And Rang byung rdo rje, *Rdzogs pa chen po'i dbang gsum pa* [Three empowerments of the great completion], 355–85.
258. Rang byung rdo rje, *Nges don phyag rgya chen po'i smon lam ldeb*, vol. *a*, 621.
259. Rang byung rdo rje, *Mgur rnam*, 56–57; Rang byung rdo rje, *Mgur 'bum*, vol. *ca*, 229–31.
260. David Jackson wrote an article and then book about this debate; the article is titled "Sa-skya Paṇḍita the Polemicist," and the book is *Enlightenment by a Single Means*. Jan-Ulrich Sobisch talks about this debate and the importance of guru devotion in the Kagyü tradition in "Guru-Devotion in the Bka' brgyud pa Tradition: The Single Means to Realisation." Julia Stenzel also addresses it in her article "The Mahāmudrā of Sakya Paṇḍita."
261. Gamble, *Reincarnation in Tibetan Buddhism*, 245–47. I describe the performance of a song by Rangjung Dorje at Radreng (Rwa sgreng) Monastery

in which he teases his Sakya colleagues about their understanding of emptiness.

262. Rang byung rdo rje, *Yul nyer bzhi'i ngo 'dzin ldeb dang gsang sngags rdo rje theg pa gsungs pa'i tshul* [Recognizing the twenty-four places], 530–35.

263. Toni Huber discusses the controversy over relocating *pīṭhas* to the Plateau in "Where Exactly Are Cāritra, Devikoṭa and Himavat," 121–65.

264. Rangjung Dorje does dedicate some songs to students, but he does not reflect on how important they are to him. Zhönnu Bum (Gzhon nu 'bum) of Lha Teng (Lha stengs) is addressed in Rang byung rdo rje, *Mgur rnam*, 150–53; and *Rang byung rdo rje'i gsung mgur,* 373–75. One song is dedicated to Shérap Sengé (Shes rab seng ge). See Rang byung rdo rje, *Mgur rnam*, 161; and Rang byung rdo rje, *Mgur 'bum*, vol. *ca*, 381–82. Another is dedicated to Könchok Sengé (Dkon mchog seng ge). See Rang byung rdo rje, *Mgur rnam*, 162–63; and Rang byung rdo rje, *Mgur 'bum*, vol. *ca*, 382–83).

265. Rang byung rdo rje, *Tshigs bcad ma*, 397; and Si tu paṇ chen, *Zla ba chu shel*, 376.

266. Their names in Tibetan are: G.yag sde Paṇ chen; Klong chen rab 'byams pa; and Dol po pa Shes rab rgyal mtshan. There is ample evidence for a connection between the first two of these students and Rangjung Dorje. Yakdé Pachen (1299–1378) is quoted in Situ Paṇchen's biography describing his interactions with Rangjung Dorje. See Si tu paṇ chen, *Zla ba chu shel*, 372. And Longchenpa (Klong chen pa) wrote a letter to Rangjung Dorje that has been studied by S. Arguill're. See *Profusion de la vaste sphere: Klong-chen rab 'byams, Tibet, 1308–1364*, 49–68. Dölpopa Shérap Gyaltsen is mentioned in Situ Paṇchen's list of students and also in his biography of Rangjung Dorje. See Si tu Paṇ chen, *Zla ba chu shel*, 375–76 and 399. But there are no descriptions of their relationship from Rangjung Dorje's time.

267. Rang byung rdo rje, *Bden gnas chen po bde chen gyi bstod pa*. vol. *ca*, 40–43.

268. Rang byung rdo rje, *Mgur rnam,* 101–2; Rang byung rdo rje, *Mgur 'bum*, vol. *ca*, 265. The idea of Tibet as the head of all rivers is described in Brandon Dotson, "Complementarity and Opposition in Early Tibetan Ritual," 41–67.

269. Rang byung rdo rje, *Mgur rnam*, 104; Rang byung rdo rje, *Mgur 'bum*, vol. *ca*, 268.

270. Rang byung rdo rje, *Tshigs bcad ma*, 397.

271. Gtsug lag phreng ba, *Mkas pa'i dga' ston*, 933.

272. Rang byung rdo rje, *Tshigs bcad ma*, 397–98.

273. Gtsug lag phreng ba, *Mkas pa'i dga' ston*, 933.
274. Rang byung rdo rje, *Tshigs bcad ma*, 403.
275. Chos dbyings rdo rje. Irmgard Mengele discusses this in "The Artist's Life," 33–63.
276. Rang byung rdo rje, *Tshigs bcad ma*, 403.
277. Rang byung rdo rje, 403.
278. Gtsug lag phreng ba, *Mkas pa'i dga' ston*, 935.
279. Gtsug lag phreng ba, 404.
280. Rang byung rdo rje, *Mgur rnam*, 146–48; Rang byung rdo rje, *Gsung 'gur thor bu*, vol. *ca*, 369–71.
281. *bcud len*. See chapter fourteen of the current volume.
282. In the context of this song, *cakras* (Tib. *'khor lo*) are places within the subtle body where energy acts in a circular motion. In most tantric yogas, the yogis visualize seven *cakras* between the top of their head and the base of their spine.
283. Here he uses the Indic word *sudhīra*, transliterated into Tibetan.
284. Rang byung rdo rje, *Mgur rnam*, 157–60; Rang byung rdo rje, *Mgur 'bum*, vol. *ca*, 378–80.
285. G.yag sde paṇ chen (1299–1378)—quoted in Si tu paṇ chen, *Zla ba chu shel*, 372—describes Rangjung Dorje during this stay at Tshal: "He explained the vast ocean of sūtras and tantras to spiritual friends (i.e., monk teachers) during the day and granted empowerments, subsequent empowerments, and profound instructions to tāntrikas at night. When he was not doing either of these, he granted audiences to many people, replying with advice to various envoys."
286. Petech, *Central Tibet and the Mongols*, 80–82.
287. Petech describes the Shalu myriarch's flight in *Central Tibet and the Mongols*, 93. For an alternate (probably incorrect and definitely partisan) version of events, see Gtsug lag phreng ba, *Mkas pa'i dga' ston*, 935. He says that after Rangjung Dorje predicted it, Mongol troops did invade.
288. Gamble, *Reincarnation in Tibetan Buddhism*, 235–37.
289. Rang byung rdo rje, *Mgur rnam*, 173–74; Rang byung rdo rje, *Mgur 'bum*, vol. *ca*, 391–92.
290. Rang byung rdo rje, *Mgur rnam*, 174–75; Rang byung rdo rje, *Mgur 'bum*, vol. *ca*, 392–95.
291. Rang byung rdo rje, *Tshigs bcad ma*, 404.
292. For a photo of a bridge across the Sok River (Sog chu), see Jones Tung,

A Portrait of Lost Tibet, 115, plate 54. Ilya Tolstoy and Brooke Dolan took the photo in 1949.

293. Rang byung rdo rje, *Tshigs bcad ma*, 404.
294. Rang byung rdo rje, 405; see also: Tshe dbang rgyal, *Lho rong chos 'byung*, 241; Gtsug lag phreng ba, *Mkas pa'i dga' ston*, 938; and Si tu paṇ chen, *Zla ba chu shel*, 381.
295. Rang byung rdo rje, *Tshigs bcad ma*, 405; Kun dga' rdo rje, *Deb ther dmar po*, 101; Gtsug lag phreng ba, *Mkas pa'i dga' ston*, 938; and Si tu paṇ chen, *Zla ba chu shel*, 382.
296. Rang byung rdo rje, *Mgur rnam,* 172; Rang byung rdo rje, *Mgur 'bum*, vol. *ca*, 390.
297. Gamble, *Reincarnation in Tibetan Buddhism*, 238–42.
298. Rang byung rdo rje, *Mgur rnam,* 177.4–5; Rang byung rdo rje, *Gsung 'gur thor bu*, vol. *ca*, 394.3–4.
299. Situ Paṇchen included this edict in his retelling of Rangjung Dorje's liberation story. See Si tu paṇ chen, *Zla ba chu shel*, 382–83.
300. Si tu paṇ chen, *Zla ba chu shel*, 382–83. This edict is discussed in Hugh Richardson, "The Karma-Pa Sect: A Historical Note," 343; Petech, *Central Tibet and the Mongols*, 86; and Schwieger, *The Dalai Lama and the Emperor of China*, 19.
301. Wylie, "Reincarnation: A Political Innovation in Tibetan Buddhism," 582–86.
302. Rang byung rdo rje, *Tshigs bcad ma*, 407; Kun dga' rdo rje, *Deb ther dmar po*, 101; Gtsug lag phreng ba, *Mkas pa'i dga' ston*, 938; and Si tu paṇ chen, *Zla ba chu shel*, 382–83.
303. Rangjung Dorje says that he died "on the twelfth day of the eighth month of the Monkey Year," *Tshigs bcad ma*, 407.
304. Rang byung rdo rje, 407.
305. Rang byung rdo rje, 407.
306. Rang byung rdo rje, 940. Van der Kuijp suggests it is the other way around and Rangjung Dorje put his head at the emperor's feet. See "The Kalacakra and the Patronage of Tibetan Buddhism by the Mongol Imperial Family," 35. The section in question reads: *rgyal po gur dkar chen po na gser khri la bzhugs pas rgyang ring po nas sngun bsus te zhabs la spyi bos gtugs.* A shorter version of this story is also given in Kun dga' rdo rje, *Deb ther dmar po*, 102.

307. Han, Guanghui, 北京历史人口地理 [*History of the population and geography of Beijing*], 120, 126, 128.
308. Rang byung rdo rje, *Tshigs bcad ma*, 409.
309. Kun dga' rdo rje, *Deb ther dmar po*, 102; Gtsug lag phreng ba, *Mkas pa'i dga' ston*, 940; Si tu paṇ chen, *Zla ba chu shel*, 386.
310. *tshe chu*. Gtsug lag phreng ba, *Mkas pa'i dga' ston*, 940; and Si tu paṇ chen, *Zla ba chu shel*, 388.
311. Rang byung rdo rje, *Tshigs bcad ma*, 409.
312. Rang byung rdo rje, *Tshigs bcad ma*, 409; Kun dga' rdo rje, *Deb ther dmar po*, 103; 'Gos Lo tsā ba, *Deb ther sngon po*, 39a; Gtsug lag phreng ba, *Mkas pa'i dga' ston*, 940; and Si tu paṇ chen, *Zla ba chu shel*, 388.
313. Elliot Sperling wrote several articles on the Tangut Empire and their relationship with the Kagyü and the Karmapas specifically. See Sperling, "Tsa-mi lo-tsa-ba Sangs-rgyas grags-pa and the Tangut Background to Early Mongol-Tibetan Relations," and "Karma Rol-pa'i rdo-Rje and the Re-Establishment of Karma-pa Political Influence in the 14th Century."
314. Rang byung rdo rje, *Tshigs bcad ma*, 409–10.
315. He calls the region through which he travels—now called Nang chen—Red Kham (Smar khams). This is not the region of southwestern Kham known now as Markham these days.
316. Rang byung rdo rje, *Tshigs bcad ma*, 410; Gtsug lag phreng ba, *Mkas pa'i dga' ston*, 940; and Si tu Pan chen, *Zla ba chu shel*, 389.
317. 'Gos Lo tsā ba, *Deb ther sngon po*, 51b; and Kun dga' rdo rje, *Deb ther dmar po*, 107.
318. Rang byung rdo rje, *Tshigs bcad ma*, 410.
319. Schaeffer used the *Deb ther dmar po* as his source for this event and, therefore, suggested that Tselpa Künga Dorje (Tshal pa Kun dga' rdo rje) himself described them as an eyewitness. See *The Culture of the Book in Tibet*, 27. This event can be read about in Kun dga' rdo rje, *Deb ther dmar po*, 96. But I have explained how I disagree with this assessment, as I think the section on the Karmapas in the *Deb ther dmar po* was a later addition to this text. See Gamble, *Reincarnation in Tibetan Buddhism*, 275–76.
320. Rang byung rdo rje, *Tshigs bcad ma*, 410.
321. Harrison, "A Brief History of the Tibetan Bka' 'gyur," 70–94.
322. *Dhyāna* (Tib. *bsam gtan*) is a specific type of concentration developed

through concentrated mental calming to make the mind steady enough to perform other yogas.

323. Rang byung rdo rje, *Mgur rnam*, 202–3; and Rang byung rdo rje, *Gsung 'gur thor bu*, vol. *ca*, 414–15. See chapter seventeen of this book where this poem is translated in full.

324. *log pa'i brtson 'grus*, literally "perverted effort."

325. For example: *Ten Teaching Topics*. Rang byung rdo rje, *Mgur rnam*, 69–70; and Rang byung rdo rje, *Gsung 'gur thor bu*, vol. *ca*, 240–41.

326. I discuss this process in much detail in Gamble, *Reincarnation in Tibetan Buddhism*, 105–32.

327. Kun dga' rdo rje, *Deb ther dmar po*, 104; Gtsug lag phreng ba, *Mkas pa'i dga' ston*, 941–42; and Si tu paṇ chen, *Zla ba chu shel*, 394.

328. Gtsug lag phreng ba, *Mkas pa'i dga' ston*, 943; and Si tu paṇ chen, *Zla ba chu shel*, 395.

329. Gtsug lag phreng ba, *Mkas pa'i dga' ston*, 943; and Si tu paṇ chen, *Zla ba chu shel*, 395.

330. Tib. Gim mi shan. Chen Qingying established this link in his analysis of Rangjung Dorje's two journeys to the capitals. See "Ka ma pa Rang jiong duo ji," 97. He also notes that the Yuan Annals records several earthquakes in the Mount Jiming area during this period. One large earthquake in 1334 transformed the top of Mount Jiming into a lake. See "Ka ma pa Rang jiong duo ji," 84. These events are also described in Rang byung rdo rje, *Tshigs bcad ma*, 411; Tshe dbang rgyal, *Lho rong chos 'byung*, 241; Gtsug lag phreng ba, *Mkas pa'i dga' ston*, 941 and 943; and Si tu paṇ chen, *Zla ba chu shel*, 393.

331. Rang byung rdo rje, *Tshigs bcad ma*, 411. A similar project based on Rangjung Dorje's *Ston pa'i skyes rabs* was undertaken at Shalu (Zhwa lu) Monastery in Tsang (Gtsang). These murals were the subject of Sarah Richardson's excellent doctoral thesis, which she completed in 2016, entitled "Painted Books for Plaster Walls: Visual Words in the Fourteenth Century Murals at the Tibetan Buddhist Temple of Shalu."

332. The colophon records it as, "The eighth day of the second month of the Rabbit Year [1339]." See Rang byung rdo rje, *Tshigs bcad ma*, 412.

333. Rang byung rdo rje, *Mgur rnam*, 205.1–6; and Rang byung rdo rje, *Gsung 'gur thor bu*, vol. *ca*, 416.

334. Rang byung rdo rje, *Tshigs bcad ma*, 412.

335. Rang byung rdo rje, 412. It reads, "the fourteenth day of the sixth month of the Rabbit Year [1339]."
336. Rang byung rdo rje, 413.
337. Tshe dbang rgyal, *Lho rong chos 'byung*, 243; Kun dga' rdo rje, *Deb ther dmar po*, 105; Gtsug lag phreng ba, *Mkas pa'i dga' ston*, 945.
338. Tshe dbang rgyal, *Lho rong chos 'byung*, 243; Kun dga' rdo rje, *Deb ther dmar po*, 105; Gtsug lag phreng ba, *Mkas pa'i dga' ston*, 945; and Si tu paṇ chen, *Zla ba chu shel*, 398.
339. Rang byung rdo rje, *Tshigs bcad ma*, 407.
340. Rang byung rdo rje, 413.
341. Gtsug lag phreng ba, *Mkas pa'i dga' ston*, 945; and Si tu paṇ chen, *Zla ba chu shel*, 398.
342. Rang byung rdo rje, *Tshigs bcad ma*, 410; Tshe dbang rgyal, *Lho rong chos 'byung*, 241; Kun dga' rdo rje, *Deb ther dmar po*, 103; 'Gos Lo tsā ba, *Deb ther sngon po*, 39b; Gtsug lag phreng ba, *Mkas pa'i dga' ston*, 940–41; and Si tu paṇ chen, *Zla ba chu shel*, 390.
343. Rang byung rdo rje, *Sngar pa'i skye bor rnam thar*, 354–58.
344. I discuss this text in some detail in Gamble, *Reincarnation in Tibetan Buddhism*, 135–48. Daniel Berounský also discusses this type of narrative more broadly in two articles: See "Entering Dead Bodies and the Miraculous Power of the Kings, Part 1" (2010) and "Entering Dead Bodies and the Miraculous Power of the Kings, Part 2" (2011).
345. *zhing skyong 'gro ma nyi shu rtsa lnga*. I discuss these beings in chapter one of this book.
346. Nyi ma'i snying po.
347. Rgyal ba mchog dbyangs of Ngan lam.
348. Kamalaśīla [ca. 740–795 CE].
349. Potowa's name is most often spelled Po to ba in Tibetan, but in this instance, it is spelled Pu to ba. The dates of his life are disputed. The most common dates given for him are 1027–1105, but he may also have been born in 1027.
350. Kha rag sgom chung.
351. Sne zur chen po.
352. Chos kyi dbang phyug.
353. The three seats of the Karmapas—Tsurpu (Mtshur phu), Karma, and Kampo Nénang (Kam po gnas nang)—are often associated with the three

bodies of a realized buddha. Rangjung Dorje's early works refer to this idea, but after he is stopped from visiting Kampo Nénang, he stopped referring to it.

354. *Srog snying*, or "life force," is usually thought to be handed down from parents to children. See Gamble, *Reincarnation in Tibetan Buddhism*, 142–43.
355. This reversal of the internal energy suggests mastery of sexual energy.
356. These guardians of the body are, in order: (1) Rdo rje thog 'bebs ma (Vajra Descending), (2) Rdo rje dpal 'bar ma (Vajra Very Strong), (3) Rdo rje stobs mo che (Vajra Strong Victory), (4) Rdo rje mthu rgyal ma (Vajra Powerful Victor), (5) Rdo rje dung sgra ma (Vajra Roaring Conch). Each of these beings is giving him personal abilities.
357. These are four of the twelve protectresses (*bstan ma bcu gnyis*) who were subjugated by Padmasambhava. They are all related to places in Tibet. These places sometimes move. The places listed above were most probably the ones that were associated with them during Rangjung Dorje's time. Their names and meaning are as follows: (1) Bdag chen mo rdo rje kun grags ma (Vajra Known-by-all); (2) Gangs kyi yum chen rdo rje kun tu bzang (Great Snow Mother, Vajra Samantabhadrī); (3) Dpal ldan lha ri rdo rje ya ma skyong (Divine Mountain, Yama's Vajra Protector); (4) 'Brog chen 'khor 'dul rdo rje bgegs gtso (Vajra Gek, Great Pastures' Tamer). The last of them here is a *gek* (*bgegs*). A gek is one of the many classes of indigenous Tibetan spirits.
358. The Tibetan for these names is as follows: (1) Btud la 'gro bzang ma (Stooped and Good); (2) Mi g.yo rdo rje glang bzang ma (Immovable, Good Vajra, Willow); (3) Bkra bshis rdo rje tshe ring ma (Auspicious, Long-life Vajra); (4) Stag gzig rdo rje khyung mgo (Tajik, Garuḍa-head, Vajra). The first three of these are three of the five sisters of long life (*tshe ring mched lnga*); the last could refer to either of the other two from this group Mthing gi zhal bzang ma or Cod pan mgrin bzang ma. But the use of the term *stag gzig*, meaning Tajik and often used to refer to the Persian Plateau in Tibetan sources, could be used to suggest a site on the far west of the Tibetan Plateau.
359. These are four of the twelve protectresses (*bstan ma bcu gnyis*), who are alternately called the "Four Female Yakṣiṇīs" (*bdud 'dul bzhi*). They are, in order: (1) Gangs dkar sha med rdo rje spyan gcig ma (Vajra, One-Eye, Skeletal, Snow White); (2) Gser chen mkha' lding ma rdo rje rlung mo

che (Great Golden Garuḍa, Vajra Great Wind); (3) Kha rag khyung btsun rdo rje dpal gyi yum (Noble Garuḍa of Kharag, Illustrious Vajra Mother); (4) Rma ri rab 'byams rdo rje grags mo rgyal (Great Ma Pomra Snow Mountain, Vajra Renowned Victor).

360. These four are not in the usual list of the twelve protectresses. They suggest "doors" or borders to the neighboring countries of Nepal, Persia, Mongolia, and Tangut. They are (1) Sa tri rdo rje 'bri bzangs ma (Vajrasatri, Wholesome Female Yak); (2) Tāg sha dung gi rdo rje sgo mo che (Great Conch-Vajra of the Tāgshi (Tajik or Persian) Door); (3) Chags so rdo rje stobs mo che (Chags, Vajra Lady (with) Great Power); (4) Gha gha rdo rje ral gri ma (Ghagha, Vajra Sword).

361. These are four more of the twelve protectresses (*bstan ma bcu gnyis*). Their alternate name is the "Four sman mo" (*sman mo bzhi*): (1) Kong btsun de mo rdo rje bod khams skyong (Lady of De mo in Kong po, Vajra protector of Tibet); (2) Btsan la la ro rdo rje sman gcig ma (La la tog btsan spirit, Vajra Singular Sman mo); (3) Ma btsun khug chos rdo rje g.yar mo bsil (Noble Lady of Khug chos, Cool G.yar mo's Vajra Lady); (4) G.yu yi sked snyan rdo rje si le ma (Vajra Silema, Turquoise Vajra Poetry).

362. This seems to be an archaic meaning for the Tibetan word *khul*, which makes little sense unless it means "convince" in this context. The Tibetan reads: *nged kyis khyed te ma khul na. rogs kyang mang du sbran no skad. rogs ci ltar sbron bgyis pas.*

363. Ber nag can. The primary protector of the Karmapa lineage.

364. The four protectors of hidden lands: (1) Badzra-satri; (2) Rdo rje bu skyong li btsun (Vajra Li, protector of children); (3) Rdo rje phu chu sman gcig ma (Vajra Waterfall, the singular *sman mo*); (4) Rdo rje g.yu chung ma (Vajra Small Turquoise).

365. Here I am reading *tshem* as *tshems*.

366. Or, alternately, the victory banner of tigers and leopards.

367. Rang byung rdo rje, *Mgur rnam*, 3–7; and Rang byung rdo rje, *Mgur 'bum*, vol. *ca*, 185–88. Sections of my translation of this poem are included within Gamble, *Reincarnation in Tibetan Buddhism,* 177–80. This song has been translated previously by Kurtis Schaeffer in his study of Saraha's work in Tibet. See *Dreaming the Great Brahmin*, 41–42.

368. Shaw, "Srisailam: Centre of the Siddhas," 161–78.

369. *brda'*.

370. The *Mgur rnam* says *bsnyon pa*, which means "the denier." This is probably the misspelling of the homonym *smyon pa*, which is the *Mgur 'bum*'s spelling.
371. Rang byung rdo rje, *Ri chos dngos grub phreng ba.* vol. *ca*, 55–62.
372. Rang byung rdo rje uses the term *ri khrod*, mountain wandering, to describe Tilopā's sojourns in not-always-mountainous, uninhabited areas. It would, therefore, be legitimate to translate this term as "wilderness wandering" or something similar. But as the Tibetan word *ri* means "mountain," I have translated it as "mountain." The word choice reflects Rangjung Dorje's mountainous environment and something of his conception of mountains.
373. Blo 'dro rin chen is the bodhisattva who abides in Tuṣita. See chapter one of this volume and Gamble, *Reincarnation in Tibetan Buddhism,* 137. This is the only time I have seen Marpa associated with this emanation tradition.
374. These are some of the qualities associated with the completion of the mahāmudrā path. For more details, see Kongtrul, *The Treasury of Knowledge*, 208.
375. This is a common way for Rangjung Dorje to refer to himself.
376. Reading *ltos gos* as *lto go.*
377. There seems to be a couple of spelling anomalies in the last lines of this verse. The text reads: *'phra'u yi rnam tog ma lus dang. mthar thug phyag rgya chen po gnyis. nor dogs yod pas gzobs las mdzod.* This translation reads this as: *phra'u yi rnam tog ma lus dang. mthar thug phyag rgya chen po* **nyid**. *nor dogs yod pas gzobs las mdzod.*
378. As far as I can ascertain, the expression being translated here, *ngo bo chen po nyid*, is rare, and when it is used, it is used in the negative. A search of the Buddhist Digital Resource Center only points to two different uses of it. One of these is this text, and the other is in *Bcom ldan 'das ma'i man ngag gi rjes su 'brang ba zhes bya ba'i rnam par bshad pa*, in the Bstan 'gyur (*Sde dge*, TBRC W23703, vol. 94, 4–641), in which it is used in the negative. Rangjung Dorje's use of this term may be put down to the young age at which he composed this text.
379. Aśvaghoṣa and Rang byung rdo rje, *Sangs rgyas bcom ldan 'das kyi skyas rabs brgya pa*, 444–47.
380. This text is analyzed in Carol Meadows, *Arya-Sura'Arya Compendium of the Perfections: Text, Translation and Analysis of the Paramitasamasa*. And parts of it are translated in Peter Khoroche, *Once the Buddha Was a Monkey: Ārya*

Śūra's Jātakamālā. For more information about the Jātaka tradition more generally, see Naomi Appleton, *Narrating Karma and Rebirth: Buddhist and Jain Multi-life Stories*.

381. Jagatī Śrī is a reconstruction of a Sanskrit name from the Tibetan name 'Gro ba'i dpal mo. I cannot find another version of this story in Sanskrit.
382. There is a discussion of a *jātaka* in which the Buddha-to-be is born as a princess. See Derris, "'My Sister's Future Buddhahood': A Jātaka of the Buddha's Lifetime as a Woman," 13–25. Reiko Ohnuma discusses another jātaka in which the Buddha-to-be was a woman in "The Story of Rūpavatī: A Female Past Birth of the Buddha," 103–46. And Naomi Appleton talks about the general presentation of women in the Jātaka tradition in "Temptress on the Path: Women as Objects and Subjects in Buddhist Jataka Stories," 103–15.
383. The kalapingka bird is associated with beautiful singing in the Sanskrit literary tradition.
384. This word "performance" translates the expression *spyod pa byed pa*.
385. Aśvaghoṣa and Rang byung rdo rje, *Sangs rgyas bcom ldan 'das kyi skyas rabs brgya pa*, 461–64.
386. Rnam rgyal sgra dbyangs.
387. *Rang byung rdo rje, Mgur rnam,* 60–63; Rang byung rdo rje, *Mgur 'bum*, vol. *ca*, 232–35.
388. I talk about these *pīṭhas* and provide further references to other work on them in Gamble, *Reincarnation in Tibetan Buddhism*, 112–17.
389. Toni Huber has written about this mountain extensively in *The Cult of Pure Crystal Mountain: Popular Pilgrimage and Visionary Landscape in Southeast Tibet*.
390. *Sahaja* (Tib. *lhan cig tu skye ba*) is a Sanskrit and Apabhraṃśa term meaning "to arise with" or "to be born along with." It is particularly associated with Saraha's writing and reflects his presentation—and the presentation of the *mahāmudrā* tradition more generally—that the nature of the mind is awakened and that the realization of this nature is the path to Buddhahood. Buddhahood arises along with the realization of the mind's nature.
391. This refers to the "fundamental knowledge" (Tib. *gzhi shes pa*; Skt. *sārvajñatā*), which is described in the *Mngon par rtogs pa'i rgyan* (Skt. *Abhisamaya-alaṅkāra*). It relates to the types of wisdom attained by *śrāvakas* and *pratyekabuddhas*.

392. The section up to here is not included within the Rang byung rdo rje, *Mgur rnam*.
393. This translation follows the *Mgur 'bum*, which uses the word *gzer ma*, "nail," in place of the *Mgur rnam*'s *zer*, "to be said" or "rays (of light)."
394. The five sciences (sometimes also called the five major sciences) include linguistic science (Skt. *Śabdavidgyā*; Tib. *sgra rig pa*), logical science (Skt. hetuvidyā; *gtan tshigs rig pa*); medical science (Skt. *cikitsāvidyā*; *gso ba rig pa*); science of fine arts and crafts (Skt. *śilpakarmasthānavidyā*; Tib. *bzo rig pa*); science of the dharma (Skt. *adhyātmavidyā*; *nang don rig pa*). For more information, see Jonathan Gold's *The Dharma's Gatekeepers* (Albany: SUNY), 14–24. See note 221.
395. See note 373.
396. This reading follows the *Mgur 'bum*, which says *the tshom*, "doubt." The *Mgur rnam* reads *tho bo*, which means "a marker stone" and does not make sense in this context.
397. Rang byung rdo rje, *Mgur rnam*, 9–14; Rang byung rdo rje, *Mgur 'bum*, vol. *ca*, 191–95.
398. *sgom*.
399. This follows the *Mgur rnam*. The *Mgur rnam* says *phyogs med kyi ri khros 'grim 1 ang*, which could be translated as: "homeless, wander the mountains." This makes much less sense and is a repeat of a previous verse.
400. The expression used here is *rnal byor spyod ba*, which means "the performance of yogis" but is also a pun on the philosophical school called the Rnal 'byor spyod ba, or, in Sanskrit, Yogācāra.
401. Within the texts that describe the mahāmudrā, the term "introduction" (Tib. *ngo sprod pa*) usually refers to the process of introducing a student to the nature of their own mind, which is said to be synonymous with the mahāmudrā.
402. Rang byung rdo rje, *Mtshur phu'i bstod pa thung ba*, vol. *ca*, 53–55.
403. Timothy Thurston discusses the secular tradition of songs dedicated to specific places in "An Introduction to Tibetan *Sa bstod* Speeches in A mdo," 49–73.
404. Rang byung rdo rje, *Rang byung rdo rje'i gsung 'bum*, vol. *ca*, 32–110.
405. *bstod pa*.
406. I talk about these practices in chapter two and three of this book, and in Gamble, *Reincarnation in Tibetan Buddhism*, 120–30, 209–14.

407. For more on the *kāvya* tradition in Tibet, see Matthew Kapstein, "The Indian Literary Identity in Tibet," 747–802.

408. See note 231.

409. See, for example, Hookham, *The Buddha Within*, 136; Stearns, *The Buddha from Dolpo*, 47–48; and Mathes, *A Direct Path to the Buddha Within*, 51–75.

410. See Cyrus Stearns, *The Buddha from Dolpo*.

411. Mathes's analysis of Rangjung Dorje's combination of these different translations is very good. See *A Direct Path to the Buddha Within*, 51–57.

412. Skt. *dharmatā*; Tib. *chos nyid*.

413. In their translations of the colophon, Brunnhölzl (in *Luminous Heart* 2009, 201) and Schaeffer (in *Enlightened Heart* 1995, 177) write that this song was written for "the great meditator, master Ngarma, and his servant." I have written *Darma* because the scribe of the *Rang byung rdo rje'i mgur rnam* consistently draws his Tibetan letter *da* shorter than his Tibetan letter *nga*. What's more, Rangjung Dorje had a teacher named Dar ma.

414. Stod lung rgyal mdo.

415. *Polygonatum*, also known as Solomon's seal, is a flowering plant that is found throughout the Himalaya and Tibet.

416. This is reading *ljong* as *ljongs*.

417. *Orchis mascula*, also known as early purple orchid, is a widespread type of flowering plant in the orchid family that contains no nectar.

418. According to Dan Martin, "*Sngo-'od-ldan* (presumably *'od ldan sngo*) is another name for the herb rtag-tu-ngu." See "For Love or Religion?" 353n27. Sarat Chandra Das's *Tibetan-English Dictionary*, 533–34, describes this *rtag tu ngu* as a "medicinal flower on which dew is formed at all times on account of which it is said to be always in tears. It grows on high altitudes in Tsari the most easternly district of Central Tibet." This is presumably also the *phyag rdo rtag ngu* described by Christa Kletter and Monika Kriechbaum in their book *Tibetan Medicinal Plants*, 281. None of these references give the botanical name for this plant. I translate *sngo* as "plant" as opposed to "blue" because later in the text it says there are three types of it that are three different colors.

419. Reading *ro kha* as taste.

420. This is reading *zil phrom ldan* as *zil khrom ldan*, short for *zil pa khrom me*. There are many misspelled homophones throughout Rangjung Dorje's Gzung 'bum. The consistency suggests that there may have been alter-

native spellings for some of these words at the time the manuscripts that were the source for this Gzung 'bum were scribed.

421. This refers to the four root precepts (*rtsa ba bzhi*) for monastics: not killing, stealing, lying, or engaging in sexual misconduct.

422. Tib. *gser mdog a ru ra*. This term most probably refers to the Indian gooseberry, the botanical name for which is *Phyllanthus emblica*.

423. This is reading *skye dug* as *skye dgu*. *Skye dug* does not make much sense in this instance.

424. Or Vairocana's position.

425. Reading *ta* as *rta*.

426. Reading *lnga* as *rnga*, which is used elsewhere in the literature to indicate the passing of time.

427. *sku mnye*. For the basics of this form of massage, see Tarthang Tulku, *Tibetan Relaxation: Kum Nye Massage and Movement*.

428. (*A pa ra'*) *dzi ta*, also known as *shu dag dkar po, rubus niveus*.

429. Reading *si 'bru* as *se 'bru*.

430. Reading *'khru* as *mkhris*.

431. *Tha ram*, or *Plantago major*, is a broadleaf, widely distributed medicinal plant.

432. *Me tog bya rkang*, probably *Delphinium brunonianum*, which grows across the Himalaya.

433. Reading *rgyam mtshan* as *rgyal mtshan*.

434. *skyu ru ra*. Once again, *Phyllanthus emblica*.

435. Rang byung rdo rje, *Nges don phyag rgya chen po'i smon lam ldeb*, vol. *a*, 617–22.

436. Chos kyi 'byung gnas, "Nges don phyag rgya chen po'i smon lam gyi 'grel pa grub pa mchog gi zhal lung," 803–916. This text has been translated in Sherab Dorje (trans.), *The Eigth Situpa on the Third Karmapa's Mahamudra Prayer*. The Eighth Situpa was also known as Bstan pa nyin byed, so attribution of this text is sometimes confusing.

437. Rang byung rdo rje, *Mgur rnam*, 202–3; and Rang byung rdo rje, *Gsung 'gur thor bu*, vol. *ca*, 414–15.

Bibliography

Tibetan Works

Rangjung Dorje's Collected Works

Rang byung rdo rje. *Rang byung rdo rje'i gsung 'bum* [Rangjung Dorje's Collected Works]. 16 vols. Mtshur phu (Tsurpu), Tibet: Mkhan po lo yag bkra shis, 2006.

VOLUME *KHA*

Ston pa'i skyes rabs [Birth stories of the teacher], 1–666.

VOLUME *GA*

Mi la bzhad pa rdo rje'i gsung mgur mdzod nag ma zhes pa karma pa rang byung rdo rjes phyogs gcig tu bkod pa [The songs of Mila Zhepa Dorje called the Black Collection, collated by Rangjung Dorje], 1–774.

VOLUME *NGA*

Bka' brgyud gyi gser phreng [Kagyü golden rosary], 1–352.

Dus gsum mkhyen pa seng ge sgra'i rnam bar thar pa'o [Lion's roar: Düsum Khyenpa's liberation story], 158–220.

Bla ma rin po che'i rnam par thar pa'o: Karma pa'i rnam thar [Liberation story of Lama Rinpoche, the Karmapa's liberation story], 256–87.

Dpal chen Rang byung rdo rje'i rnam thar [Rangjung Dorje's liberation story], 353–76.

VOLUME *CA*

Mtshur phu'i bstod pa bzhugs so: gnas kyi tshul gsal bar byed pa snyang ngag gyi me tog gsal ba'i sgron me rdzogs [A praise to Tsurpu: The lamp that illuminates the flower of poetic decoration], 32–40.

Bden gnas chen po bde chen gyi bstod pa [A praise to the solitary, great sacred site of Dechen], 40–43.

Dus bzi'i gnas la bsngags pa [Extolling the seasons in this sacred site], 43–49.

Rong btsan kha ba dkar po'i bstod pa [Adorning Mount Meru, a subtle illumination of this sacred site: A praise to Khawa Karpo], 49–53.

Mtshur phu'i bstod pa thung ba [A short praise to Tsurpu], 53–55.

Mgur 'bum [Collected songs], 85–297.

Rang byung rdo rje'i gsung 'gur [sic] thor bu [Miscellaneous songs], 359–416.

VOLUME *JA*

Dbu ma chos dbyings bstod pa'i rnam par bshad pa la [An explanation of (Nāgārjuna's) *In Praise of Dharmadhātu*], 1–125.

Rnam shes dang ye shes bstan pa'i bstan bcos [Distinction between consciousness and wisdom], 269–76.

De bzhin gshegs pa'i snying po bstan pa'i bstan bcos [Pointing out the tathāgatagarbha], 282–90.

Zab mo nang don gyi gzhung [Profound inner principles], 308–60.

Zab mo nang don gyi 'grel pa [Autocommentary on profound inner meaning], 361–634.

VOLUME *THA*

Yul nyer bzhi'i ngos 'dzin ldeb [Recognising the twenty-four places], 530–33.

VOLUME *A*

Phyag rgya chen po gang gA ma'i gzhung gi sa bcad [Outline of the texts of the Ganga Mahāmudrā], 159–60.

Phyag rgya chen po gang gA ma'i 'grel pa [sic] [Commentary on the Ganga Mahāmudrā], 161–75.

Rgyal po do ha'i sab cad [Outline of the *King Dohā*], 177–80.

Bstun mo do ha'i sab cad [Outline of the *Queen Dohā*], 180–85.

Do ha mdzod kyi bsdud don bcad la ldeb [Condensation of the meaning of the *Dohā-kośa*], 185–91.

Ra mo shag gi bcus len [Exctacting the essence of Solomon's seal], 636–37.

Dbang po lag gi bcus len [Exctacting the essence of early purple orchid], 637–39.

'Od ldan ngo'I bcus len [Exctacting the essence of a lustrous plant], 639–41.

Other Tibetan Works

Aśvaghoṣa and Rang byung rdo rje. *Sangs rgyas bcom ldan 'das kyi skyas rabs brgya pa.* Beijing: Mi rig dpe sprun khang, 1995.

Karma Pak shi (1204–1283). *Grub chen karma pakshi'i bka' 'bum. Autobiographical Writings of the Second Karma-pa Karma-Pakṣi and Spyi lan rin mo. A Defence of the Bka'-brgyud-pa Teachings Addressed to G.yag-sde Paṇ-chen.* Gangtok: Gonpo Tseten, 1978.

(Tshal pa) Kun dga' rdo rje (1309–1364). *Deb ther dmar po* [Red annals]. Pe cin: Mi rigs dpe skrung khang, 1981.

Mkha' spyod dbang po (1350–1405). *Mkha' spyod dbang po'i gsung 'bum.* 4 vols. Gangtok: Gonpo Tseten, 1978.

Mkha' spyod dbang po. *Rang byung rdo rje'i rnam thar tshigs bcad ma 2.* s.n.; s.d. (TBRC: W2CZ7973).

Rwa Lo tsā ba. "Chos rje Dus gsum khyen pa'i skyes rabs rin po che ser gling le'u bco brgyad pa". In *Dbel lden dus gsum mkhyen pa'i zhal gdams gces btul,* edited by Jamgon Kongtrul Labrang, 33–72. Kalimpong: Karmapa 900, 2010.

'Gos Lo tsā ba gzhon nu dpal (1392–1481), *Deb ther sngon po* [Blue annals]. Edited by Lokesh Chandra. New Delhi: International Academy of Indian Culture, 1974.

Chos kyi 'byung gnas. "Nges don phyag rgya chen po'i smon lam gyi 'grel pa grub pa mchog gi zhal lung." In *Thabs grol,* 803–916. Zi ling: Mtsho sngon mi rigs dpe skrun khang, 2004.

Jamgön Kongtrul Labrang, ed. *Dbel lden dus gsum mkhyen pa'i zhal gdams gces btul.* Kalimpong: Karmapa 900, 2010.

Rdo rje rgyal po (1110–1170), "'Gro mgon phag mo gru pa'i skyes rabs kyi skor la chos tshan lnga gzhugs so." In *Rdo rje'i rgyal po gsung 'bum.* Kathmandu: Khanpo Shedrup Tenzin and Lama Thinley Namgyal, 2003.

Gtsug lag phreng ba (1504–1566). *Chos 'byung mkas pa'i dga' ston* [Feast for scholars]. Varanasi: Vajra Vidya Publishing, 2003.

Gtsang smyon He ru ka (1452–1507). *Sgra bsgyur Mar pa lo tsa'i rnam par thar pa mthong ba don yod.* Varanasi: E. Kalsang, 1970.

Tshe dbang rgyal (1697–1763). *Lho rong chos 'byung.* Lhasa: Bod ljongs bod yig dpe rnying dpe skrun khang, 1994.

Rang byung rdo rje. *Rang byung rdo rje' mgur nam.* Bidung, Tashigang: Kunchhap, 1983.

Rin chen rdo rje and Tshe ring chos 'phel, eds. *Gnas chen kha ba dkar po'i bsang mchod dang gnas yig*. Yunnan: Mi rigs dpe skrun khang, 2006.

Si tu paṇ chen chos kyi byung gnas and 'Be lo tshe dban kun khyab. *Bka' brgyud gser 'phreng rnam thar zla ba chu shel gyi 'phreng ba*, 2 vols. Varanasi, India: Vajra Vidya, 2004.

Other Sources

Allsen, Thomas. *Culture and Conquest in Mongol Eurasia*. Cambridge: Cambridge University Press, 2004.

Amitai, Reuven, and David Morgan. *The Mongol Empire and Its Legacy*. Leiden: Brill, 2000.

Appleton, Naomi. *Narrating Karma and Rebirth: Buddhist and Jain Multi-life Stories*. Cambridge: Cambridge University Press, 2014.

———. "Temptress on the Path: Women as Objects and Subjects in Buddhist Jataka Stories." In *New Topics in Feminist Philosophy of Religion*, edited by Pamela Anderson, 103–15. Dordrecht: Springer, 2009.

Arguill're, S. *Profusion de la vaste sphere: Klong-chen rab 'byams, Tibet, 1308–1364*. Paris: Peeters Publishing, 2007.

Atwood, Christopher P. *Encyclopedia of Mongolia and the Mongol Empire*. New York: Facts on File Inc., 2004.

Aufschaiter, Peter. "Land and Places of Milarepa." *East and West* 26 (1976): 175–89.

Berounský, Daniel. "Entering Dead Bodies and the Miraculous Power of the Kings: The Landmark of Karma Pakshi's Reincarnation in Tibet, Part 1." *Mongolo-Tibetica Pragensia' 10: Linguistics, Ethnolinguistics, Religion, and Culture* 3, no. 2 (2010): 7–33.

———. "Entering Dead Bodies and the Miraculous Power of the Kings: The Landmark of Karma Pakshi's Reincarnation in Tibet, Part 2." *Mongolo-Tibetica Pragensia' 11: Ethnolinguistics, Sociolinguistics, Religion, and Culture* 4, no. 2 (2011): 7–29.

Brunnhölzl, Karl. *The Center of the Sunlit Sky: Madhyamaka in the Kagyü Tradition*. Ithaca, NY: Snow Lion, 2004.

———. *In Praise of Dharmadhātu: Nāgārjuna and the Third Karmapa, Rangjung Dorje*. Ithaca, NY: Snow Lion, 2007.

———. *Luminous Heart: The Third Karmapa on Consciousness, Wisdom, and Buddha Nature*. Ithaca, NY: Snow Lion, 2009.

Callahan, Elizabeth M. Introduction to *The Profound Inner Principles* by Rangjung Dorje, The Third Karmapa, xiii–lii. Boston: Shambhala Publications, 2014.

Chen Qingying. "Ka ma pa Rang jiong duo ji liang ci jin jing shi lue." *Zhongguo Zangzue* 3 (1988): 89–99.

Childs, Geoff. "Refuge and Revitalization: Hidden Himalayan Sanctuaries (Sbas-yul) and the Preservation of Tibet's Imperial Lineage," *Acta Orientalia* 60 (1999): 126–58.

Das, Sarat Chandra. *A Tibetan-English Dictionary with Sanskrit Synonyms*. Calcutta: Government of Bengal, Bengal Secretariat Book Depot, 1902.

Davidson, Ronald. *Tibetan Renaissance: Tantric Buddhism in the Rebirth of Tibetan Culture*. New York: Columbia University Press, 2005.

de Nebesky-Wojkowitz, Rene. *Oracles and Demons of Tibet: The Cult and Iconography of the Tibetan Protective Deities*. New Delhi: Book Faith India, 1996.

Derris, Karen. "'My Sister's Future Buddhahood': A Jātaka of the Buddha's Lifetime as a Woman." In *Eminent Buddhist Women*, edited by Karma Leskshe Tsomo, 13–25. Albany: State University of New York, 2014.

Dorje, Rangjung. *The Profound Inner Principles*. Translated by Elizabeth M. Callahan. Boston: Shambhala Publications, 2014.

Dorje, Sherab, trans. *The Eighth Situpa on the Third Karmapa's Mahamudra Prayer.* Ithaca: Shambhala Publications, 2004.

Dotson, Brandon. "Complementarity and Opposition in Early Tibetan Ritual." *Journal of the American Oriental Society* 128, no. 1 (2008): 41–67.

Ehrhard, Franz-Karl. *Buddhism in Tibet & the Himalayas: Texts & Traditions*. Kathmandu: Vajra Publications, 2013.

———. *Die Statue und der Tempel des Arya Va-ti bzang-po: Ein Beitrag zur Geschichte und Geographie des Tibetischen Buddhismus*. Wien: Wiesbaden, 2004.

Gamble, Ruth. *Reincarnation in Tibetan Buddhism: The Third Karmapa and the Invention of a Tradition*. New York: Oxford University Press, 2018.

Garry, Ron. "Kumārarāja." *Treasury of Lives* (2007), http://www.treasuryoflives.org/biographies/view/Kumaradza/4043.

Gerke, Barbara. "Engaging the Subtle Body: Re-Approaching *Bla* Rituals among Himalayan Tibetan Societies." In *Soundings in Tibetan Medicine: Anthropological and Historical Perspectives*, edited by Mona Schrempf, 191–212. Leiden and Boston: Brill, 2007.

Gold, Jonathan. *The Dharma's Gatekeepers: Sakya Paṇḍita on Buddhist Scholarship in Tibet*. New York: State University Press, 2007.

Gyatso, Janet. *Apparitions of the Self: The Secret Autobiographies of a Tibetan Visionary*. New Delhi: Motilal Banarsidass Publications, 2001.

Han, Guanghui (韩光辉). 北京历史人口地理 [History of the population and geography of Beijing] (in Chinese). Beijing: Peking University Press, 1996.

Harrison, Paul. "A Brief History of the Tibetan Bka' 'gyur." In *Tibetan Literature: Studies in Genre*, edited by Jose Ignacio Cabezón and Roger R. Jackson, 70–94. Ithaca, NY: Snow Lion Publications, 1996.

Hirshberg, Daniel. *Remembering the Lotus-Born: Padmasambhava in the History of Tibet's Golden Age*. Boston: Wisdom Publications, 2016.

Hookham, Susan K. *The Buddha Within: Tathagatagarbha Doctrine According to the Shentong Interpretation of the Ratnagotravibhaga*. Albany: State University of New York Press, 1991.

Hopkins, Jeffrey. "The Tibetan Genre of Doxography: Structuring a Worldview." In *Tibetan Literature: Studies in Genre*, edited by Jose Ignacio Cabezón and Roger R. Jackson, 170–217. Ithaca, NY: Snow Lion Publications, 1996.

Huber, Toni. *The Cult of Pure Crystal Mountain: Popular Pilgrimage and Visionary Landscape in Southeast Tibet*. Oxford: Oxford University Press, 1999.

———. "Where Exactly Are Cāritra, Devikoṭa and Himavat? A Sacred Geography Controversy and the Development of Tantric Buddhist Pilgrimage Sites in Tibet." *Kailash* 16, nos. 3–4 (1990): 121–65.

Jackson, David. *Enlightenment by a Single Means: Tibetan Controversies on the 'Self Sufficient White Remedy' (Dkar Po Chig Thub)*. Wien and Verlag: Der Österreichischen Akademie Der Wissenschaften, 1994.

———. "Sa-skya Paṇḍita the Polemicist: Ancient Debates and Modern Interpretations." *Journal of the International Association of Buddhist Studies* 13, no. 2 (1990): 17–116.

———. *Two Biographies of Śākyaśrībhadra: The Eulogy by Khro phu Lo tsā ba and Its 'Commentary' by Bsod nams dpal bzang po*. Stuttgart: Franz Steiner Verlag, 1990.

Jones Tung, Rosemary. *A Portrait of Lost Tibet*. Berkeley: University of California Press, 1996.

Kapstein, Matthew. "The Indian Literary Identity in Tibet." In *Literary Cultures in History: Reconstructions from South Asia*, edited by Sheldon Pollock, 747–802. Berkeley: University of California Press, 2003.

Khoroche, Peter. *Once the Buddha Was a Monkey: Ārya Śūra's Jātakamālā*. Chicago and London: University of Chicago Press, 1989.

Kletter, Christa, and Monika Krichbaum. *Tibetan Medicinal Plants*. Boca Raton: CRC Press, 2001.

Kongtrul, Jamgön. *The Treasury of Knowledge: Book Eight, Part Four: Esoteric Instructions*. Translated by Sarah Harding. Ithaca, NY: Snow Lion Publications, 2007.

Kragh, Ulrich Timme. "Prolegomenon to the Six Doctrines of Nā ro pa: Authority and Tradition." In *Mahāmudrā and the Bka' brgyud Tradition*, edited by Roger R. Jackson and Matthew T. Kapstein, 131–78. Andiast: International Institute for Tibetan and Buddhist Studies GmbH, 2011.

Li, Brenda. "A Critical Study of the Life of the 13th-Century Tibetan Monk U rgyan pa Rin chen dpal Based on His Biographies." PhD diss., University of Oxford, 2011.

Lindtner, Christian. *Nāgārjuniana: Studies in the Writings and Philosophy of Nāgārjuna*. Copenhagen: Akademisk Forlag, 1982.

Manson, Charles E. "Elastic Time, Magical Memories: Multifarious Lives of Karmapas." Unpublished.

———. "Introduction to the Life of Karma Pakshi (1204/6-1283)." *Bulletin of Tibetology* 45, no. 1 (2009): 22–52.

Martin, Dan. "For Love or Religion? Another Look at a 'Love Song' by the Sixth Dalai Lama." *Zeitschrift der Deutschen Morgenländischen Gesellschaft* 138, no. 2 (1988): 349–63.

Mathes, Klaus-Dieter. *A Direct Path to the Buddha Within: Go Lotsāwa's Mahāmudrā Interpretation of the Ratnagotravibhāga*. Boston: Wisdom Publications, 2008.

Meadows, Carol. *Arya-Sura'Arya Compendium of the Perfections: Text, Translation and Analysis of the Paramitasamasa*. Ann Arbor: Indica et Tibetica, Verlag University Microfilms International, 1986.

Mengele, Irmgard. "The Artist's Life." In *The Black Hat Eccentric: Artistic Visions of the Tenth Karmapa*, edited by Karl Debreczeny, 33–63. New York: Rubin Museum of Art, 2012.

Nyingpo, Yudra. *The Great Image: The Life Story of Vairochana the Translator*. Translated by Ani Jinba Palmo. Boston: Shambhala Publications, 2004.

Ohnuma, Reiko. "The Story of Rūpavatī: A Female Past Birth of the Buddha." *Journal of the International Association of Buddhist Studies* 23, no. 1 (2000): 103–46.

Pakhoutova, Elena. "A Wondrous Great Accomplishment: A Painting of an Event." In *The Arts of Tibetan Painting. PIATS 2010: Proceedings of the Twelfth*

Seminar of the International Association of Tibetan Studies, Vancouver, 2010. Online Publication: Asian Arts, http://www.asianart.com/articles/pakhoutova/index.html.

Petech, Luciano. *Central Tibet and the Mongols: the Yüan-Sa-skya period of Tibetan history*. Roma: Istituto italiano per il Medio ed Estremo Oriente, 1990.

Quintman, Andrew. "Toward a Geographic Biography: Milarepa's Life in the Tibetan Landscape." *Numen* 55, no. 4 (2008): 363–410.

———. *The Yogin and the Madman: Reading the Biographical Corpus of Tibet's Great Saint Milarepa*. New York: Columbia University Press, 2013.

Ricard, Matthieu. *The Life of Shabkar: The Autobiography of a Tibetan Yogin*. Albany: SUNY Press, 1994.

Richardson, Hugh E. "The Karma-Pa Sect: A Historical Note." *Journal of the Royal Asiatic Society* 90, nos. 3–4 (1958): 139–64.

Richardson, Sarah. "Painted Books for Plaster Walls: Visual Words in the Fourteenth-Century Murals at the Tibetan Buddhist Temple of Shalu." PhD diss., University of Toronto, 2016.

Roberts, Peter Alan. *Mahamudra and Related Instructions*. Somerville, MA: Wisdom Publications, 2011.

Robinson, James B. *Buddha's Lions: The Lives of the Eighty-Four Siddhas*. Berkeley: Dharma Publishing, 1979.

Ruegg, David Seyfort. *The Literature of the Madhyamaka School of Philosophy in India*: *Volume 1, A History of Indian literature: Buddhist and Jaina Literature*. Vienna: Otto Harrassowitz Verlag, 1981.

Schaeffer, Kurtis. *The Culture of the Book in Tibet*. New York: Columbia University Press, 2009.

———. *Dreaming the Great Brahmin: Creative Traditions of the Buddhist Poet-Saint Saraha*. Oxford and New York: Oxford University Press, 2005.

———. "The Enlightened Heart of Buddhahood: A Study and Translation of the Third Karma pa Rang byung rdo rje's work on Tathagatagarbha, The De bzhin gshegs pa'i snying po gtan la dbab pa." MA thesis, University of Washington, 1995.

Schwieger, Peter. *The Dalai Lama and the Emperor of China*. New York: Columbia University Press, 2015.

Seegers, Manfred. "Lord of the Teachings: The Life and Works of the Third Karmapa, Rang byung rdo rje." MPhil diss., University of Canterbury, 2009.

Shaw, R. "Srisailam: Centre of the Siddhas." *South Asian Studies* 13, no. 1 (1997): 161–78.

Smith, E. Gene. *Among Tibetan Texts: History and Literature of the Himalayan Plateau*. New York: Simon and Schuster, 2001.

Sobisch, Jan-Ulrich. "Guru-Devotion in the Bka' brgyud pa Tradition: The Single Means to Realisation." In *Mahāmudrā and the Bka' brgyud Tradition*, edited by Roger R. Jackson and Matthew T. Kapstein, 211–57. Andiast, Switzerland: International Institute for Tibetan and Buddhist Studies, 2011.

Sørensen, Per K., Guntram Hazod, and Tsering Gyalpo. *Rulers on the Celestial Plain: Ecclesiastic and Secular Hegemony in Medieval Tibet. A Study of Tshal Gung-thang*. Wien: Arbeitskreis für Tibetische und Buddhistische Studien, 2007.

Sperling, Elliot. "Karma Rol-pa'i rdo-Rje and the Re-Establishment of Karma-pa Political Influence in the 14th Century." In *Tibet after Empire: Culture, Society and Religion between 850–1000*, edited by Cristoph Cüppers, Rob Mayer, and Michael Walter, 229–44. Lumbini: Lumbini International Research Institute, 2004.

———. "Tsa-mi lo-tsa-ba Sangs-rgyas grags-pa and the Tangut Background to Early Mongol-Tibetan Relations." In *Tibetan Studies: Proceedings of the 6th Seminar of the International Association for Tibetan Studies, Fagernes*, edited by Per Kværne, 801–24. Oslo: Institute for Comparative Research in Human Culture, 1992.

Stearns, Cyrus. *The Buddha from Dolpo: A Study of the Life and Thought of the Tibetan Master Dolpopa Sherab Gyaltsen*. Albany: State University of New York Press, 1999.

Stenzel, Julia. "The Mahāmudrā of Sakya Paṇḍita." *Indian International Journal of Buddhist Studies* 14 (2014): 199–228.

Templeman, David. "Iranian Themes in Tibetan Tantric Culture: The *Ḍākinī*." In *Religion and Secular Culture in Tibet*, edited by Hank Blezer, 114–29. Netherlands: Brill, 2002.

Thakchöe, Sonam. "Reification and Nihilism: The Three-Nature Theory and Its Implications." In *Madhyamaka and Yogacara: Allies Or Rivals?*, edited by Jay L. Garfield and Jan Westerhoff, 72–110. New York: Oxford University Press, 2015.

Thurston, Timothy. "An Introduction to Tibetan *Sa bstod* Speeches in Amdo." *Asian Ethnology* 71, no. 1 (2012): 49–73.

Tulku, Tarthang. *Tibetan Relaxation: Kum Nye Massage and Movement*. New York: Thorsons, 2003.

van der Kuijp, Leonard W. J. "The Dalai Lamas and the Origins of Reincarnate Lamas." In *The Dalai Lamas: A Visual History*, edited by Martin Brauen, 15–31. Chicago: Serindia Publications, 2005.

———. "The Kalacakra and the Patronage of Tibetan Buddhism by the Mongol Imperial Family." In *Central Eurasian Studies Lectures*, edited by Federica Venturi. Lecture 4, 1–62. Bloomington: Department of Central Eurasian Studies, 2004.

———. "The Monastery of Gsang-phu Ne'u-thog and Its Abbatial Succession from ca. 1073 to 1250." *Berliner Indologische Studien* 3 (1987): 103–27.

———. "On the *Lives* of Sakyasribhadra." *Journal of the American Oriental Society* 114, no. 4 (1995): 599–616.

Vitali, Roberto. "Grub chen U rgyan pa and the Mongols of China." In *Studies on the History and Literature of Tibet and the Himalayas*, edited by Roberto Vitali, 31–64. Kathmandu: Vajra Publications, 2012.

Waldron, William S. *The Buddhist Unconscious: The Ālaya-vijñāna in the Context of Indian Buddhist Thought*. London: Routledge, 2003.

Wylie, Turrell. "Reincarnation: A Political Innovation in Tibetan Buddhism." In *Contributions on Tibetan and Buddhist Religion and Philosophy: Proceedings of the Csoma de Koros Symposium*, edited by Louis Ligeti, 579–86. Wien: Arbeitskreis für Tibetische und Buddhistische Studien, Universität Wien, 1983.

Yamamoto, Karl. *Vision and Violence: Lama Zhang and the Politics of Charisma in Twelfth-Century Tibet*. Leiden and Boston: Brill, 2012.

Zivkovic, Tanya. *Death and Reincarnation in Tibetan Buddhism: In-Between Bodies*. London: Routledge, 2013.

Index

LIVES OF THE MASTERS

"Since the time of Buddha Shakyamuni himself, Buddhists have been accustomed to recollect the lives of great teachers and practitioners as a source of inspiration from which we may still learn. The Lives of the Masters series continues this noble tradition, recounting the stories, wisdom, and experience of many accomplished Buddhists over the last 2,500 years. I am sure readers will find the accounts in this series inspirational and encouraging."

His Holiness the Dalai Lama

"The lives of the most important Buddhist masters in history written by the very best of scholars in elegant and accessible prose—who could ask for more?"

Jose Cabezón, *Professor of Tibetan Buddhist Studies*
University of California Santa Barbara

BOOKS IN THE SERIES

Atiśa Dīpaṃkara: Illuminator of the Awakened Mind
Gendun Chopel: Tibet's Modern Visionary
S. N. Goenka: Emissary of Insight
The Third Karmapa Rangjung Dorje: Master of Mahāmudrā
Tsongkhapa: A Buddha in the Land of Snows

Please visit www.shambhala.com
for more information on forthcoming titles.